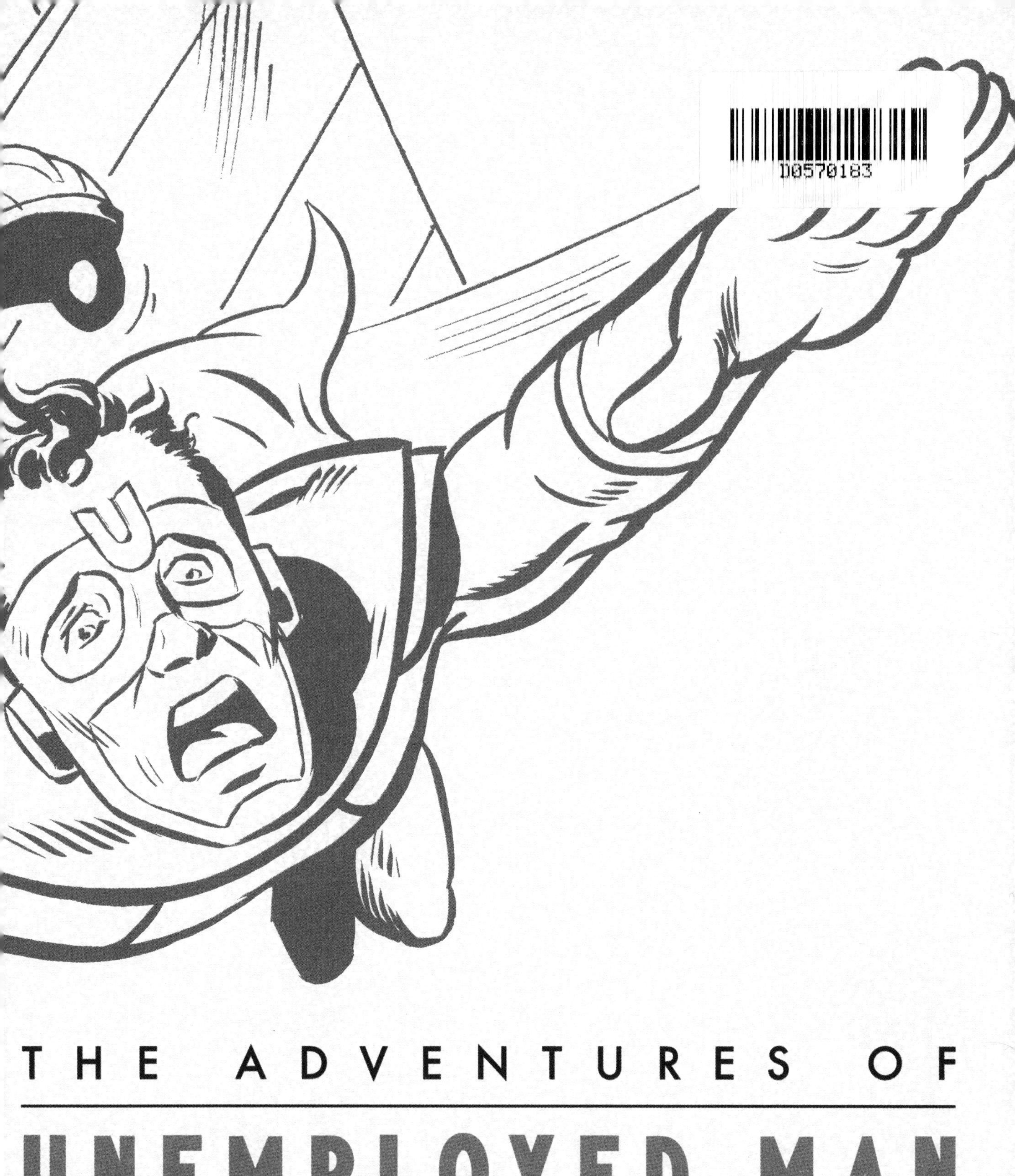

THE ADVENTURES OF

UNEMPLOYED MAN

LB

LITTLE, BROWN AND COMPANY

NEW YORK | BOSTON | LONDON

CREATED BY
ERICH ORIGEN & GAN GOLAN

WRITTEN BY
ERICH ORIGEN & GAN GOLAN

ART DIRECTION, LAYOUTS & CHARACTER DESIGN BY
GAN GOLAN

PENCILS BY

RAMONA FRADON
"The Dark Knight of Self-Help" pages 3-18
"Apply Within" pages 19-29; 36-40
Origin Story: "Wonder Mother"
*Ads: "Everyman," "Return of The
Just Great Society"*

RICK VEITCH
"Attack of the Toxic Debt Blob" pages 43-59
*Ads: "Shake The Invisible Hand,"
"Coming Soon!"*

MICHAEL NETZER
"The Dark Knight of Self-Help" pages 15,16
"Apply Within" page 24
"The Just Us League" pages 62-73; 76-78
Origin Story: "White Rage"

INKS BY

TERRY BEATTY
"The Dark Knight of Self-Help" pages 3,13-17
"Apply Within" pages 19-29; 36-40
"Attack of the Toxic Debt Blob" pages 43-59
Origin Stories: "Wonder Mother," "White Rage"
*Ads: "Shake The Invisible Hand,"
"Coming Soon!," "Everyman,"
"Return of The Just Great Society"*

INKS BY

JOE RUBINSTEIN
"The Dark Knight of Self-Help" pages 4-11
"The Just Us League" pages 62-73; 76-78

COLORS BY
LEE LOUGHRIDGE

ADDITIONAL ARTWORK BY

BENTON JEW
Fantastic Facts
Origin Story: "Good Grief"
*Ads: "Self-Pulling Bootstraps,"
"Superlotto," "Political Science Kit"*

THOMAS YEATES
Origin Story: "Master of Degrees"

SHAWN MARTINBROUGH
Origin Story: "Fellowman"

LETTERING BY

THOMAS MAUER
"The Dark Knight of Self-Help" pages 3-18
"Apply Within" pages 19-29; 36-40
Origin Story: "Fellowman"
Ads: "Shake The Invisible Hand," "Everyman"

CLEM ROBINS
"Attack of the Toxic Debt Blob" pages 43-59

TOM ORZECHOWSKI
"The Just Us League" pages 62-73; 76-78
*Origin Stories: "Wonder Mother," "Master
of Degrees," "White Rage"*

LITTLE, BROWN AND COMPANY
HACHETTE BOOK GROUP
237 PARK AVENUE, NEW YORK, NY 10017
WWW.HACHETTEBOOKGROUP.COM

FIRST EDITION: OCTOBER 2010

LITTLE, BROWN AND COMPANY IS A DIVISION OF
HACHETTE BOOK GROUP, INC. THE LITTLE, BROWN
NAME AND LOGO ARE TRADEMARKS OF HACHETTE
BOOK GROUP, INC.

THE CHARACTERS AND EVENTS
IN THIS BOOK ARE FICTITIOUS. ANY
SIMILARITY TO REAL PERSONS, LIVING OR
DEAD, IS COINCIDENTAL AND NOT
INTENDED BY THE AUTHOR.

ISBN 978-0-316-09882-3/LCCN 2010932064

10 9 8 7 6 5 4 3 2 1

RRD-OH

PRINTED BY THE WORK FORCE IN THE UNITED STATES OF AMERICA

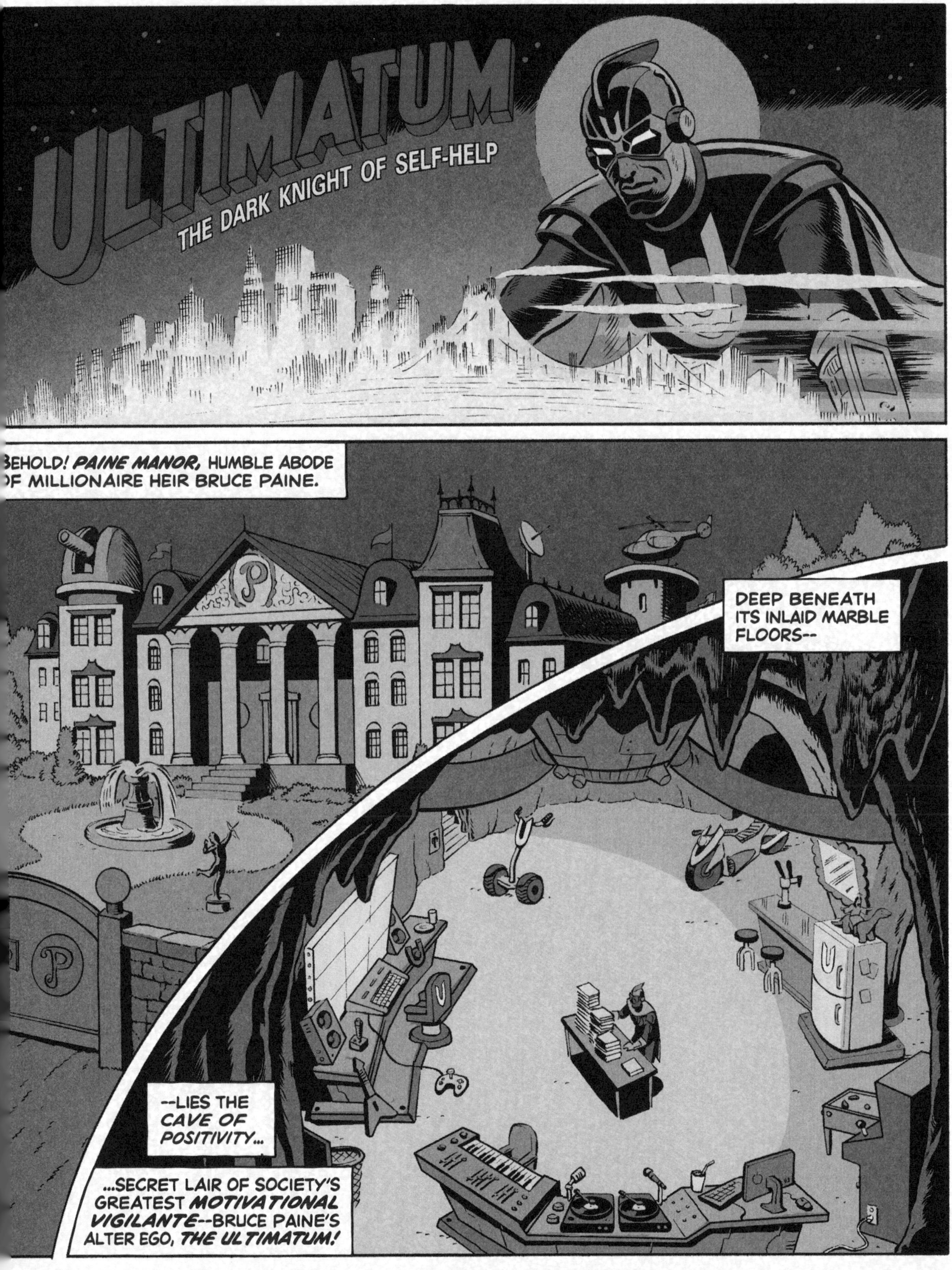

ULTIMATUM
THE DARK KNIGHT OF SELF-HELP
BEHOLD! PAINE MANOR, HUMBLE ABODE OF MILLIONAIRE HEIR BRUCE PAINE.
DEEP BENEATH ITS INLAID MARBLE FLOORS--
--LIES THE CAVE OF POSITIVITY...
...SECRET LAIR OF SOCIETY'S GREATEST MOTIVATIONAL VIGILANTE--BRUCE PAINE'S ALTER EGO, THE ULTIMATUM!

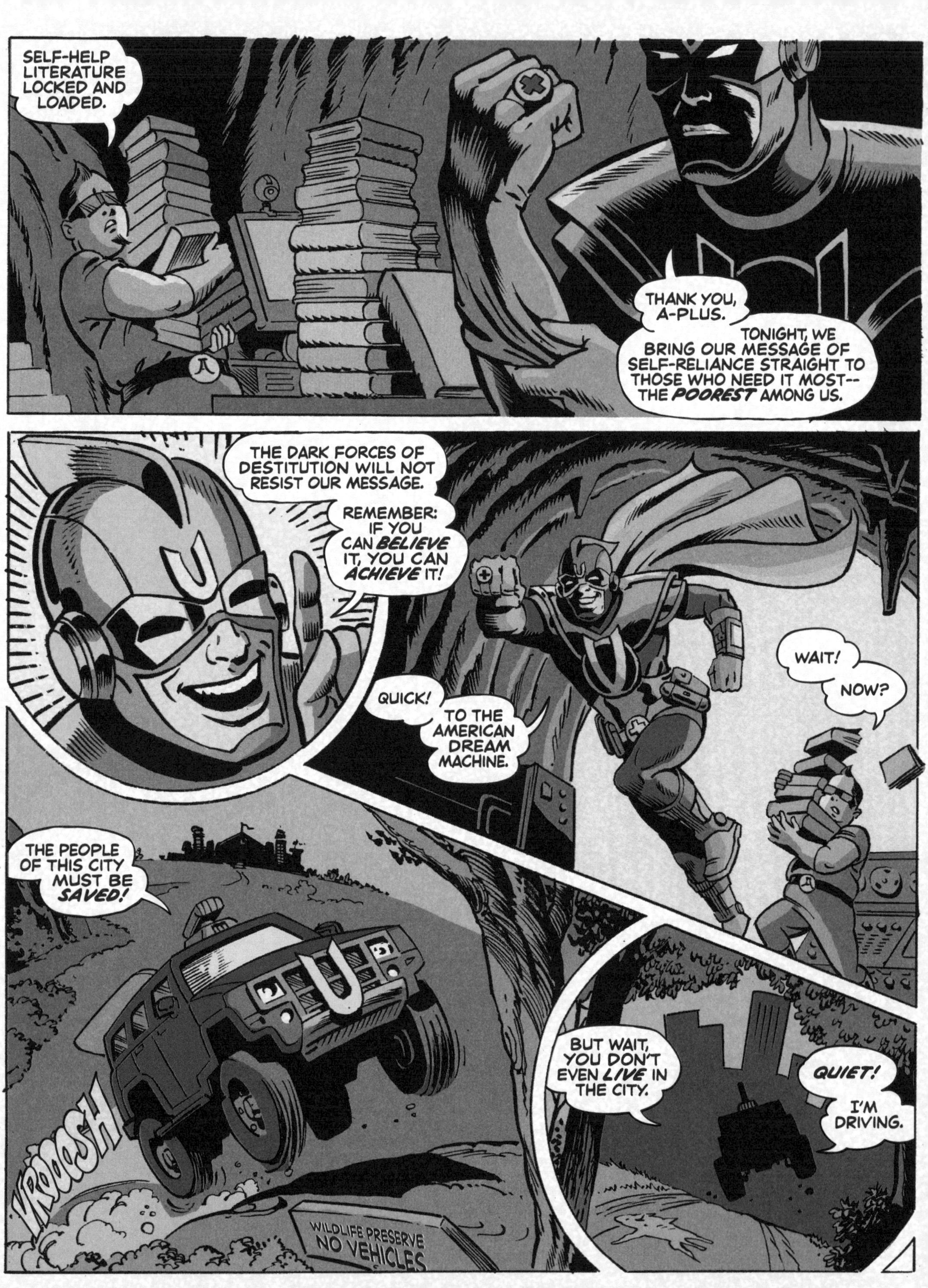
SELF-HELP LITERATURE LOCKED AND LOADED.
THANK YOU, A-PLUS.
TONIGHT, WE BRING OUR MESSAGE OF SELF-RELIANCE STRAIGHT TO THOSE WHO NEED IT MOST-- THE *POOREST* AMONG US.
THE DARK FORCES OF DESTITUTION WILL NOT RESIST OUR MESSAGE.
REMEMBER: IF YOU CAN *BELIEVE* IT, YOU CAN *ACHIEVE* IT!
QUICK!
TO THE AMERICAN DREAM MACHINE.
WAIT!
NOW?
THE PEOPLE OF THIS CITY MUST BE *SAVED!*
VROOOSH
WILDLIFE PRESERVE
NO VEHICLES
BUT WAIT, YOU DON'T EVEN *LIVE* IN THE CITY.
QUIET!
I'M DRIVING.

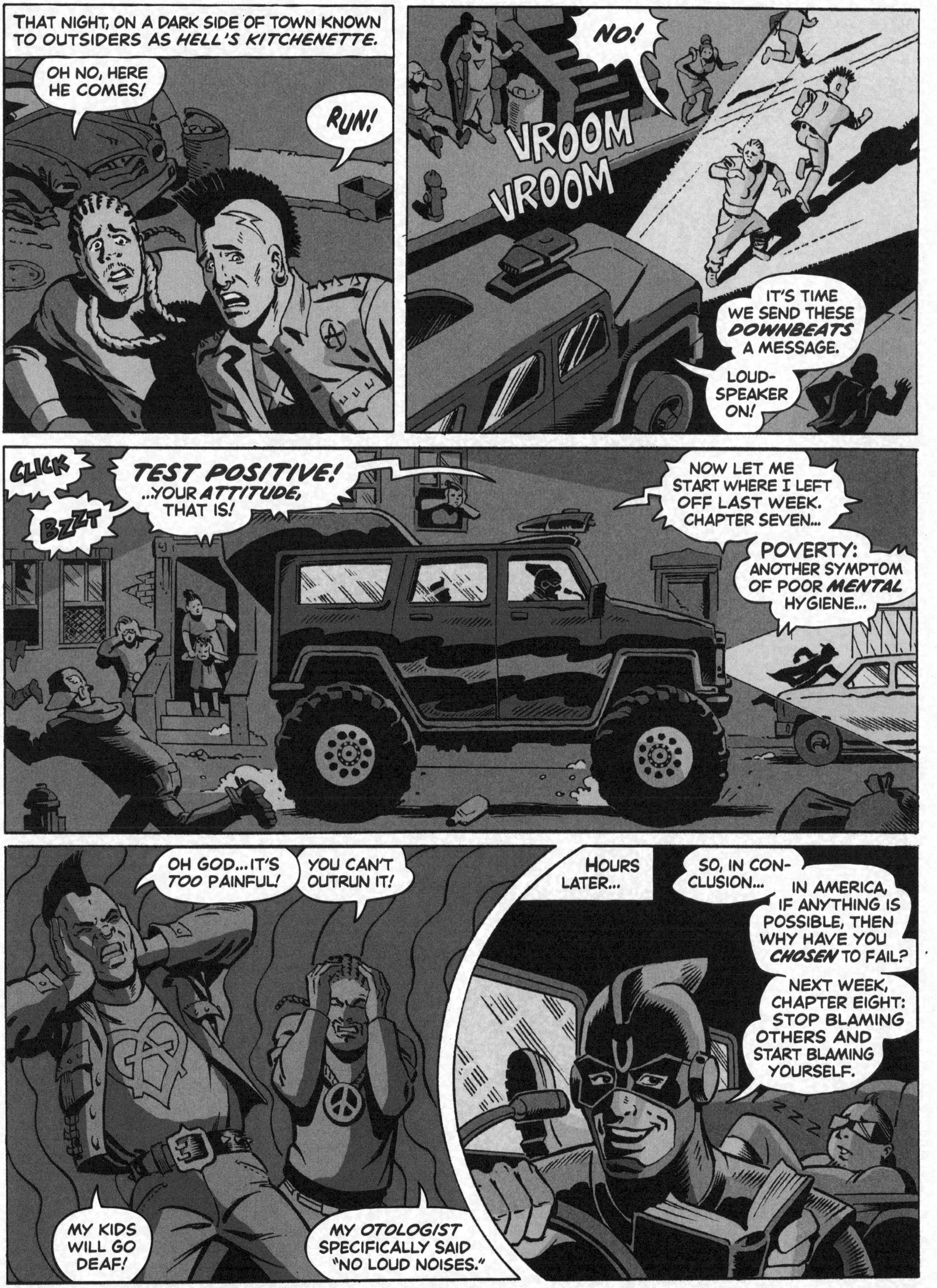
THAT NIGHT, ON A DARK SIDE OF TOWN KNOWN TO OUTSIDERS AS *HELL'S KITCHENETTE*.
OH NO, HERE HE COMES!
RUN!
NO!
VROOM VROOM
IT'S TIME WE SEND THESE *DOWNBEATS* A MESSAGE.
LOUD-SPEAKER ON!
CLICK
BZZT
TEST POSITIVE! ...YOUR *ATTITUDE,* THAT IS!
NOW LET ME START WHERE I LEFT OFF LAST WEEK. CHAPTER SEVEN...
POVERTY: ANOTHER SYMPTOM OF POOR *MENTAL* HYGIENE...
OH GOD...IT'S *TOO* PAINFUL!
YOU CAN'T OUTRUN IT!
MY KIDS WILL GO DEAF!
MY *OTOLOGIST* SPECIFICALLY SAID "NO LOUD NOISES."
HOURS LATER...
SO, IN CON-CLUSION...
IN AMERICA, IF ANYTHING IS POSSIBLE, THEN WHY HAVE YOU *CHOSEN* TO FAIL?
NEXT WEEK, CHAPTER EIGHT: STOP BLAMING OTHERS AND START BLAMING YOURSELF.

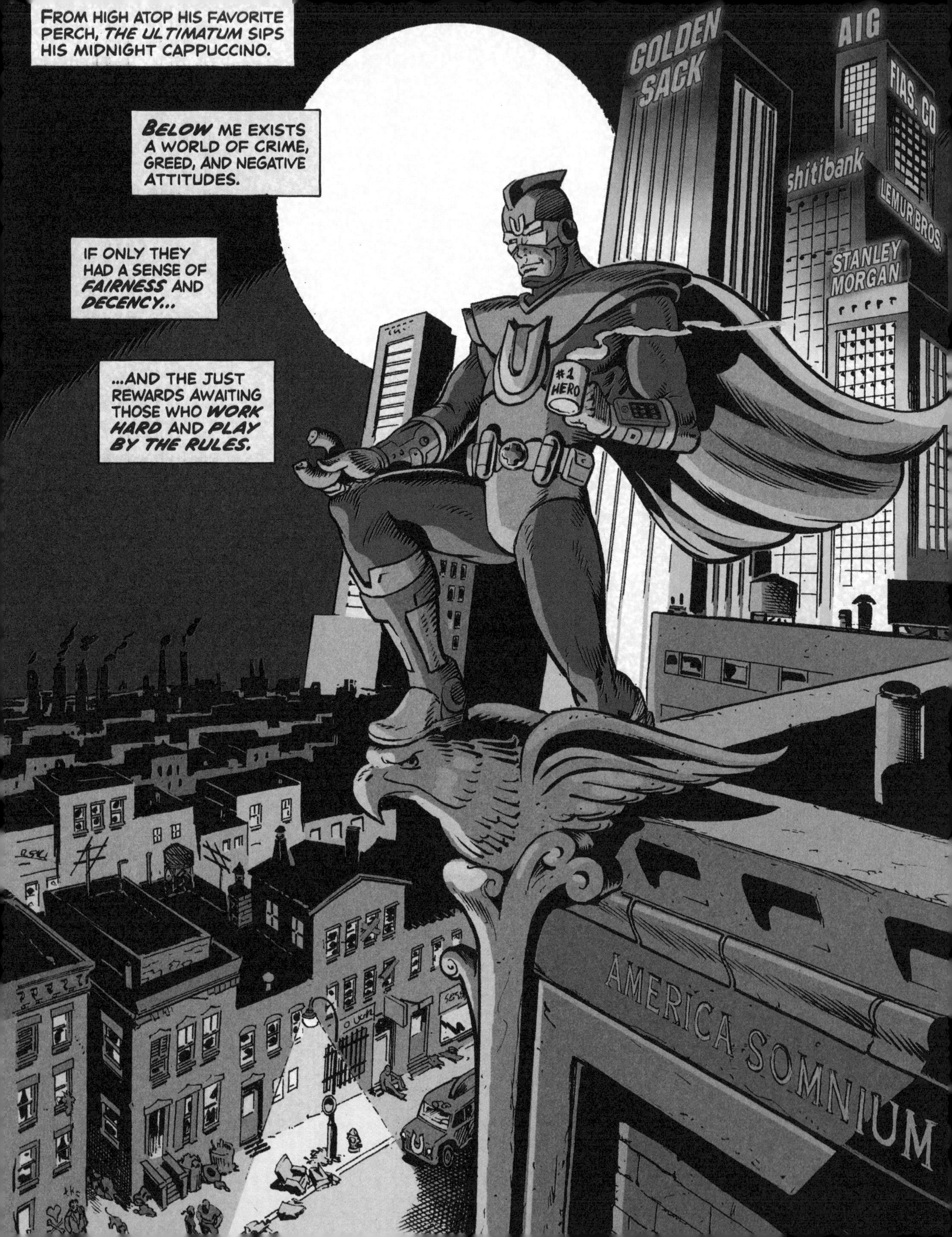
FROM HIGH ATOP HIS FAVORITE PERCH, THE ULTIMATUM SIPS HIS MIDNIGHT CAPPUCCINO.
BELOW ME EXISTS A WORLD OF CRIME, GREED, AND NEGATIVE ATTITUDES.
IF ONLY THEY HAD A SENSE OF FAIRNESS AND DECENCY...
...AND THE JUST REWARDS AWAITING THOSE WHO WORK HARD AND PLAY BY THE RULES.
GOLDEN SACK
AIG
FIAS. CO
shitibank
LEMUR BROS.
STANLEY MORGAN
#1 HERO
AMERICA SOMNIUM

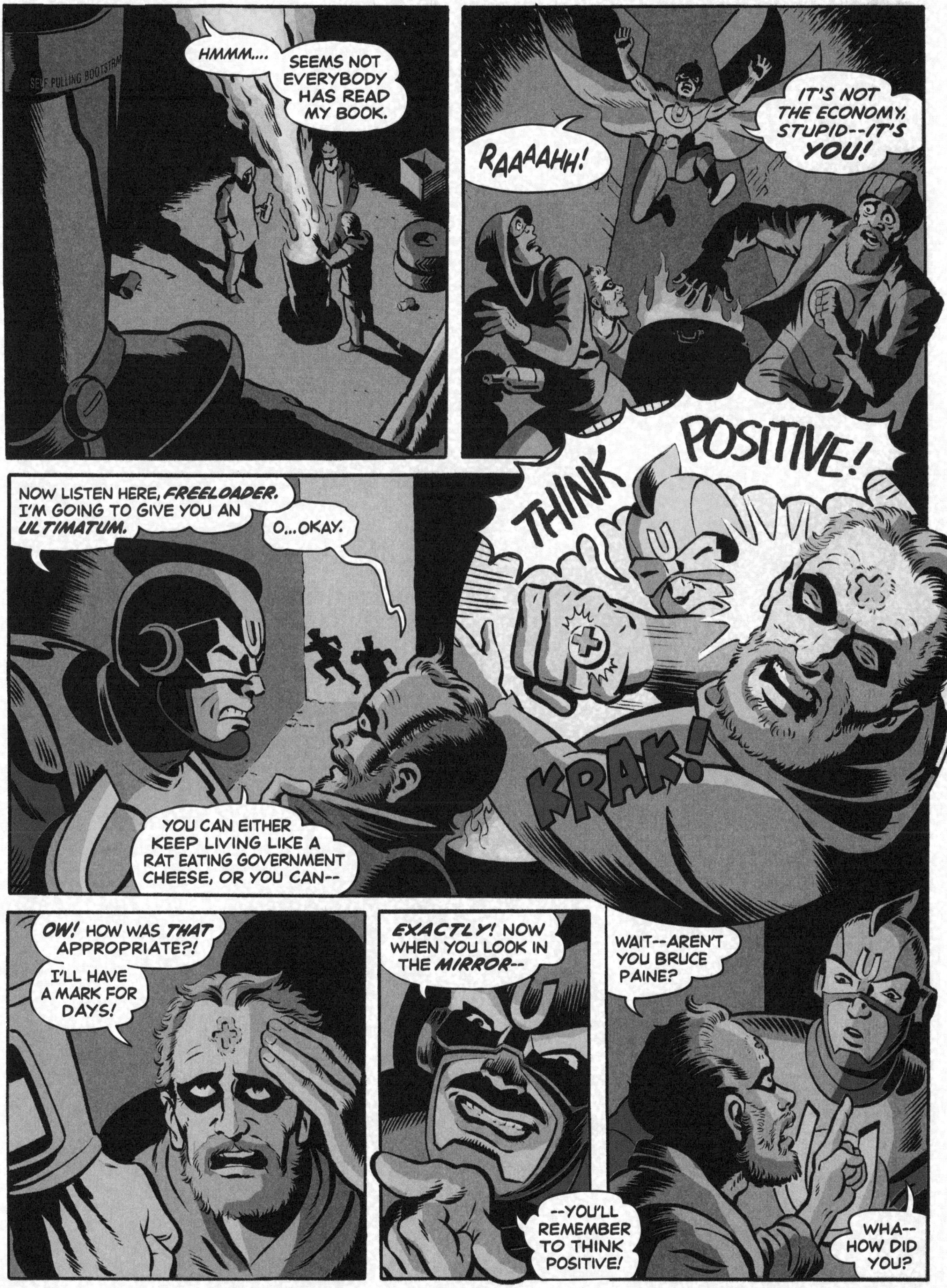

SELF PULLING BOOTSTRAP
HMMM....
SEEMS NOT EVERYBODY HAS READ MY BOOK.
RAAAAHH!
IT'S NOT THE ECONOMY, STUPID--IT'S YOU!
NOW LISTEN HERE, FREELOADER. I'M GOING TO GIVE YOU AN ULTIMATUM.
O...OKAY.
YOU CAN EITHER KEEP LIVING LIKE A RAT EATING GOVERNMENT CHEESE, OR YOU CAN--
THINK POSITIVE!
KRAK!
OW! HOW WAS THAT APPROPRIATE?!
I'LL HAVE A MARK FOR DAYS!
EXACTLY! NOW WHEN YOU LOOK IN THE MIRROR--
--YOU'LL REMEMBER TO THINK POSITIVE!
WAIT--AREN'T YOU BRUCE PAINE?
WHA-- HOW DID YOU?

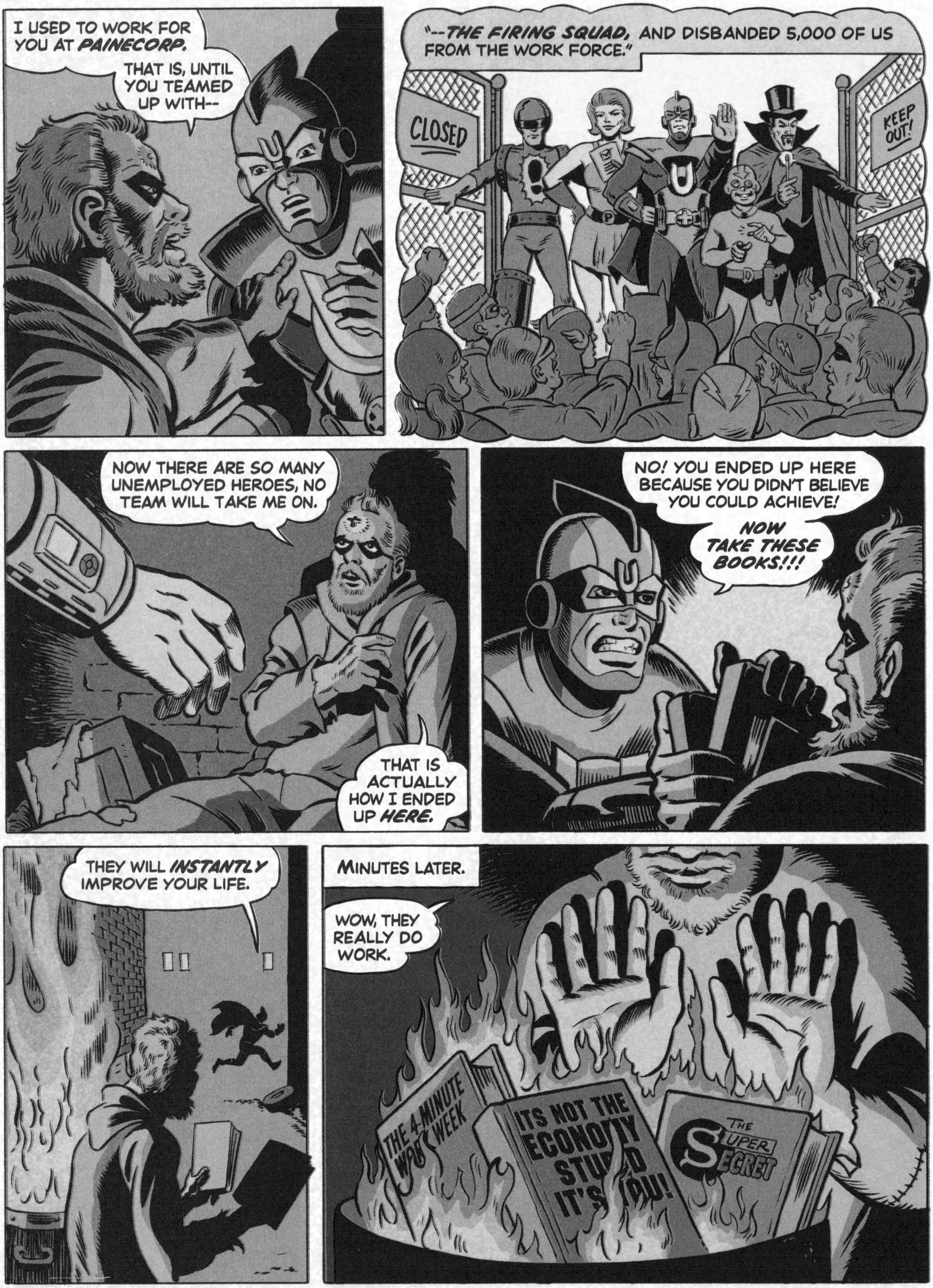
I USED TO WORK FOR YOU AT PAINECORP.
THAT IS, UNTIL YOU TEAMED UP WITH--
"--THE FIRING SQUAD, AND DISBANDED 5,000 OF US FROM THE WORK FORCE."
CLOSED
KEEP OUT!
NOW THERE ARE SO MANY UNEMPLOYED HEROES, NO TEAM WILL TAKE ME ON.
THAT IS ACTUALLY HOW I ENDED UP HERE.
NO! YOU ENDED UP HERE BECAUSE YOU DIDN'T BELIEVE YOU COULD ACHIEVE!
NOW TAKE THESE BOOKS!!!
THEY WILL INSTANTLY IMPROVE YOUR LIFE.
MINUTES LATER.
WOW, THEY REALLY DO WORK.
THE 4-MINUTE WORK WEEK
ITS NOT THE ECONOMY STUPID IT'S YOU!
THE SUPER SECRET

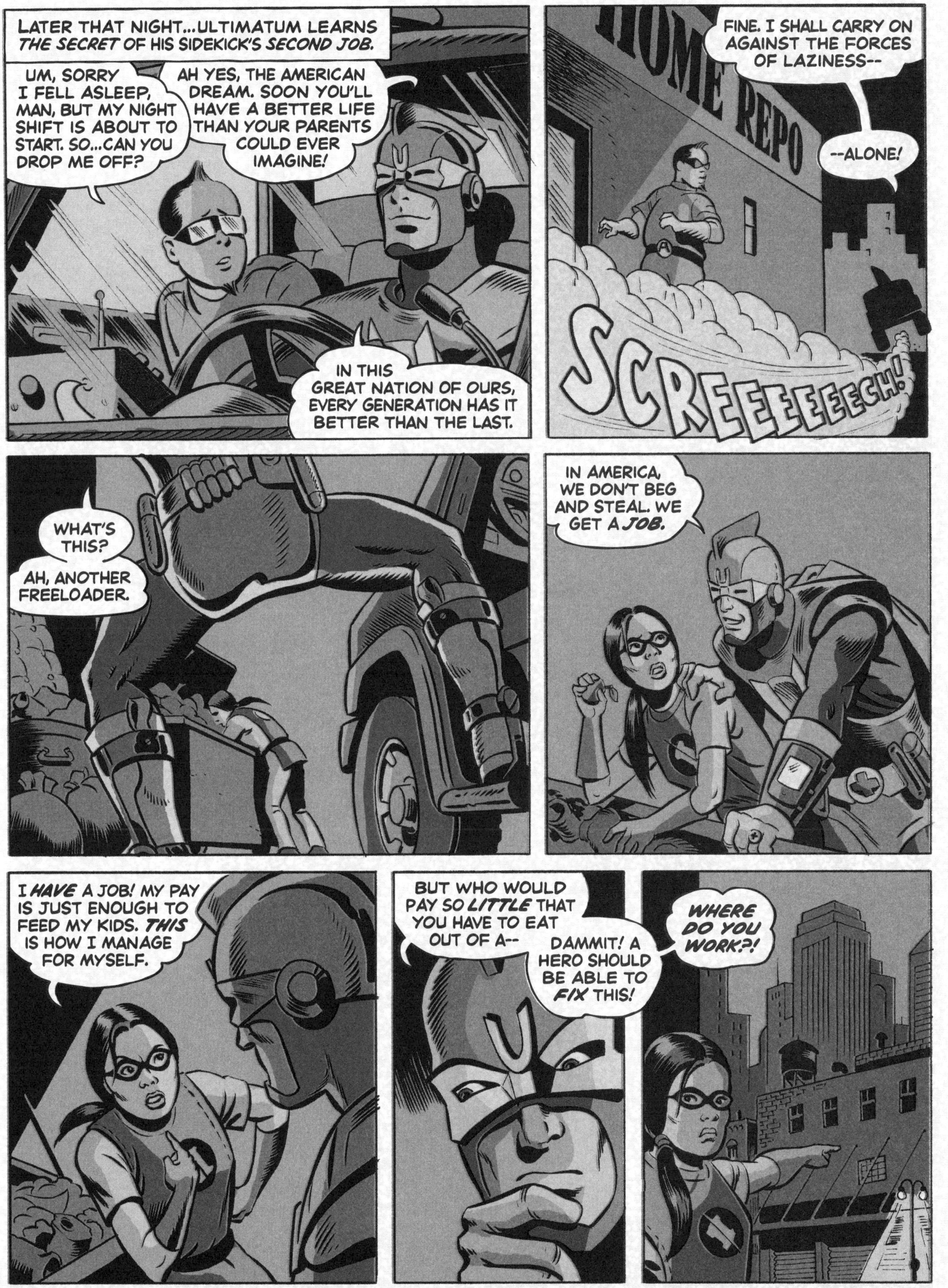

LATER THAT NIGHT...ULTIMATUM LEARNS *THE SECRET* OF HIS SIDEKICK'S *SECOND JOB.*
UM, SORRY I FELL ASLEEP, MAN, BUT MY NIGHT SHIFT IS ABOUT TO START. SO...CAN YOU DROP ME OFF?
AH YES, THE AMERICAN DREAM. SOON YOU'LL HAVE A BETTER LIFE THAN YOUR PARENTS COULD EVER IMAGINE!
IN THIS GREAT NATION OF OURS, EVERY GENERATION HAS IT BETTER THAN THE LAST.
HOME REPO
FINE. I SHALL CARRY ON AGAINST THE FORCES OF LAZINESS--
--ALONE!
SCREEEEEEECH!
WHAT'S THIS?
AH, ANOTHER FREELOADER.
IN AMERICA, WE DON'T BEG AND STEAL. WE GET A *JOB.*
I *HAVE* A JOB! MY PAY IS JUST ENOUGH TO FEED MY KIDS. *THIS* IS HOW I MANAGE FOR MYSELF.
BUT WHO WOULD PAY SO *LITTLE* THAT YOU HAVE TO EAT OUT OF A--
DAMMIT! A HERO SHOULD BE ABLE TO *FIX* THIS!
WHERE DO YOU WORK?!

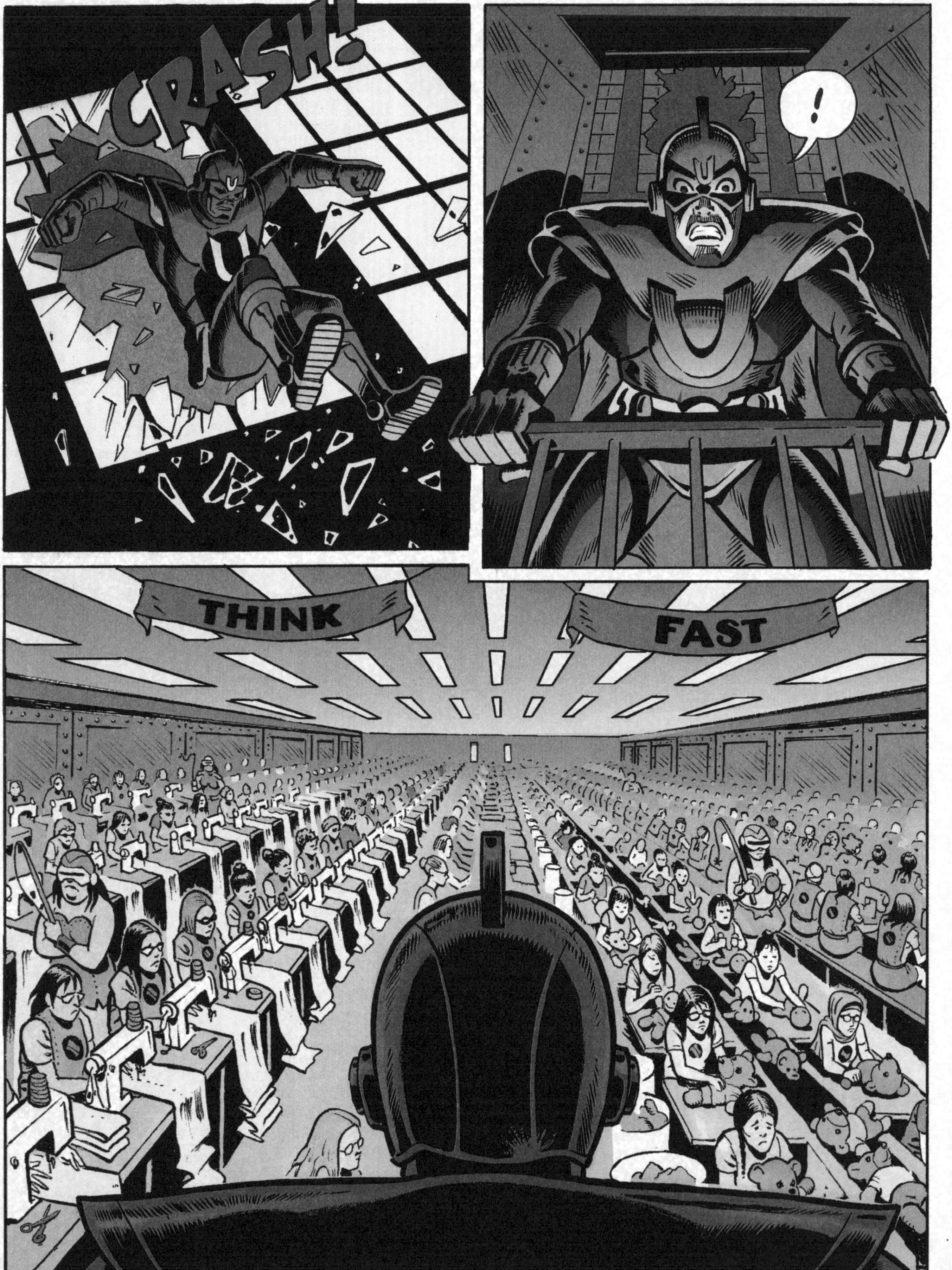
CRASH!
!
THINK
FAST

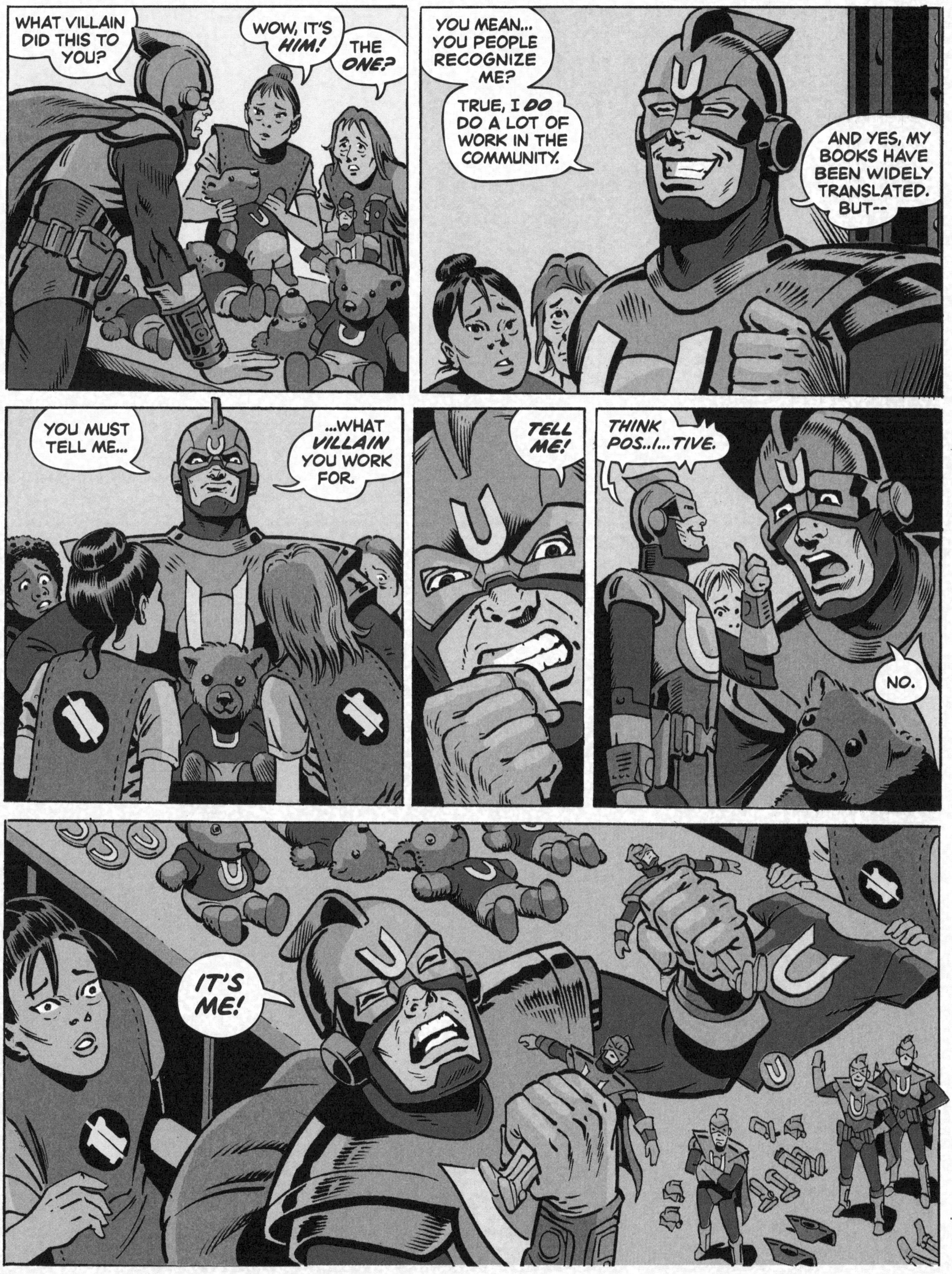
WHAT VILLAIN DID THIS TO YOU?
WOW, IT'S *HIM!*
THE *ONE?*
YOU MEAN... YOU PEOPLE RECOGNIZE ME?
TRUE, I *DO* DO A LOT OF WORK IN THE COMMUNITY.
AND YES, MY BOOKS HAVE BEEN WIDELY TRANSLATED. BUT--
YOU MUST TELL ME...
...WHAT *VILLAIN* YOU WORK FOR.
TELL ME!
THINK POS..I...TIVE.
NO.
IT'S ME!

Fantastic Facts

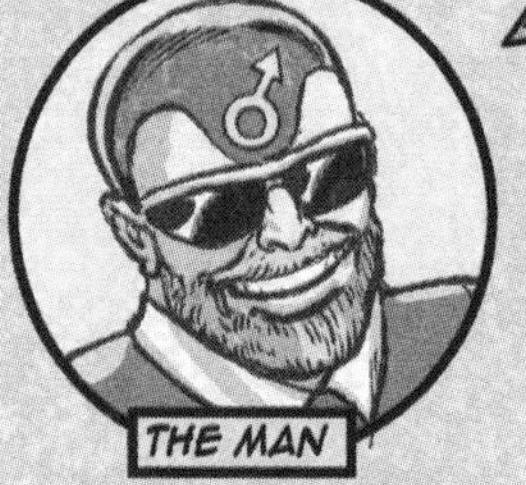
THE MAN

GRAB YOUR BOOTSTRAPS!

THIRTY YEARS AGO, CORPORATE ***CEOS*** LIKE ***THE MAN*** WERE PAID ONLY AROUND ***78 TIMES*** MORE THAN MINIMUM WAGE EARNERS. BUT THANKS TO THE HARD WORK OF ***THE JUST US LEAGUE***, TODAY'S ***CEOS*** EARN OVER ***4000 TIMES*** MORE! IN FACT, THEY CAN MAKE MORE IN ONE YEAR THAN ***AVERAGE EARNERS*** (NOT THE LOWEST) MAKE IN ***90*** YEARS! THEY'RE ***THAT*** GOOD.

REACH FOR THE SKY!

IF THE ***USA*** MAINTAINED THE SAME INCOME DISTRIBUTION WE HAD IN THE ***1970S***, HEROES IN THE WORK FORCE WOULD EARN AT LEAST THREE TIMES AS MUCH AS THEY DO TODAY -- AVERAGING ABOUT ***$120,000*** INSTEAD OF TODAY'S ***$40,000***. AS OF ***2007***, INCOME INEQUALITY WAS HIGHER THAN IN ANY YEAR ON RECORD, SAVE ONE: ***1928***. HAPPY DAYS ARE HERE AGAIN!

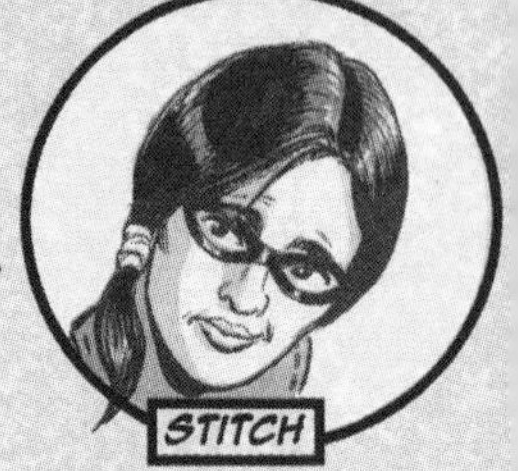
STITCH

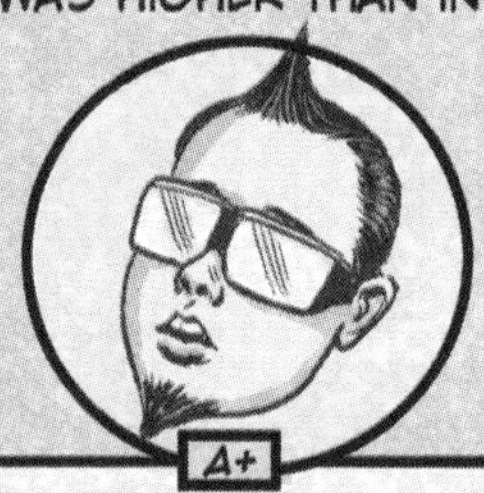
A+

DREAM BIG!

IN THE LAST ***30*** YEARS, THE AMERICAN DREAM HAS GROWN INCREASINGLY OUT OF REACH FOR MORE AND MORE PEOPLE -- UNLESS THEY DON'T LIVE IN AMERICA. TODAY A POOR CHILD BORN IN GERMANY, FRANCE, CANADA, OR SCANDINAVIA ACTUALLY HAS A BETTER CHANCE OF JOINING THE MIDDLE CLASS IN ADULTHOOD THAN A CHILD BORN POOR IN THE GOOD OL' ***US*** OF ***A***. TAKE THAT, YOU CHEESE-EATING SOCIALISTS!

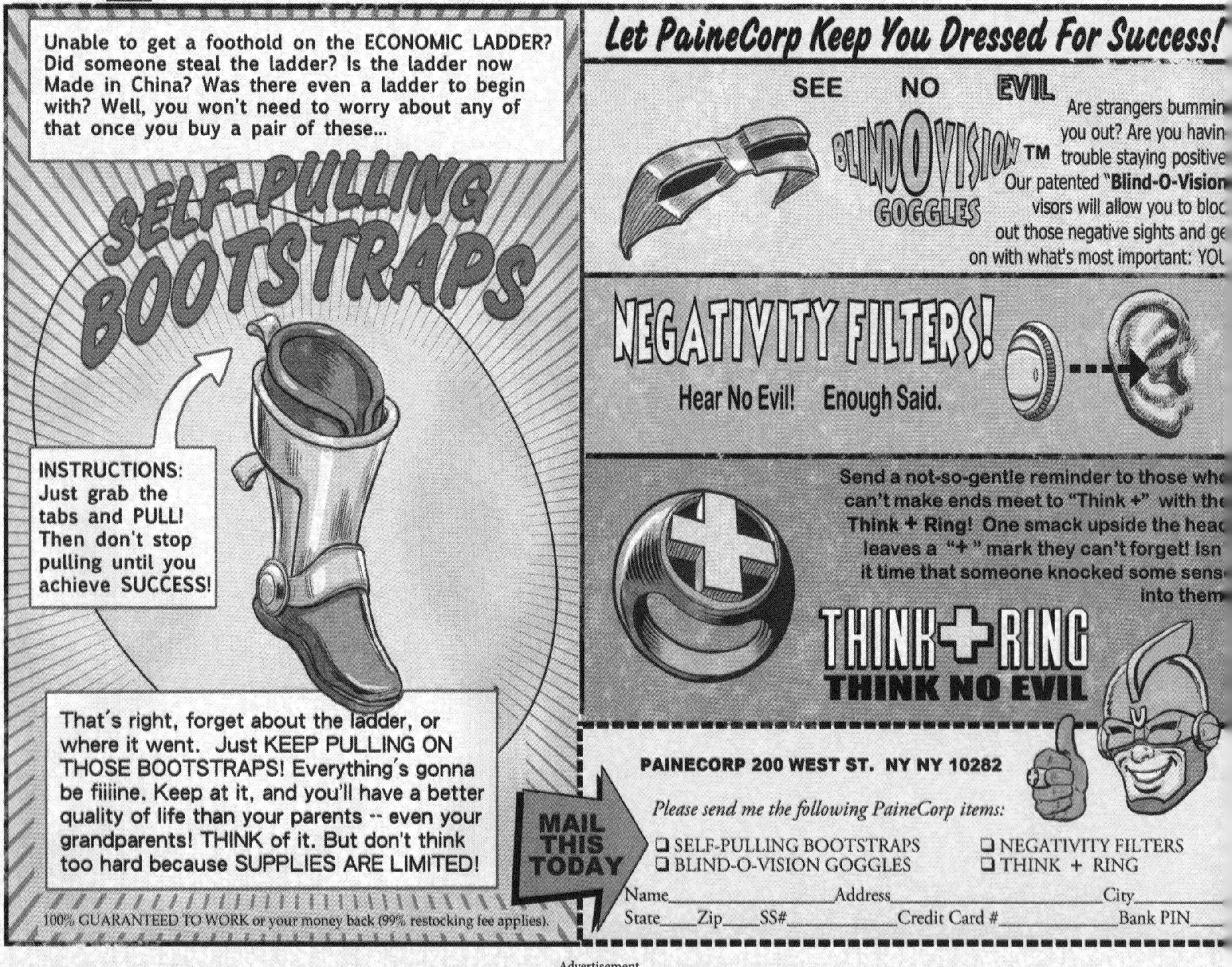
Unable to get a foothold on the ECONOMIC LADDER? Did someone steal the ladder? Is the ladder now Made in China? Was there even a ladder to begin with? Well, you won't need to worry about any of that once you buy a pair of these...
SELF-PULLING BOOTSTRAPS
INSTRUCTIONS: Just grab the tabs and PULL! Then don't stop pulling until you achieve SUCCESS!
That's right, forget about the ladder, or where it went. Just KEEP PULLING ON THOSE BOOTSTRAPS! Everything's gonna be fiiiine. Keep at it, and you'll have a better quality of life than your parents -- even your grandparents! THINK of it. But don't think too hard because SUPPLIES ARE LIMITED!
100% GUARANTEED TO WORK or your money back (99% restocking fee applies).
Let PaineCorp Keep You Dressed For Success!
SEE NO EVIL
BLIND O VISION™ GOGGLES
Are strangers bummin
you out? Are you havin
trouble staying positive
Our patented "Blind-O-Vision
visors will allow you to bloc
out those negative sights and ge
on with what's most important: YOU
NEGATIVITY FILTERS!
Hear No Evil! Enough Said.
Send a not-so-gentle reminder to those wh
can't make ends meet to "Think +" with th
Think + Ring! One smack upside the hea
leaves a "+" mark they can't forget! Isn
it time that someone knocked some sens
into them
THINK + RING
THINK NO EVIL
PAINECORP 200 WEST ST. NY NY 10282
MAIL THIS TODAY
Please send me the following PaineCorp items:
❑ SELF-PULLING BOOTSTRAPS ❑ NEGATIVITY FILTERS
❑ BLIND-O-VISION GOGGLES ❑ THINK + RING
Name______ Address______ City______
State____ Zip____ SS#______ Credit Card #______ Bank PIN______

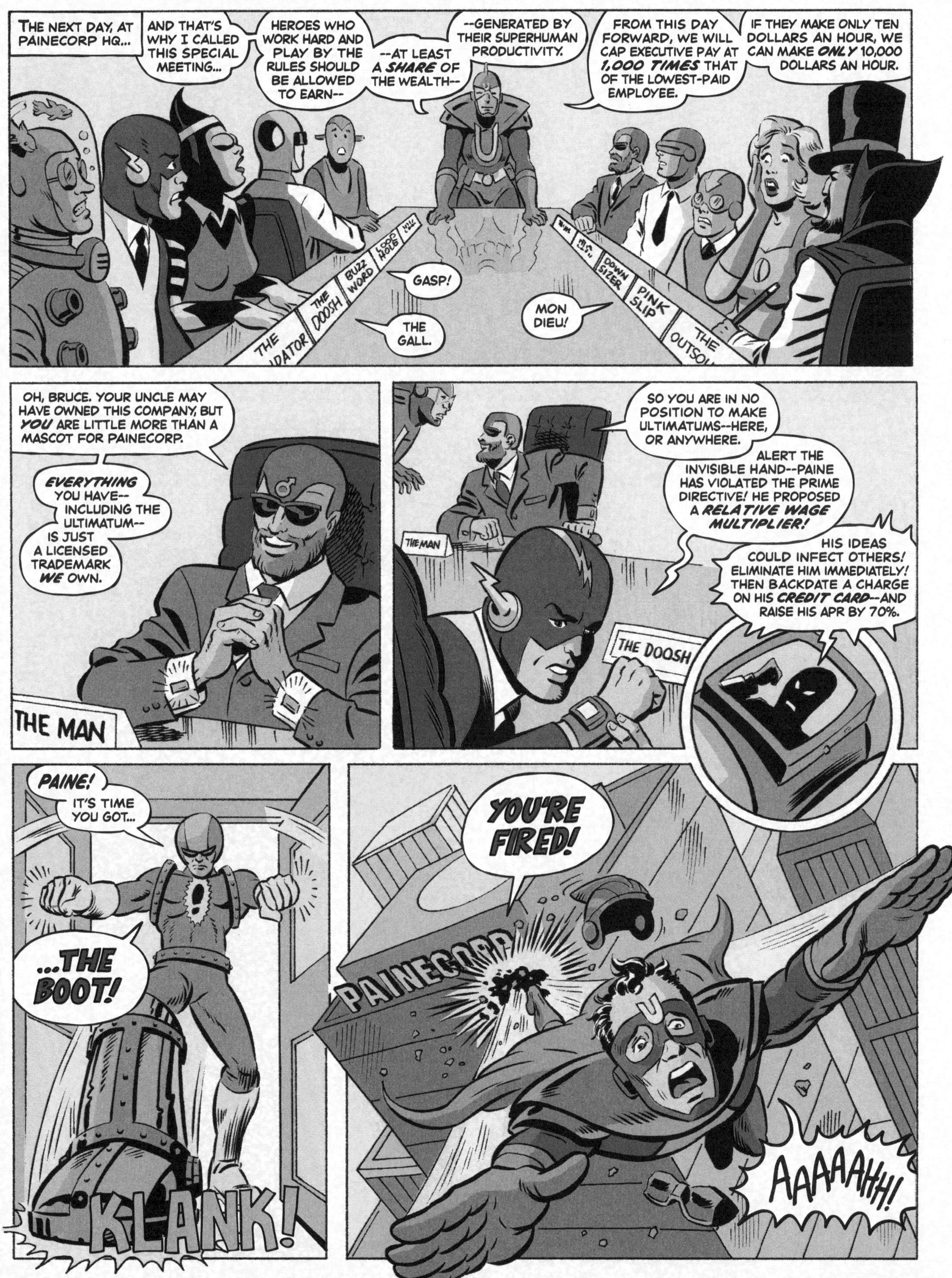
THE NEXT DAY, AT PAINECORP HQ...
AND THAT'S WHY I CALLED THIS SPECIAL MEETING...
HEROES WHO WORK HARD AND PLAY BY THE RULES SHOULD BE ALLOWED TO EARN--
--AT LEAST A SHARE OF THE WEALTH--
--GENERATED BY THEIR SUPERHUMAN PRODUCTIVITY.
FROM THIS DAY FORWARD, WE WILL CAP EXECUTIVE PAY AT 1,000 TIMES THAT OF THE LOWEST-PAID EMPLOYEE.
IF THEY MAKE ONLY TEN DOLLARS AN HOUR, WE CAN MAKE ONLY 10,000 DOLLARS AN HOUR.
GASP!
THE GALL.
MON DIEU!
THE DOOSH
BUZZ WORD
LOOP HOLE
DOWN SIZER
PINK SLIP
OH, BRUCE. YOUR UNCLE MAY HAVE OWNED THIS COMPANY, BUT YOU ARE LITTLE MORE THAN A MASCOT FOR PAINECORP.
EVERYTHING YOU HAVE-- INCLUDING THE ULTIMATUM-- IS JUST A LICENSED TRADEMARK WE OWN.
THE MAN
SO YOU ARE IN NO POSITION TO MAKE ULTIMATUMS--HERE, OR ANYWHERE.
ALERT THE INVISIBLE HAND--PAINE HAS VIOLATED THE PRIME DIRECTIVE! HE PROPOSED A RELATIVE WAGE MULTIPLIER!
HIS IDEAS COULD INFECT OTHERS! ELIMINATE HIM IMMEDIATELY! THEN BACKDATE A CHARGE ON HIS CREDIT CARD--AND RAISE HIS APR BY 70%.
THE MAN
THE DOOSH
PAINE! IT'S TIME YOU GOT...
...THE BOOT!
KLANK!
YOU'RE FIRED!
PAINECORP
AAAAAHH!

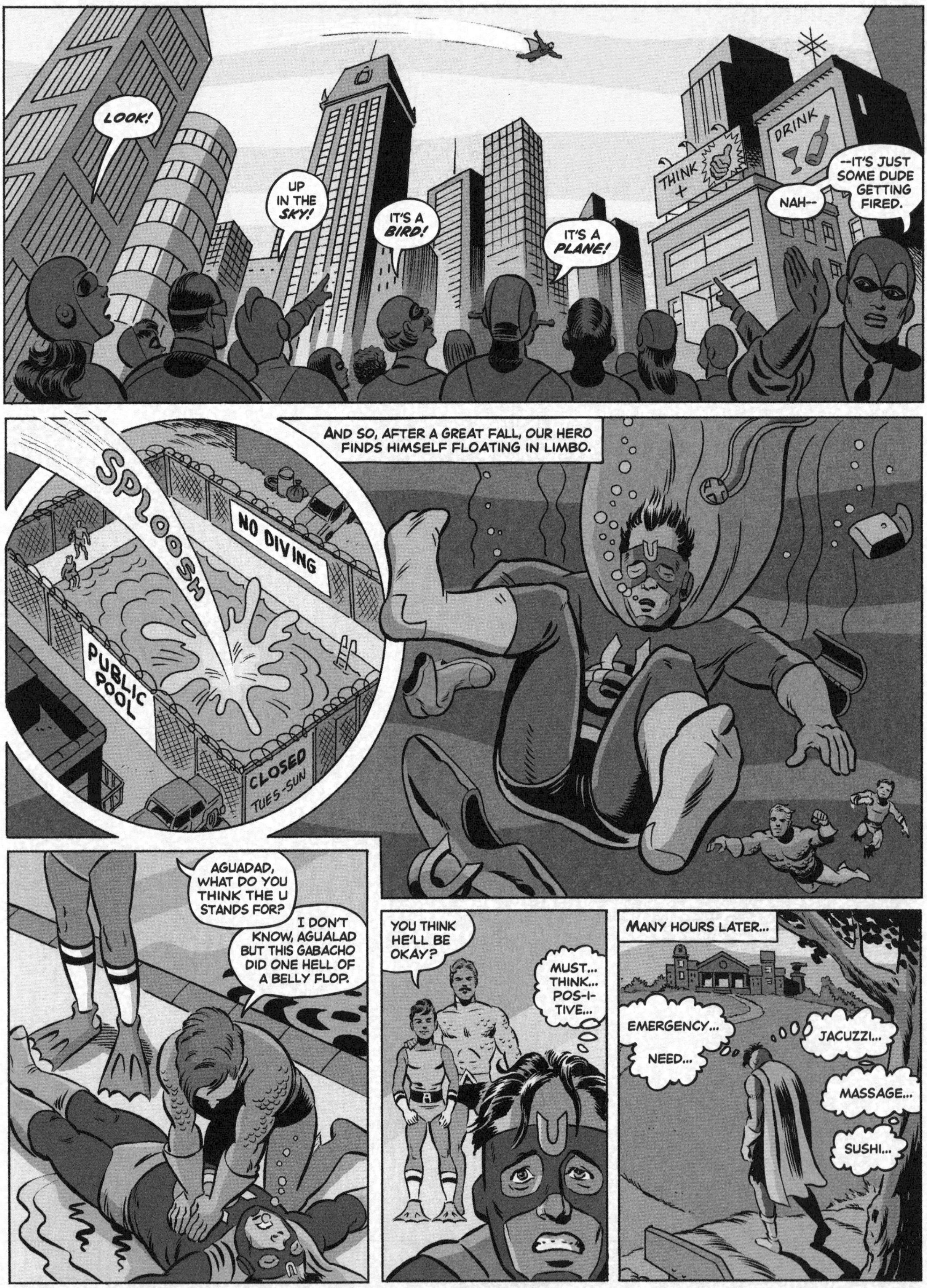
LOOK!
UP IN THE SKY!
IT'S A BIRD!
IT'S A PLANE!
THINK +
DRINK
NAH--
--IT'S JUST SOME DUDE GETTING FIRED.
AND SO, AFTER A GREAT FALL, OUR HERO FINDS HIMSELF FLOATING IN LIMBO.
SPLOOSH
NO DIVING
PUBLIC POOL
CLOSED TUES-SUN
AGUADAD, WHAT DO YOU THINK THE U STANDS FOR?
I DON'T KNOW, AGUALAD BUT THIS GABACHO DID ONE HELL OF A BELLY FLOP.
YOU THINK HE'LL BE OKAY?
MUST... THINK... POS-I-TIVE...
MANY HOURS LATER...
EMERGENCY...
NEED...
JACUZZI...
MASSAGE...
SUSHI...

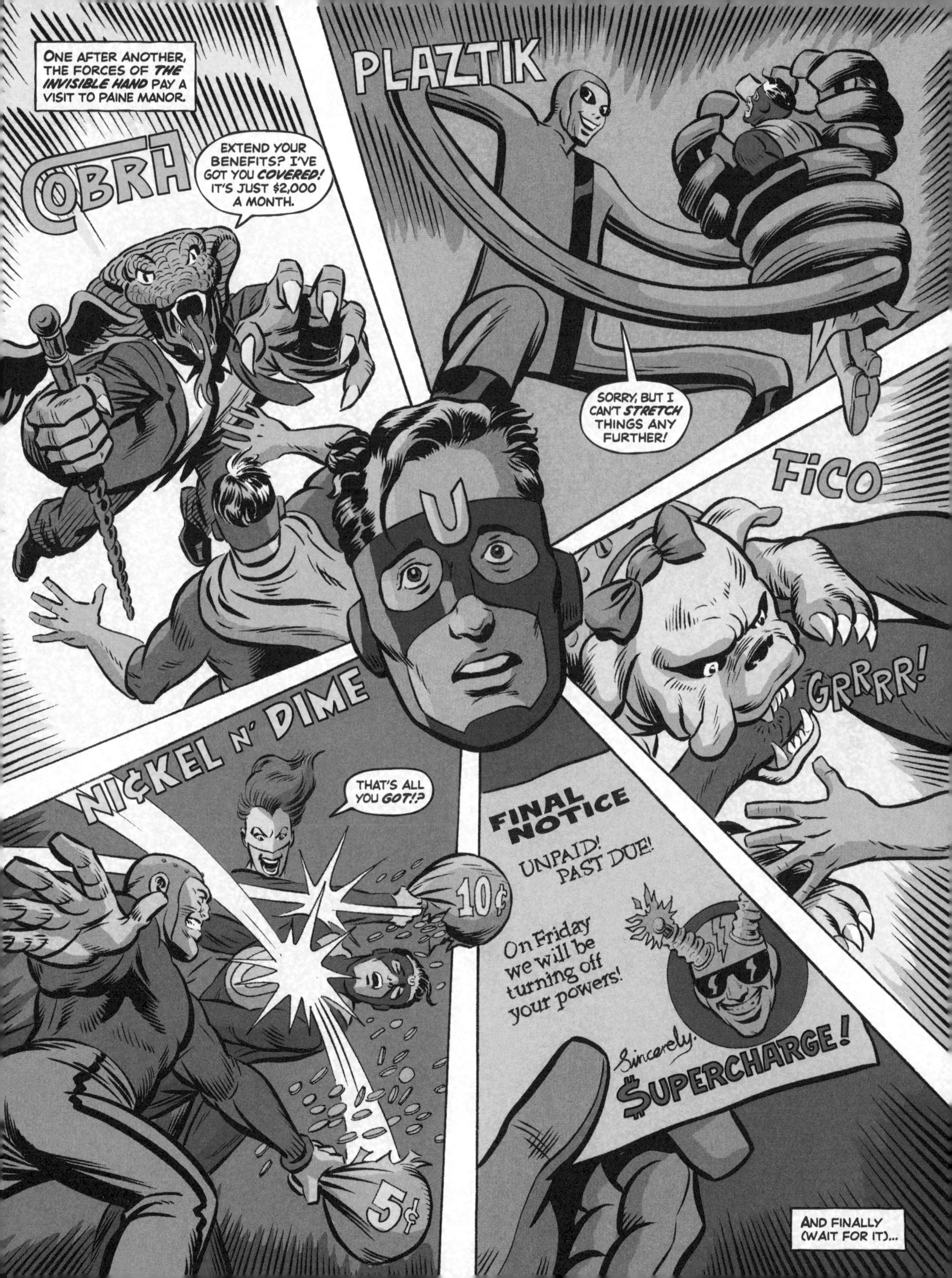
ONE AFTER ANOTHER, THE FORCES OF THE INVISIBLE HAND PAY A VISIT TO PAINE MANOR.
COBRA
EXTEND YOUR BENEFITS? I'VE GOT YOU COVERED! IT'S JUST $2,000 A MONTH.
PLAZTIK
SORRY, BUT I CAN'T STRETCH THINGS ANY FURTHER!
FICO
GRRRR!
NI¢KEL N' DIME
THAT'S ALL YOU GOT!?
10¢
5¢
FINAL NOTICE
UNPAID! PAST DUE!
On Friday we will be turning off your powers!
Sincerely,
$UPERCHARGE!
AND FINALLY (WAIT FOR IT)...

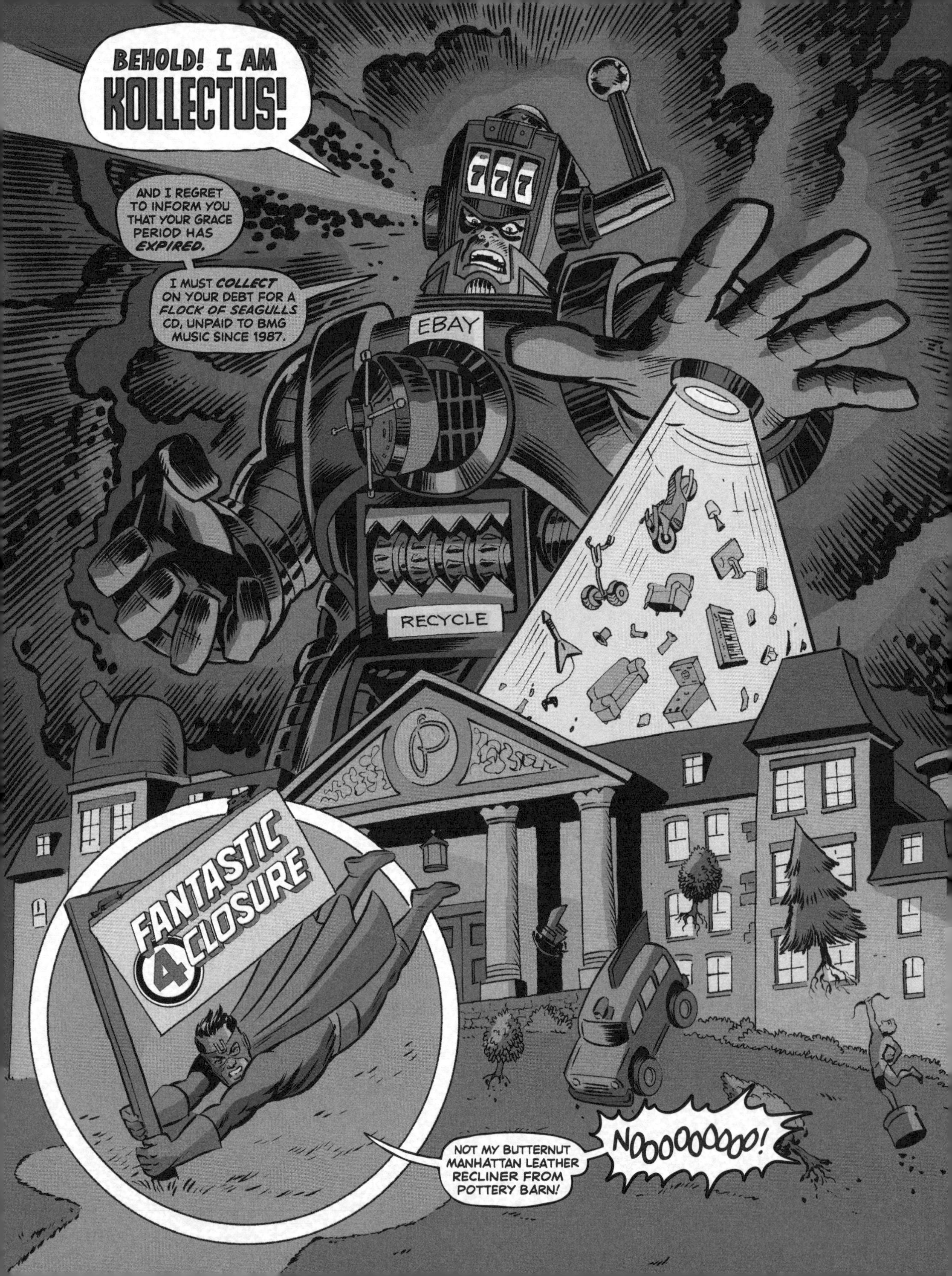

BEHOLD! I AM KOLLECTUS!
AND I REGRET TO INFORM YOU THAT YOUR GRACE PERIOD HAS *EXPIRED.*
I MUST *COLLECT* ON YOUR DEBT FOR A *FLOCK OF SEAGULLS* CD, UNPAID TO BMG MUSIC SINCE 1987.
EBAY
RECYCLE
FANTASTIC 4 CLOSURE
NOT MY BUTTERNUT MANHATTAN LEATHER RECLINER FROM POTTERY BARN!
NOOOOOOOOO!

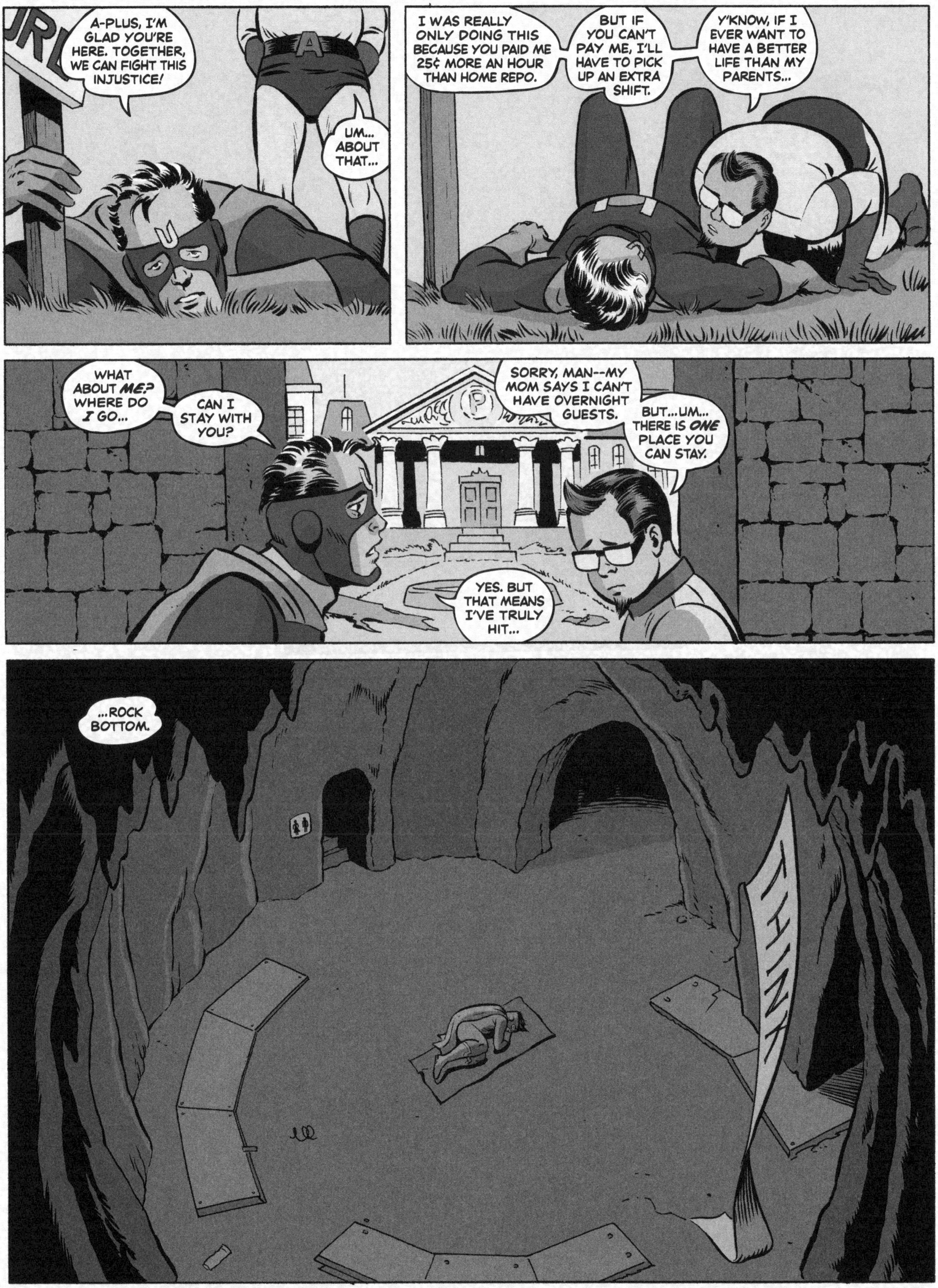
A-PLUS, I'M GLAD YOU'RE HERE. TOGETHER, WE CAN FIGHT THIS INJUSTICE!
UM... ABOUT THAT...
I WAS REALLY ONLY DOING THIS BECAUSE YOU PAID ME 25¢ MORE AN HOUR THAN HOME REPO.
BUT IF YOU CAN'T PAY ME, I'LL HAVE TO PICK UP AN EXTRA SHIFT.
Y'KNOW, IF I EVER WANT TO HAVE A BETTER LIFE THAN MY PARENTS...
WHAT ABOUT *ME?* WHERE DO *I* GO...
CAN I STAY WITH YOU?
SORRY, MAN--MY MOM SAYS I CAN'T HAVE OVERNIGHT GUESTS.
BUT...UM... THERE IS *ONE* PLACE YOU CAN STAY.
YES. BUT THAT MEANS I'VE TRULY HIT...
...ROCK BOTTOM.
THINK

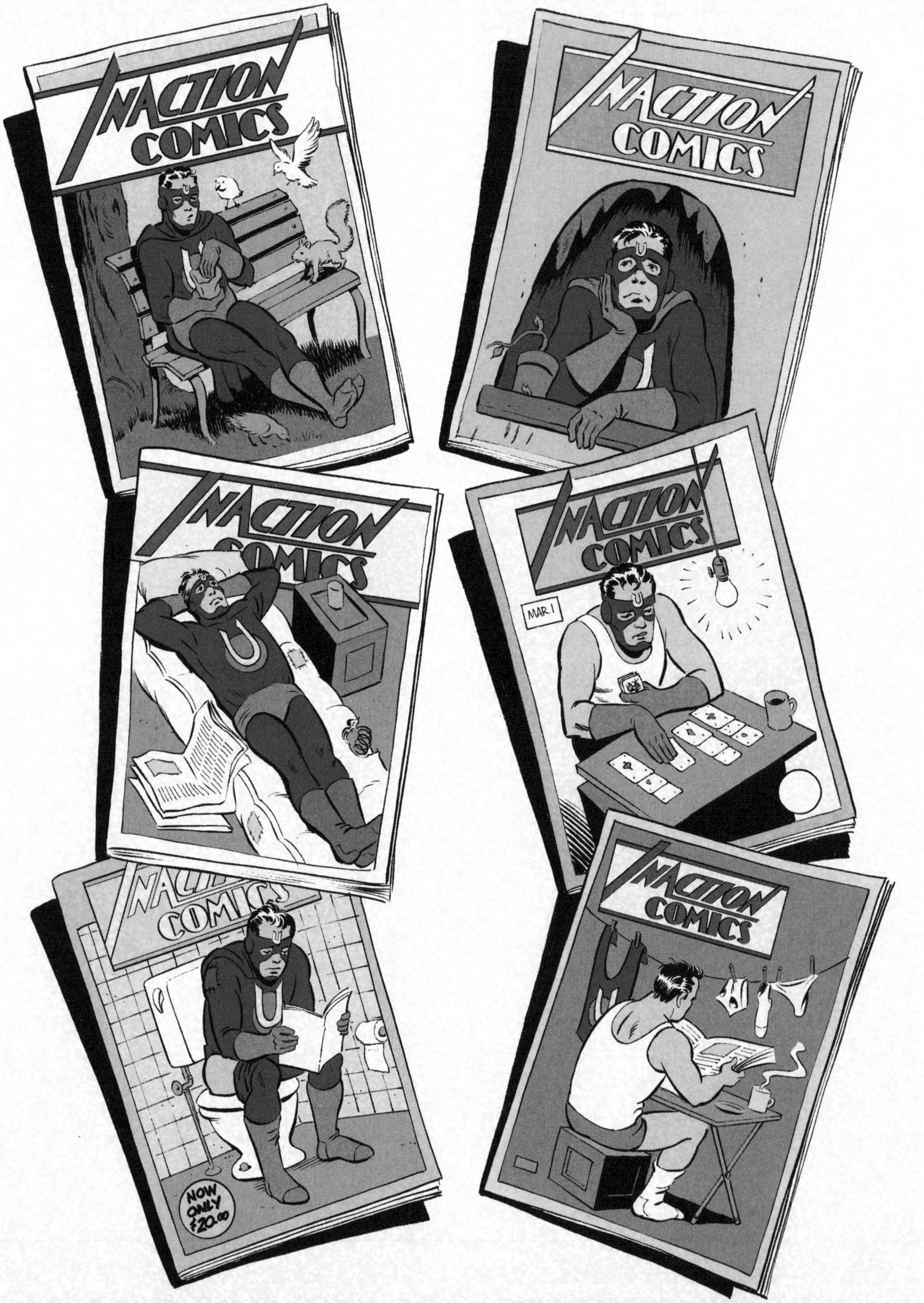
INACTION COMICS
INACTION COMICS
INACTION COMICS
INACTION COMICS
MAR. 1
INACTION COMICS
NOW ONLY $20.00
INACTION COMICS

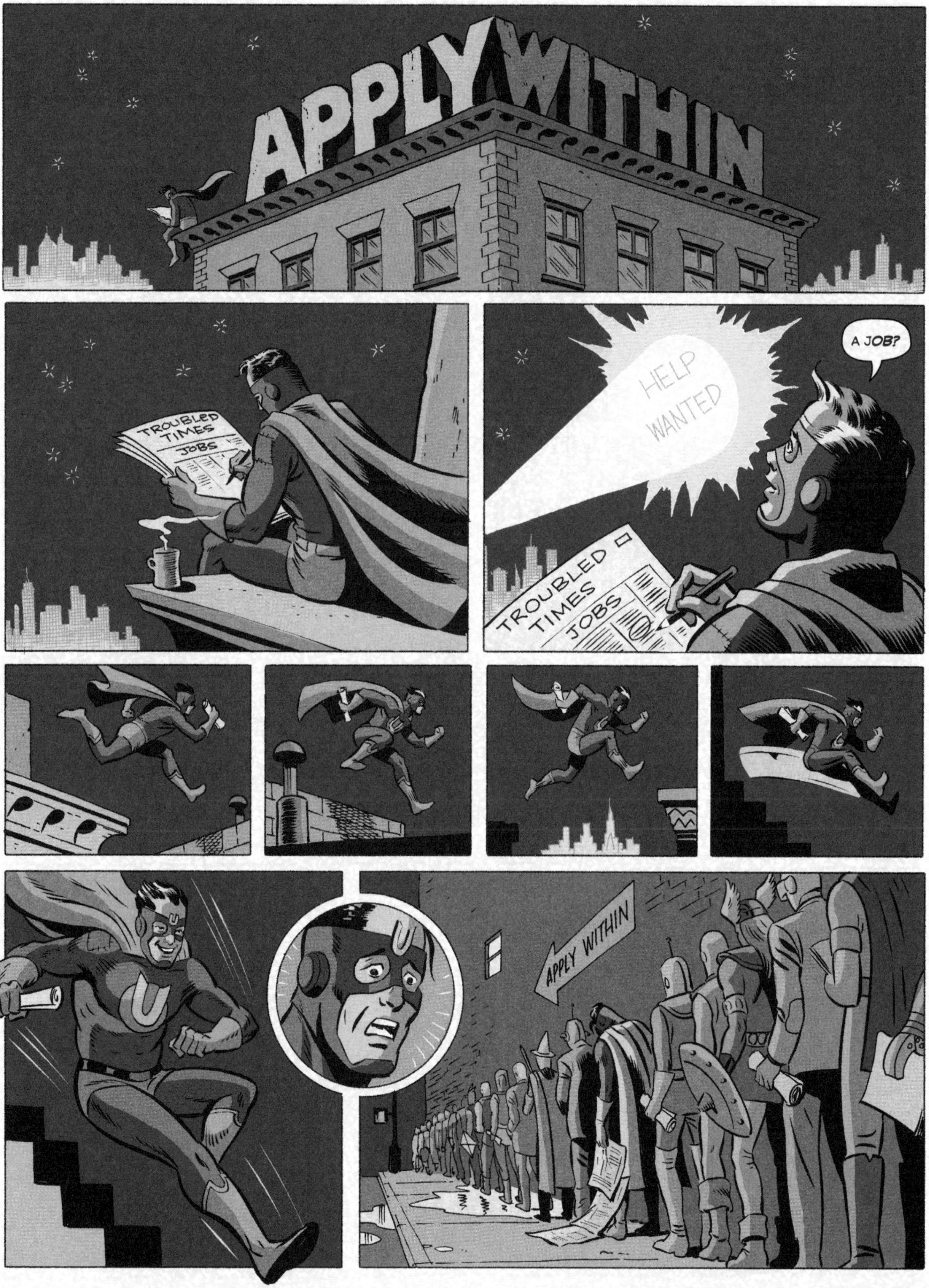
APPLY WITHIN
TROUBLED TIMES
JOBS
HELP WANTED
A JOB?
TROUBLED TIMES
JOBS
APPLY WITHIN

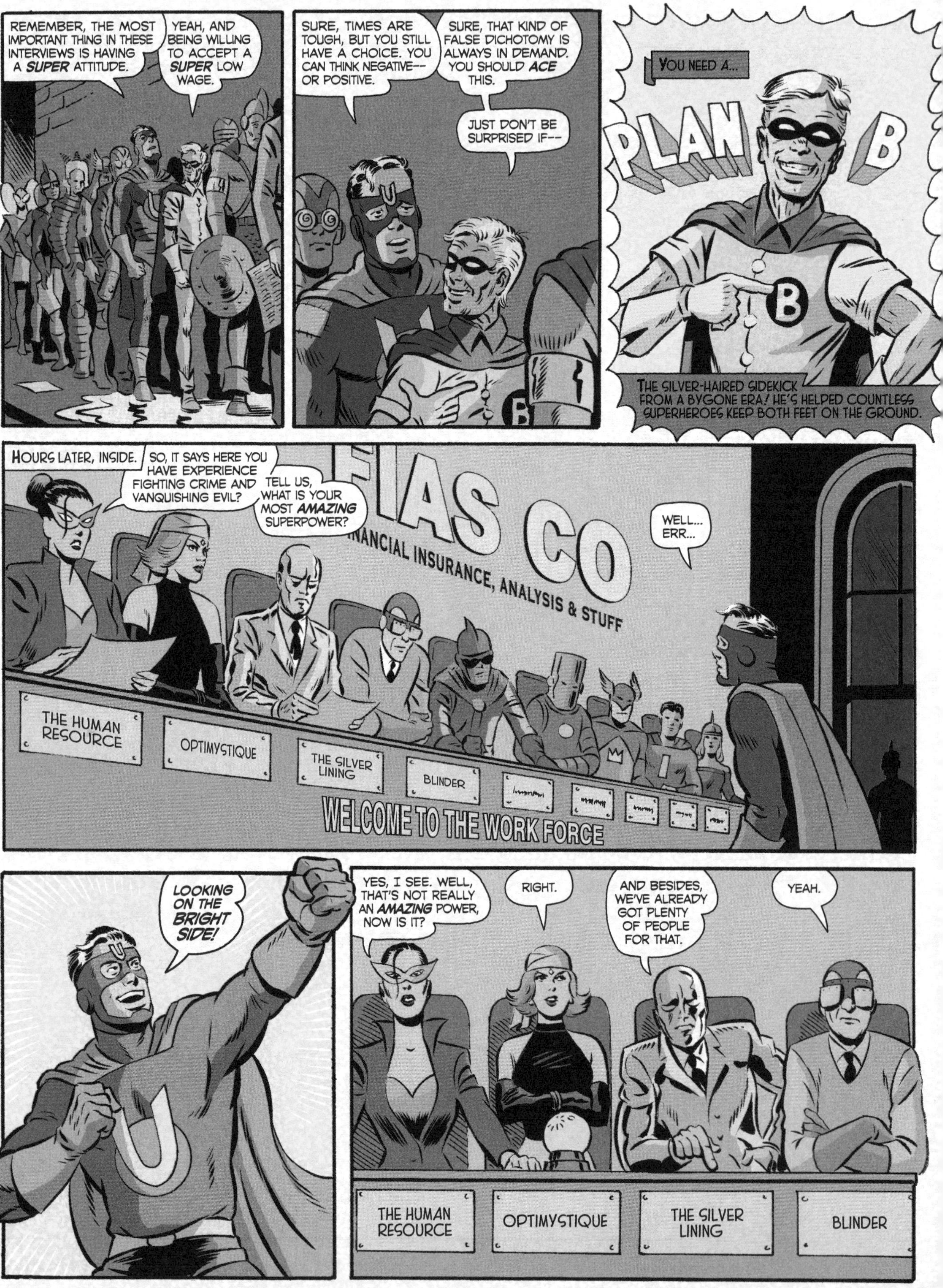

REMEMBER, THE MOST IMPORTANT THING IN THESE INTERVIEWS IS HAVING A *SUPER* ATTITUDE.
YEAH, AND BEING WILLING TO ACCEPT A *SUPER* LOW WAGE.
SURE, TIMES ARE TOUGH, BUT YOU STILL HAVE A CHOICE. YOU CAN THINK NEGATIVE-- OR POSITIVE.
SURE, THAT KIND OF FALSE DICHOTOMY IS ALWAYS IN DEMAND. YOU SHOULD *ACE* THIS.
JUST DON'T BE SURPRISED IF--
YOU NEED A...
PLAN B
B
THE SILVER-HAIRED SIDEKICK FROM A BYGONE ERA! HE'S HELPED COUNTLESS SUPERHEROES KEEP BOTH FEET ON THE GROUND.
HOURS LATER, INSIDE.
SO, IT SAYS HERE YOU HAVE EXPERIENCE FIGHTING CRIME AND VANQUISHING EVIL?
TELL US, WHAT IS YOUR MOST *AMAZING* SUPERPOWER?
FIAS CO
FINANCIAL INSURANCE, ANALYSIS & STUFF
WELL... ERR...
THE HUMAN RESOURCE
OPTIMYSTIQUE
THE SILVER LINING
BLINDER
WELCOME TO THE WORK FORCE
LOOKING ON THE BRIGHT SIDE!
YES, I SEE. WELL, THAT'S NOT REALLY AN *AMAZING* POWER, NOW IS IT?
RIGHT.
AND BESIDES, WE'VE ALREADY GOT PLENTY OF PEOPLE FOR THAT.
YEAH.
THE HUMAN RESOURCE
OPTIMYSTIQUE
THE SILVER LINING
BLINDER

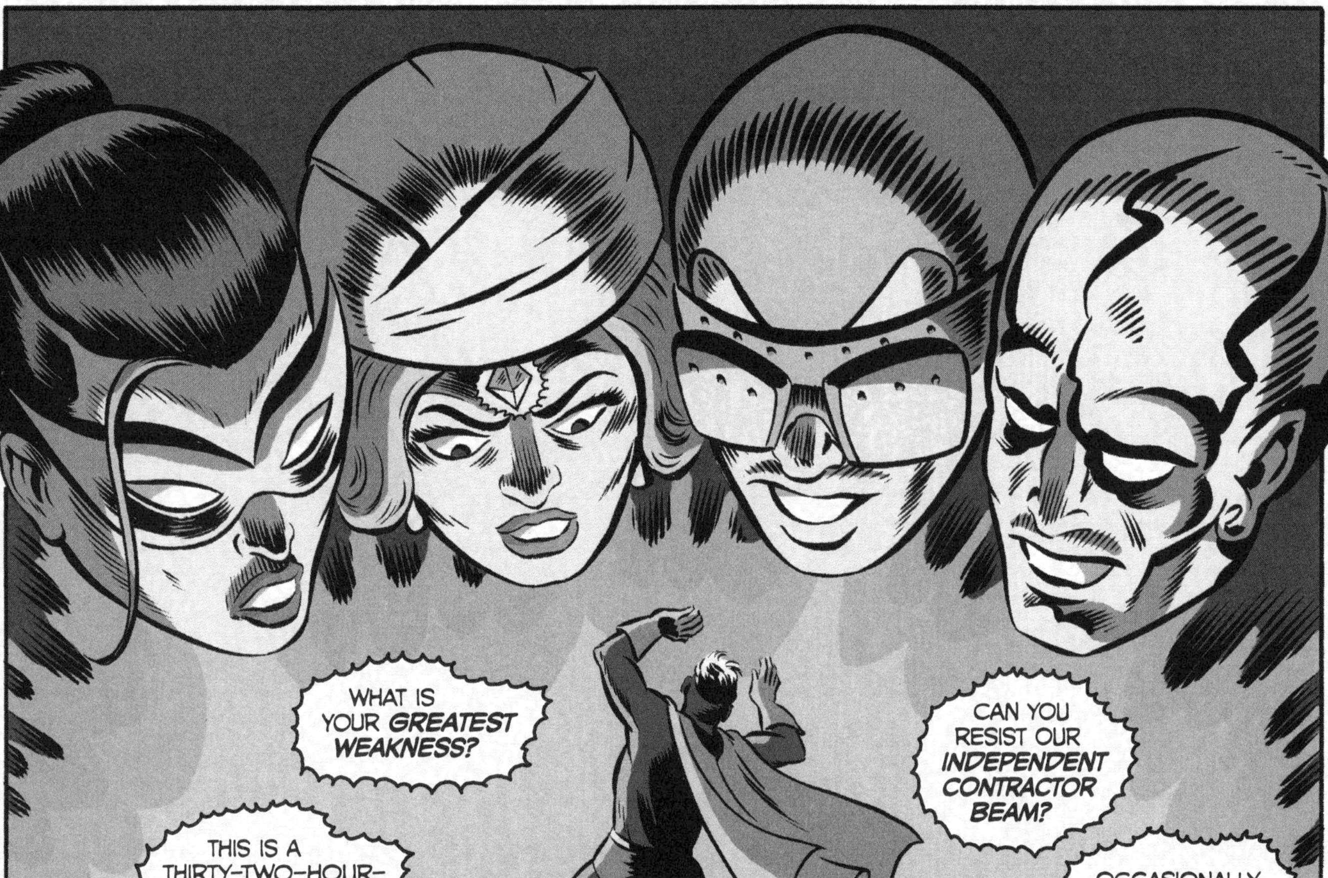
WHAT IS YOUR GREATEST WEAKNESS?
CAN YOU RESIST OUR INDEPENDENT CONTRACTOR BEAM?
THIS IS A THIRTY-TWO-HOUR-A-WEEK SALARIED POSITION.
OCCASIONALLY WE DO WORK FOR VILLAINS.
NO OVERTIME! NO BENEFITS!
IS THAT A PROBLEM?

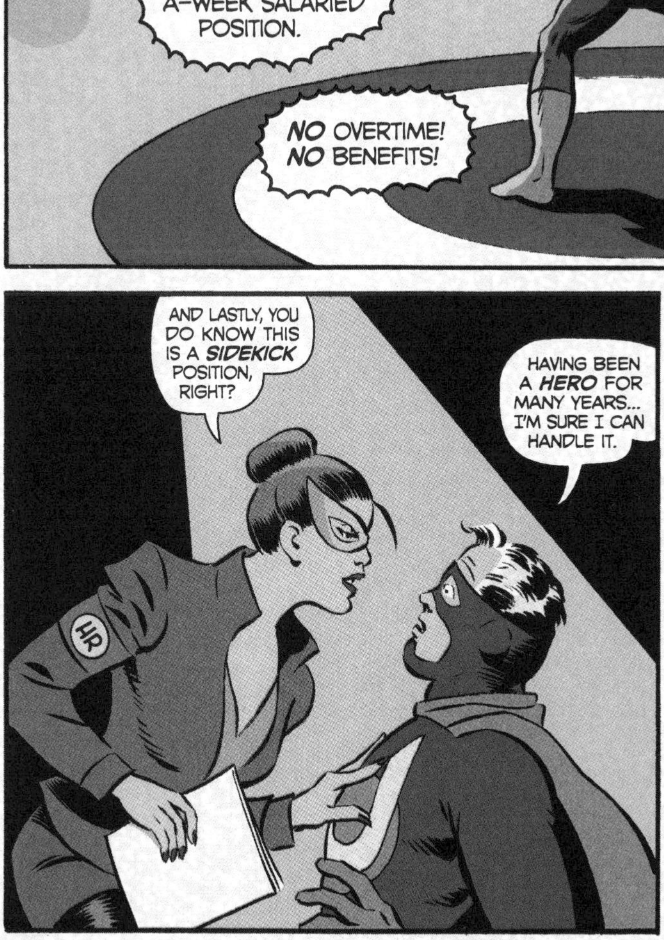
AND LASTLY, YOU DO KNOW THIS IS A SIDEKICK POSITION, RIGHT?
HAVING BEEN A HERO FOR MANY YEARS... I'M SURE I CAN HANDLE IT.

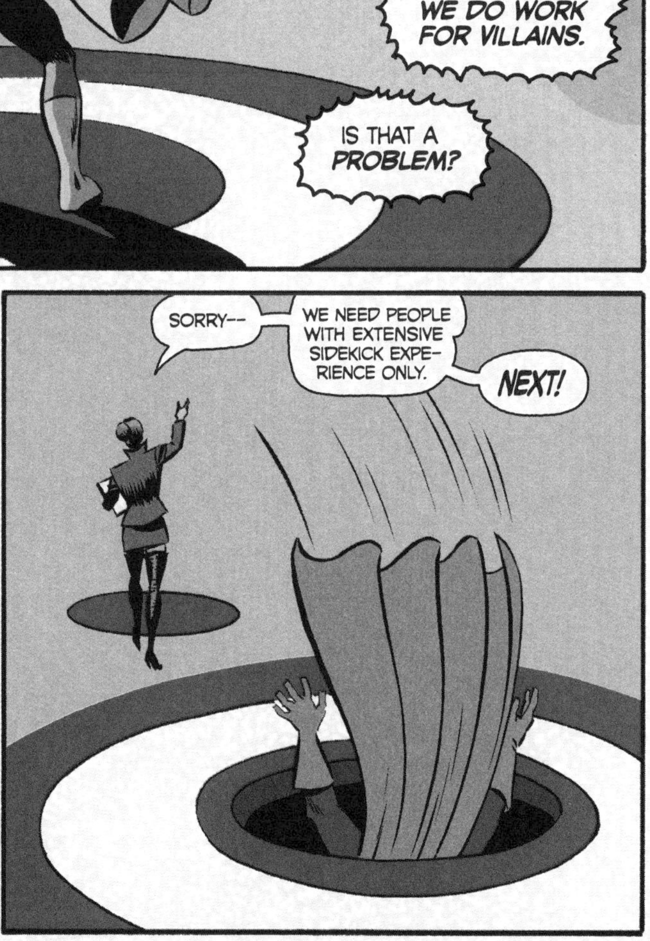
SORRY--
WE NEED PEOPLE WITH EXTENSIVE SIDEKICK EXPERIENCE ONLY.
NEXT!

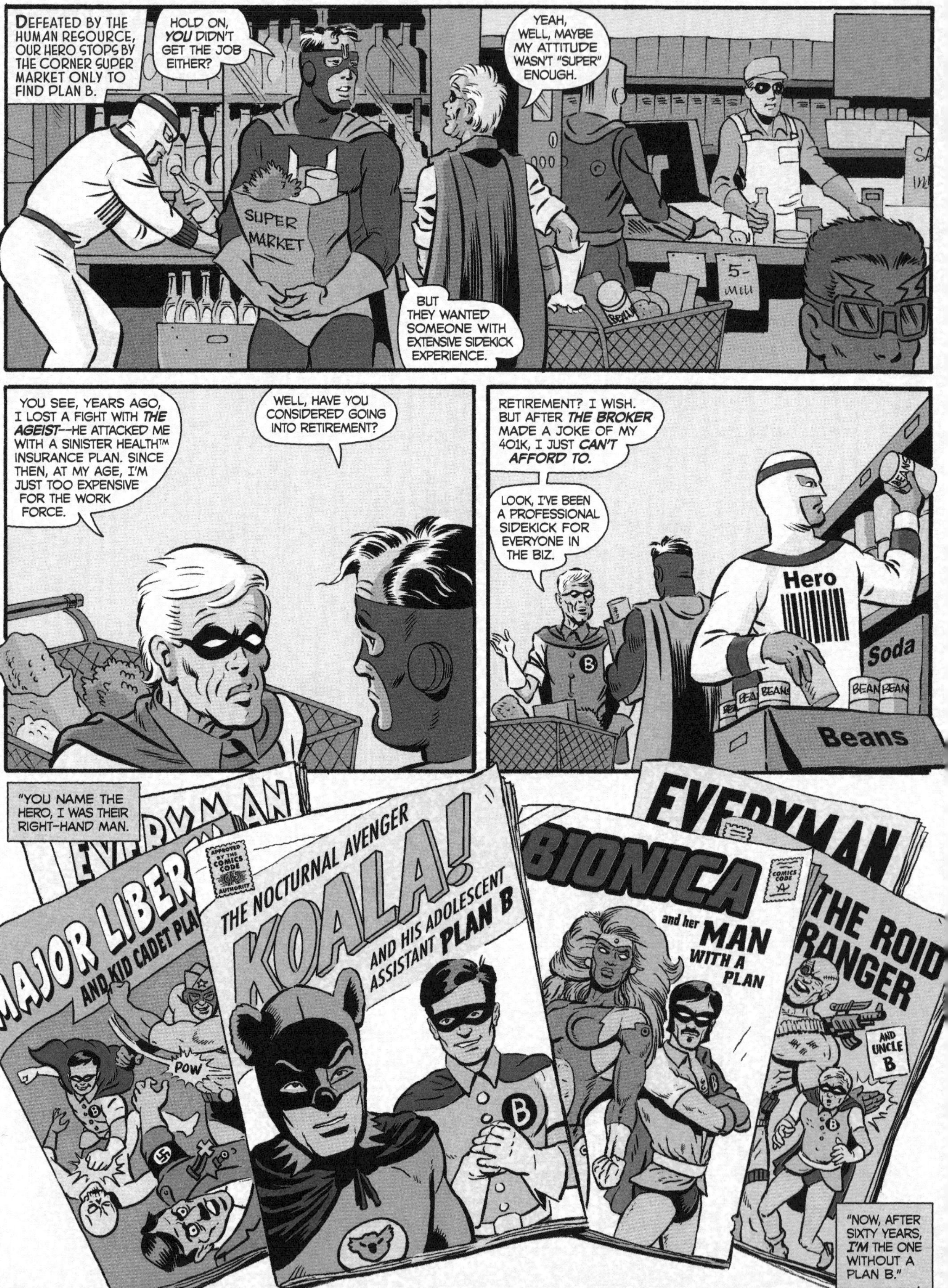
DEFEATED BY THE HUMAN RESOURCE, OUR HERO STOPS BY THE CORNER SUPER MARKET ONLY TO FIND PLAN B.
HOLD ON, *YOU* DIDN'T GET THE JOB EITHER?
YEAH, WELL, MAYBE MY ATTITUDE WASN'T "SUPER" ENOUGH.
BUT THEY WANTED SOMEONE WITH EXTENSIVE SIDEKICK EXPERIENCE.
SUPER MARKET
YOU SEE, YEARS AGO, I LOST A FIGHT WITH ***THE AGEIST***--HE ATTACKED ME WITH A SINISTER HEALTH™ INSURANCE PLAN. SINCE THEN, AT MY AGE, I'M JUST TOO EXPENSIVE FOR THE WORK FORCE.
WELL, HAVE YOU CONSIDERED GOING INTO RETIREMENT?
RETIREMENT? I WISH. BUT AFTER ***THE BROKER*** MADE A JOKE OF MY 401K, I JUST ***CAN'T AFFORD TO.***
LOOK, I'VE BEEN A PROFESSIONAL SIDEKICK FOR EVERYONE IN THE BIZ.
Hero
Soda
Beans
"YOU NAME THE HERO, I WAS THEIR RIGHT-HAND MAN.
10¢
THE NOCTURNAL AVENGER
KOALA!
AND HIS ADOLESCENT ASSISTANT PLAN B
POW
BIONICA
and her MAN WITH A PLAN
EVERYMAN
THE ROID RANGER
AND UNCLE B
"NOW, AFTER SIXTY YEARS, *I'M* THE ONE WITHOUT A PLAN B."

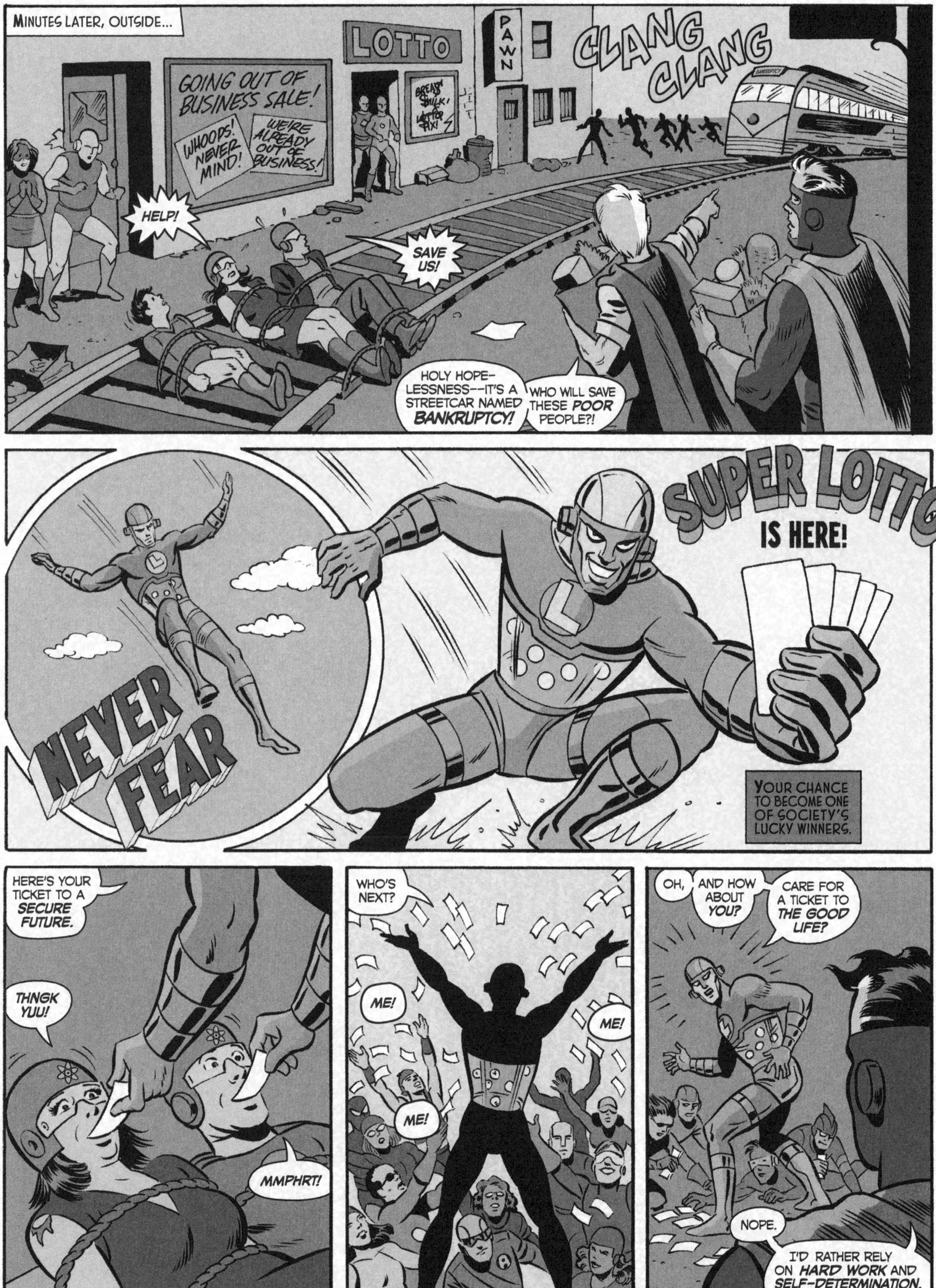
MINUTES LATER, OUTSIDE...
LOTTO
PAWN
GOING OUT OF BUSINESS SALE!
WHOOPS! NEVER MIND!
WE'RE ALREADY OUT OF BUSINESS!
CLANG CLANG
BANKRUPTCY
HELP!
SAVE US!
HOLY HOPE-LESSNESS--IT'S A STREETCAR NAMED BANKRUPTCY!
WHO WILL SAVE THESE POOR PEOPLE?!
NEVER FEAR
SUPER LOTTO IS HERE!
YOUR CHANCE TO BECOME ONE OF SOCIETY'S LUCKY WINNERS.
HERE'S YOUR TICKET TO A SECURE FUTURE.
THNGK YUU!
MMPHRT!
WHO'S NEXT?
ME!
ME!
ME!
OH,
AND HOW ABOUT YOU?
CARE FOR A TICKET TO THE GOOD LIFE?
NOPE.
I'D RATHER RELY ON HARD WORK AND SELF-DETERMINATION.

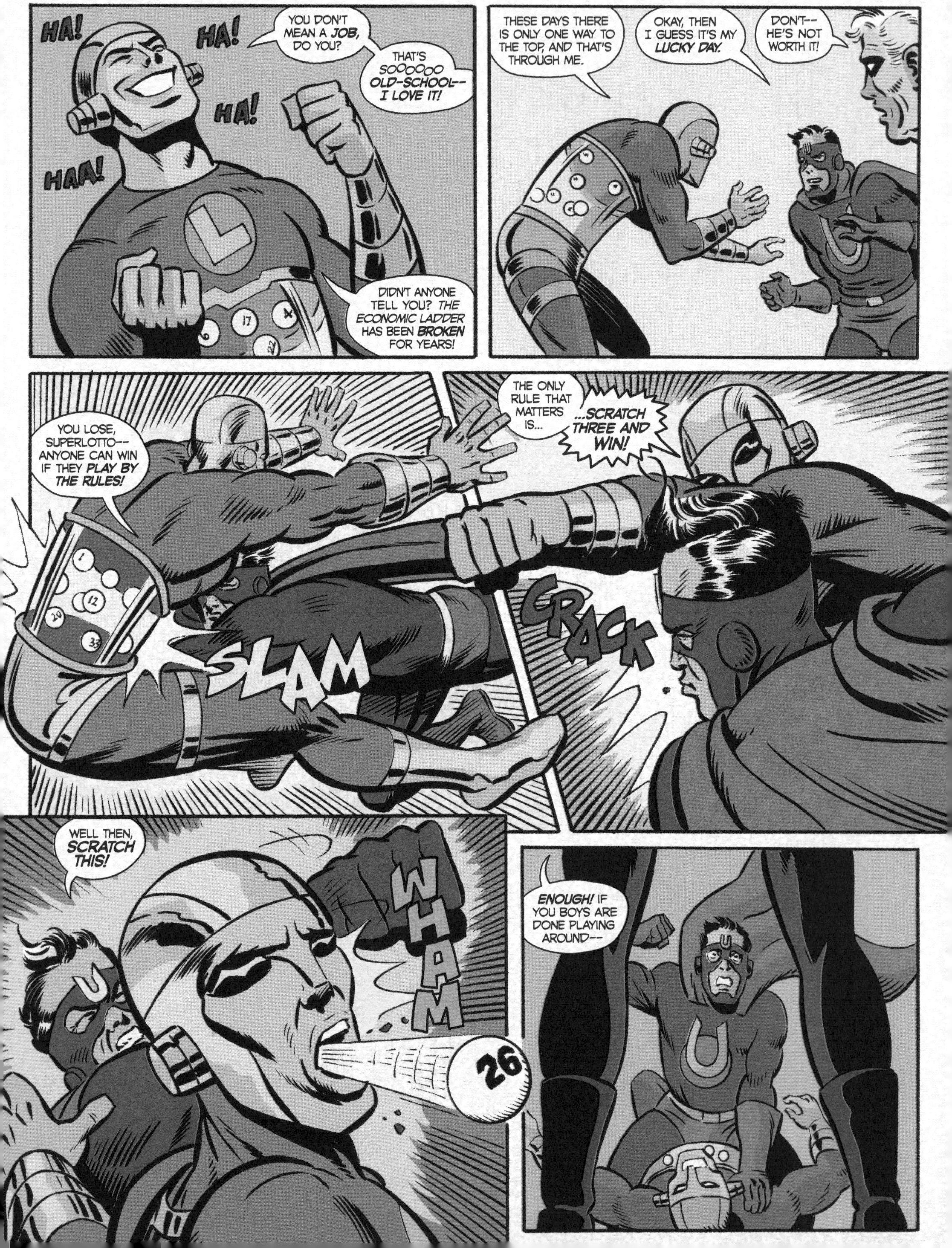
HA! HA! HA! HAA!
YOU DON'T MEAN A JOB, DO YOU?
THAT'S SOOOOOOO OLD-SCHOOL-- I LOVE IT!
DIDN'T ANYONE TELL YOU? THE ECONOMIC LADDER HAS BEEN BROKEN FOR YEARS!
THESE DAYS THERE IS ONLY ONE WAY TO THE TOP, AND THAT'S THROUGH ME.
OKAY, THEN I GUESS IT'S MY LUCKY DAY.
DON'T-- HE'S NOT WORTH IT!
YOU LOSE, SUPERLOTTO-- ANYONE CAN WIN IF THEY PLAY BY THE RULES!
SLAM
THE ONLY RULE THAT MATTERS IS...
...SCRATCH THREE AND WIN!
CRACK
WELL THEN, SCRATCH THIS!
WHAM
26
ENOUGH! IF YOU BOYS ARE DONE PLAYING AROUND--

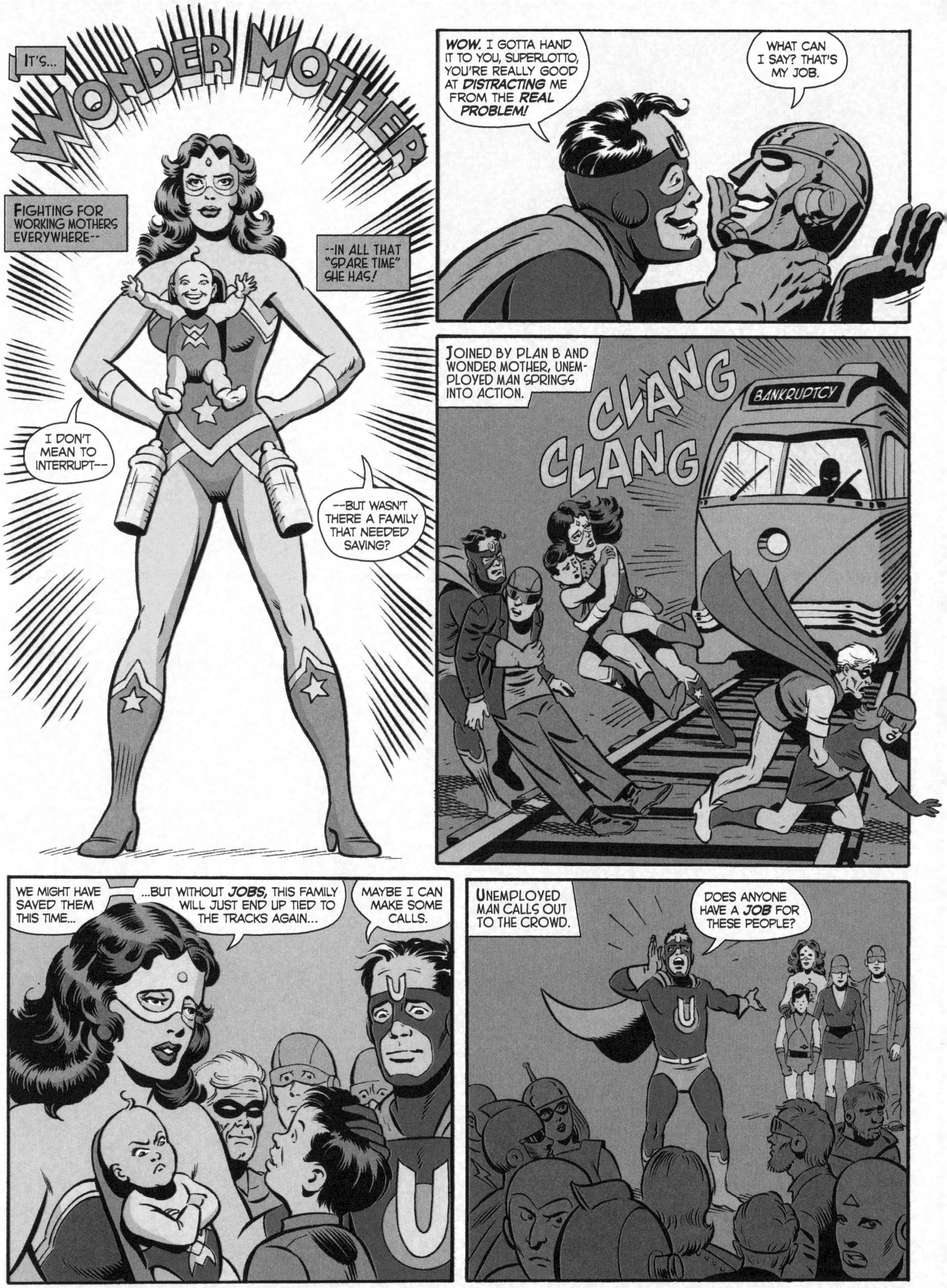

IT'S...
WONDER MOTHER
FIGHTING FOR WORKING MOTHERS EVERYWHERE--
--IN ALL THAT "SPARE TIME" SHE HAS!
I DON'T MEAN TO INTERRUPT--
--BUT WASN'T THERE A FAMILY THAT NEEDED SAVING?
WOW. I GOTTA HAND IT TO YOU, SUPERLOTTO, YOU'RE REALLY GOOD AT DISTRACTING ME FROM THE REAL PROBLEM!
WHAT CAN I SAY? THAT'S MY JOB.
JOINED BY PLAN B AND WONDER MOTHER, UNEMPLOYED MAN SPRINGS INTO ACTION.
CLANG CLANG
BANKRUPTCY
WE MIGHT HAVE SAVED THEM THIS TIME...
...BUT WITHOUT JOBS, THIS FAMILY WILL JUST END UP TIED TO THE TRACKS AGAIN...
MAYBE I CAN MAKE SOME CALLS.
UNEMPLOYED MAN CALLS OUT TO THE CROWD.
DOES ANYONE HAVE A JOB FOR THESE PEOPLE?

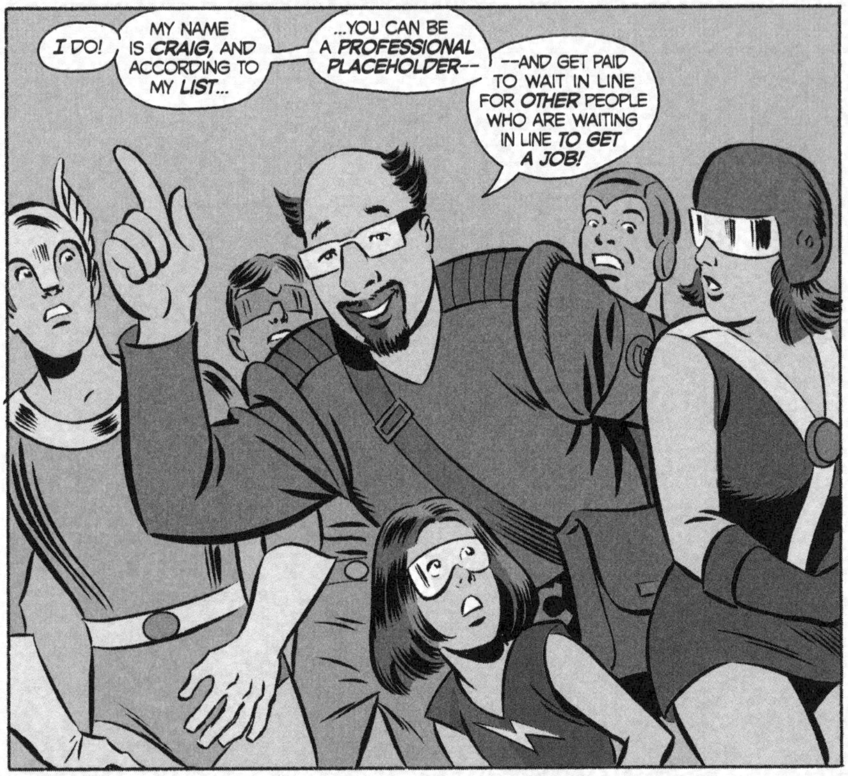
I DO!
MY NAME IS CRAIG, AND ACCORDING TO MY LIST...
...YOU CAN BE A PROFESSIONAL PLACEHOLDER--
--AND GET PAID TO WAIT IN LINE FOR OTHER PEOPLE WHO ARE WAITING IN LINE TO GET A JOB!

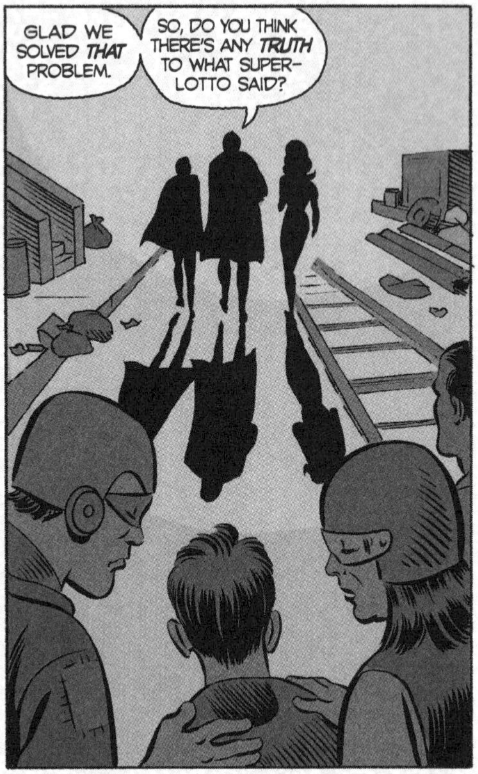
GLAD WE SOLVED THAT PROBLEM.
SO, DO YOU THINK THERE'S ANY TRUTH TO WHAT SUPER-LOTTO SAID?

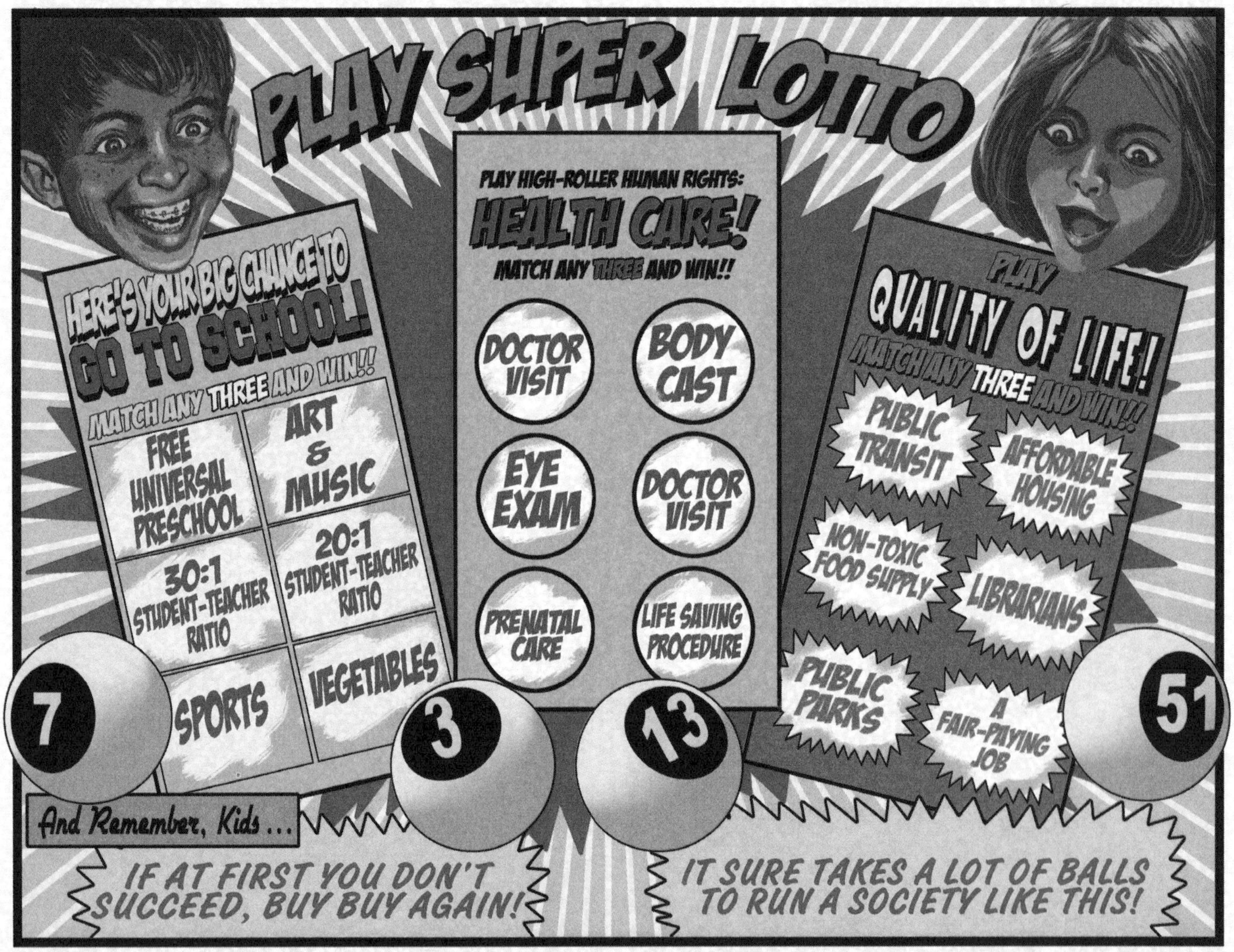
PLAY SUPER LOTTO
HERE'S YOUR BIG CHANCE TO GO TO SCHOOL!
MATCH ANY THREE AND WIN!!
FREE UNIVERSAL PRESCHOOL
ART & MUSIC
30:1 STUDENT-TEACHER RATIO
20:1 STUDENT-TEACHER RATIO
SPORTS
VEGETABLES
PLAY HIGH-ROLLER HUMAN RIGHTS:
HEALTH CARE!
MATCH ANY THREE AND WIN!!
DOCTOR VISIT
BODY CAST
EYE EXAM
DOCTOR VISIT
PRENATAL CARE
LIFE SAVING PROCEDURE
PLAY
QUALITY OF LIFE!
MATCH ANY THREE AND WIN!!
PUBLIC TRANSIT
AFFORDABLE HOUSING
NON-TOXIC FOOD SUPPLY
LIBRARIANS
PUBLIC PARKS
A FAIR-PAYING JOB
7
3
13
51
And Remember, Kids ...
IF AT FIRST YOU DON'T SUCCEED, BUY BUY AGAIN!
IT SURE TAKES A LOT OF BALLS TO RUN A SOCIETY LIKE THIS!

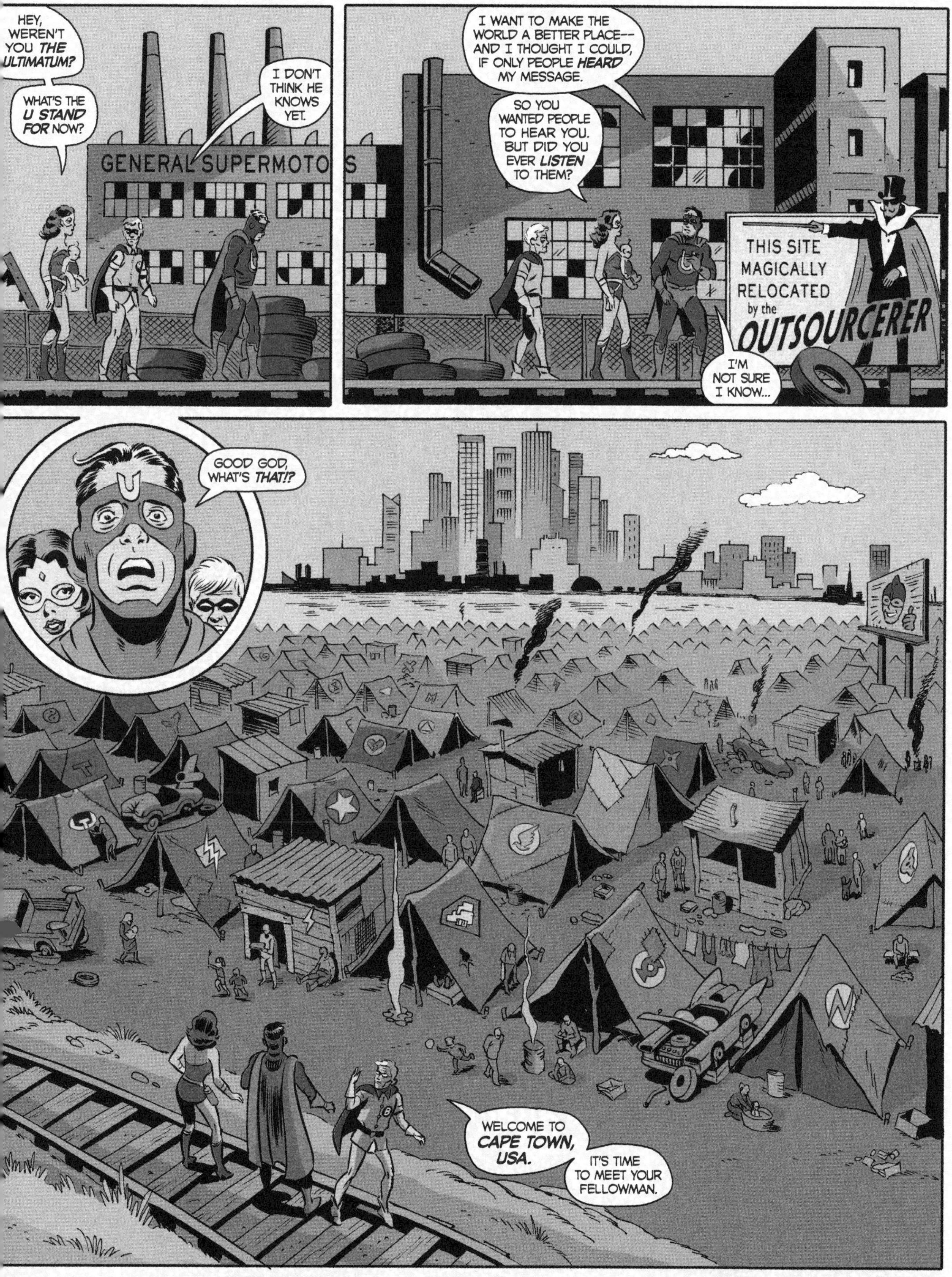
HEY, WEREN'T YOU THE ULTIMATUM?
WHAT'S THE U STAND FOR NOW?
I DON'T THINK HE KNOWS YET.
GENERAL SUPERMOTORS
I WANT TO MAKE THE WORLD A BETTER PLACE-- AND I THOUGHT I COULD, IF ONLY PEOPLE HEARD MY MESSAGE.
SO YOU WANTED PEOPLE TO HEAR YOU. BUT DID YOU EVER LISTEN TO THEM?
THIS SITE MAGICALLY RELOCATED by the OUTSOURCERER
I'M NOT SURE I KNOW...
GOOD GOD, WHAT'S THAT!?
WELCOME TO CAPE TOWN, USA.
IT'S TIME TO MEET YOUR FELLOWMAN.

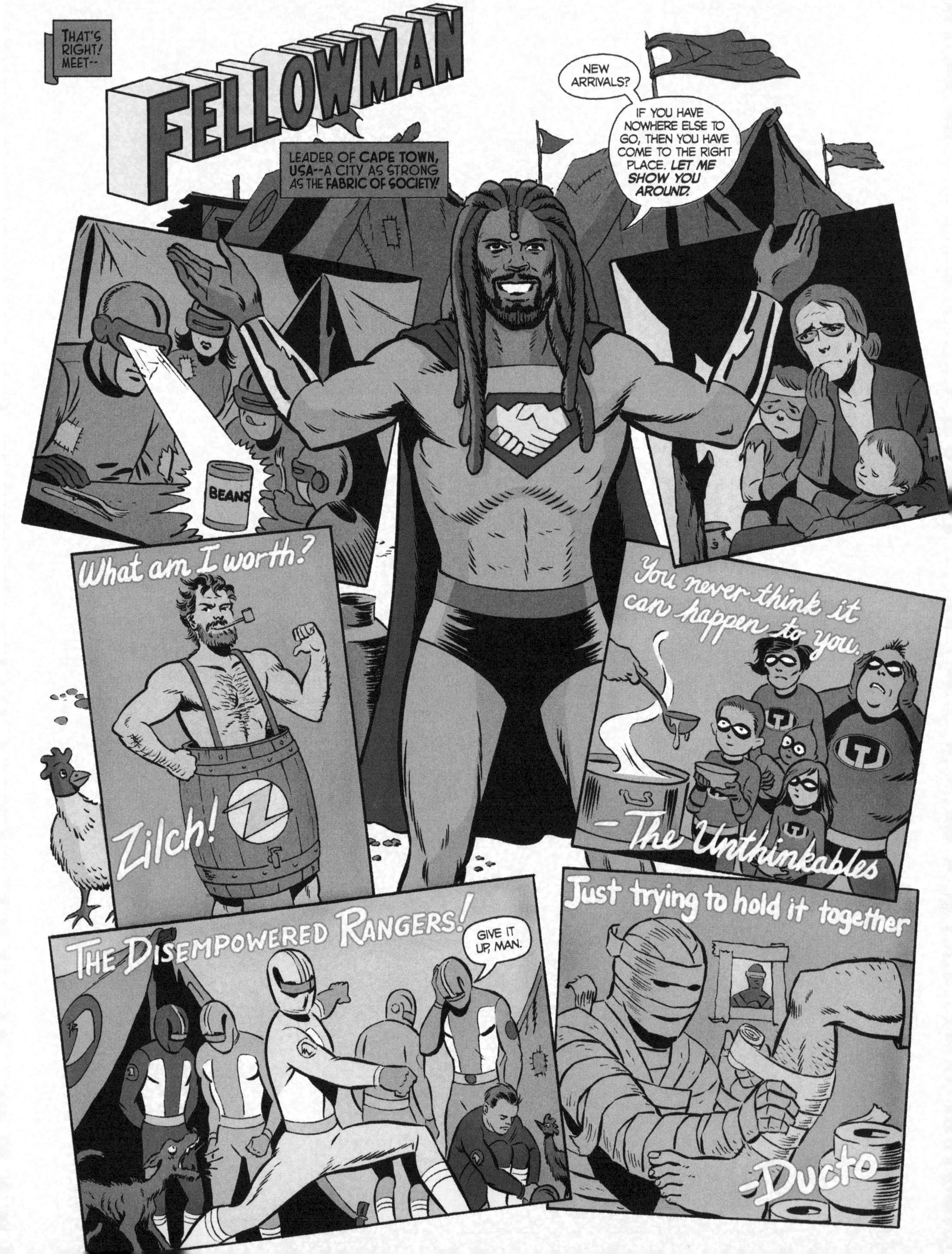
THAT'S RIGHT! MEET--
FELLOWMAN
LEADER OF CAPE TOWN, USA--A CITY AS STRONG AS THE FABRIC OF SOCIETY!
NEW ARRIVALS?
IF YOU HAVE NOWHERE ELSE TO GO, THEN YOU HAVE COME TO THE RIGHT PLACE. LET ME SHOW YOU AROUND.
BEANS
What am I worth?
Zilch!
You never think it can happen to you.
-The Unthinkables
THE DISEMPOWERED RANGERS!
GIVE IT UP, MAN.
Just trying to hold it together
-Ducto

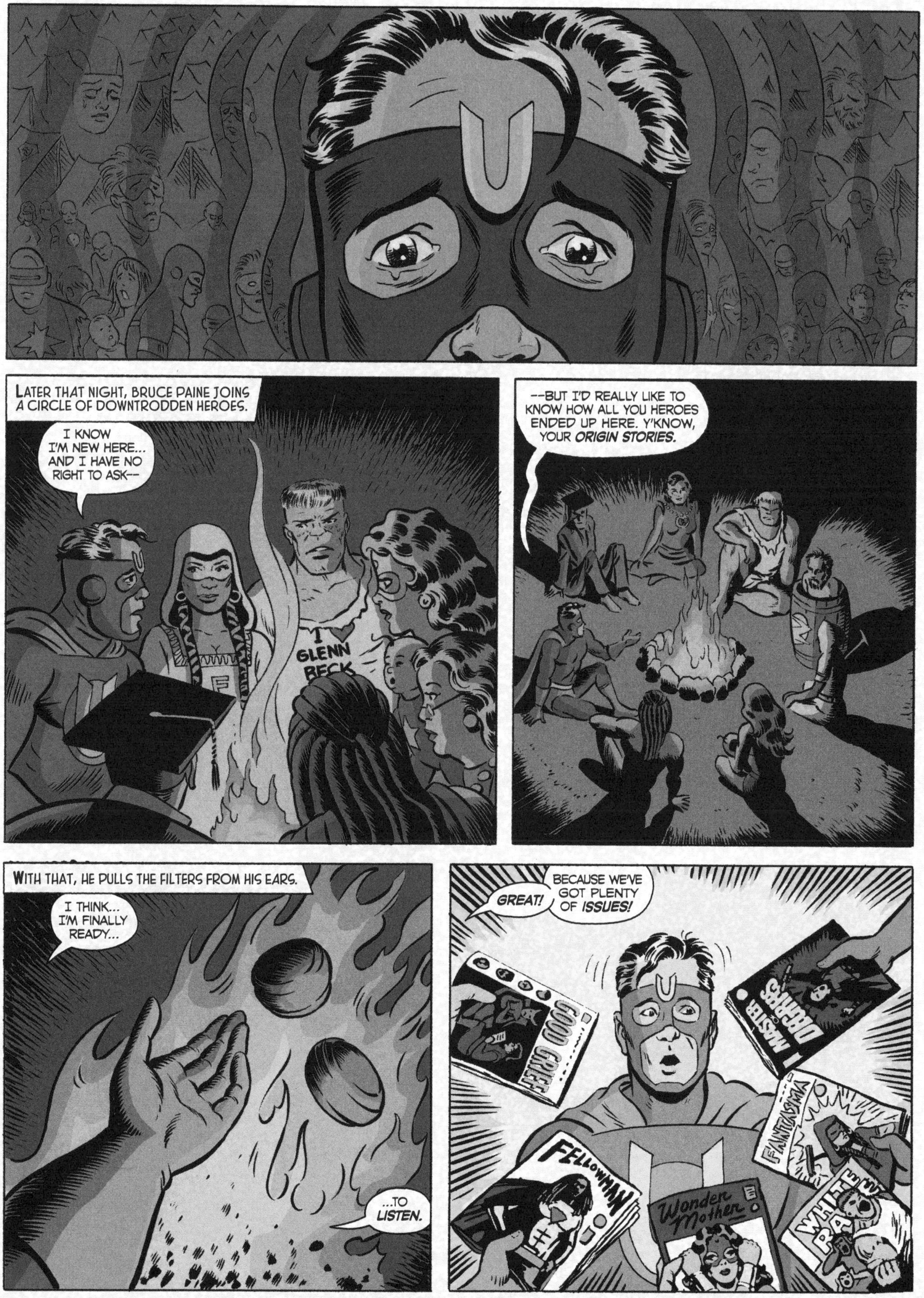

LATER THAT NIGHT, BRUCE PAINE JOINS A CIRCLE OF DOWNTRODDEN HEROES.
I KNOW I'M NEW HERE... AND I HAVE NO RIGHT TO ASK--
I ♥ GLENN BECK
--BUT I'D REALLY LIKE TO KNOW HOW ALL YOU HEROES ENDED UP HERE. Y'KNOW, YOUR *ORIGIN STORIES.*
WITH THAT, HE PULLS THE FILTERS FROM HIS EARS.
I THINK... I'M FINALLY READY...
...TO *LISTEN.*
GREAT!
BECAUSE WE'VE GOT PLENTY OF *ISSUES!*
GOOD GRIEF
FELLOWMAN
Wonder Mother

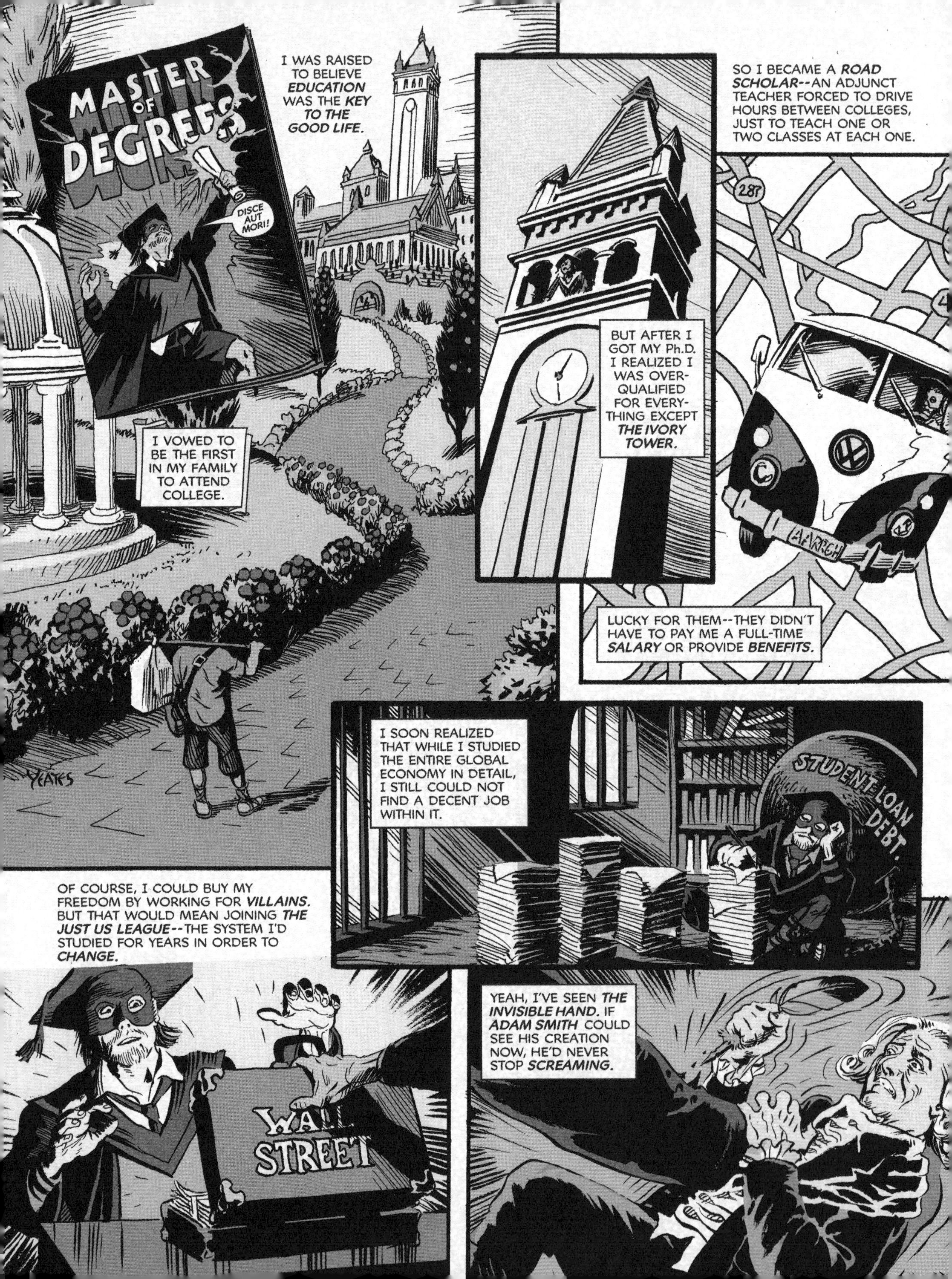
MASTER OF DEGREES
DISCE AUT MORI!
I WAS RAISED TO BELIEVE EDUCATION WAS THE KEY TO THE GOOD LIFE.
I VOWED TO BE THE FIRST IN MY FAMILY TO ATTEND COLLEGE.
YEATES
BUT AFTER I GOT MY Ph.D. I REALIZED I WAS OVER-QUALIFIED FOR EVERY-THING EXCEPT THE IVORY TOWER.
SO I BECAME A ROAD SCHOLAR--AN ADJUNCT TEACHER FORCED TO DRIVE HOURS BETWEEN COLLEGES, JUST TO TEACH ONE OR TWO CLASSES AT EACH ONE.
287
AARRGH
LUCKY FOR THEM--THEY DIDN'T HAVE TO PAY ME A FULL-TIME SALARY OR PROVIDE BENEFITS.
I SOON REALIZED THAT WHILE I STUDIED THE ENTIRE GLOBAL ECONOMY IN DETAIL, I STILL COULD NOT FIND A DECENT JOB WITHIN IT.
STUDENT LOAN DEBT.
OF COURSE, I COULD BUY MY FREEDOM BY WORKING FOR VILLAINS. BUT THAT WOULD MEAN JOINING THE JUST US LEAGUE--THE SYSTEM I'D STUDIED FOR YEARS IN ORDER TO CHANGE.
WALL STREET
YEAH, I'VE SEEN THE INVISIBLE HAND. IF ADAM SMITH COULD SEE HIS CREATION NOW, HE'D NEVER STOP SCREAMING.

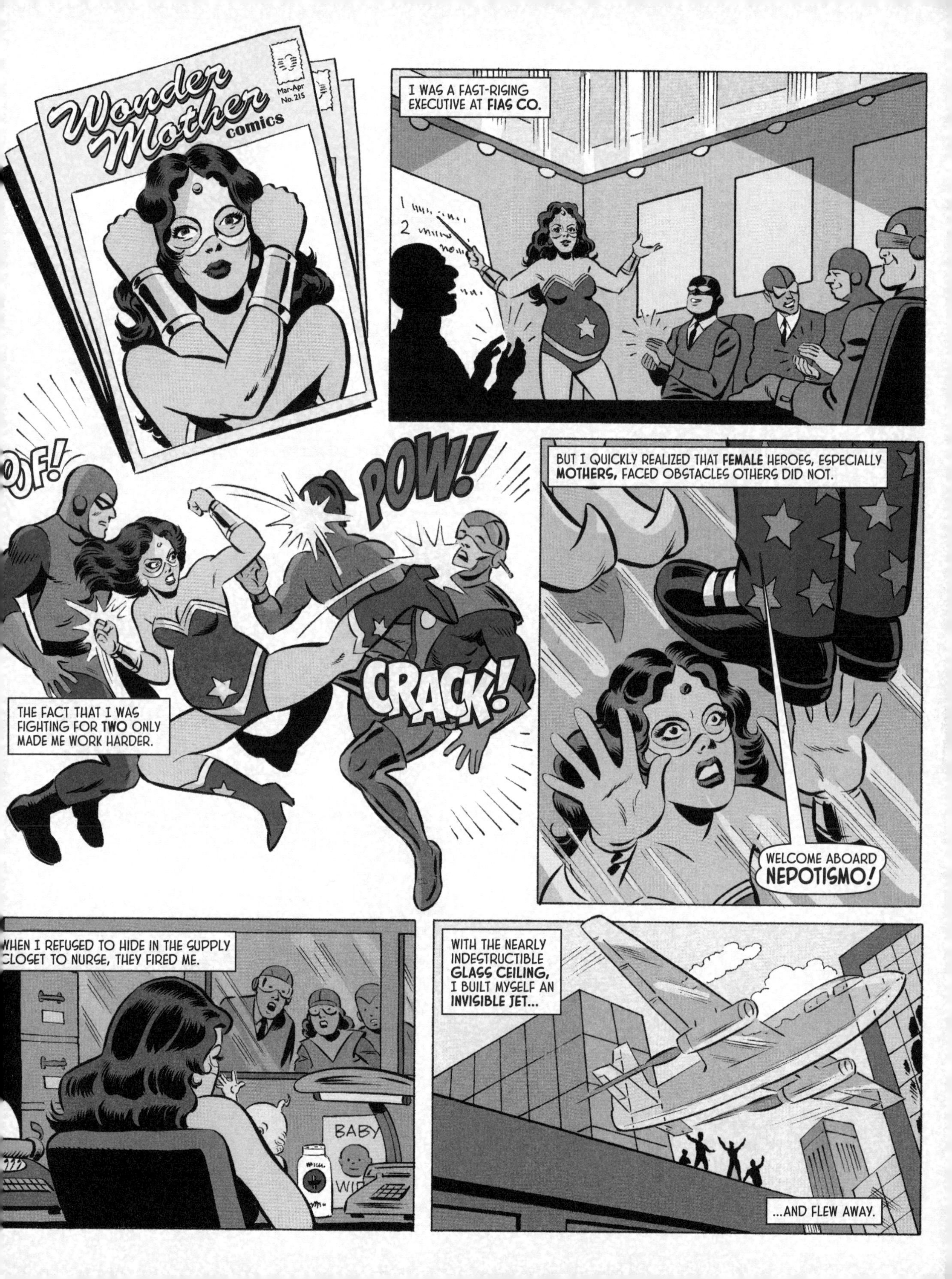
Wonder Mother comics
Mar-Apr No. 215
I WAS A FAST-RISING EXECUTIVE AT FIAS CO.
OOF!
POW!
CRACK!
THE FACT THAT I WAS FIGHTING FOR TWO ONLY MADE ME WORK HARDER.
BUT I QUICKLY REALIZED THAT FEMALE HEROES, ESPECIALLY MOTHERS, FACED OBSTACLES OTHERS DID NOT.
WELCOME ABOARD NEPOTISMO!
WHEN I REFUSED TO HIDE IN THE SUPPLY CLOSET TO NURSE, THEY FIRED ME.
BABY
WITH THE NEARLY INDESTRUCTIBLE GLASS CEILING, I BUILT MYSELF AN INVISIBLE JET...
...AND FLEW AWAY.

"I used to be a different hero, with a different name—*The Blue Line.*"

"I felt it was my duty to try and save at-risk superheroes, kids with few options and in danger of becoming villains."

"In the *Drug War*, I lost one of those boys."

"As I watched the father weep over his son's body, I tried to give what comfort I could."

"But then I looked at my partner and saw only *indifference.* To him, the kid was just another nobody who had it coming..."

"I knew the forces that push a good kid to go bad well, though."

"So I grabbed his hand...and that was the first time I discovered my power—with a touch, I could make one person feel the emotions of another."

"Soon afterward, I realized what my role had really been: Not to stop villainy, just to maintain a line that kept it out of certain places—and *inside* others."

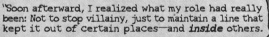

"Maybe a bullet killed that boy, but I know who pulled the trigger. *The Invisible Hand.*"

"That"'s when I gave up being *The Blue Line* and became..."

FELLOWMAN

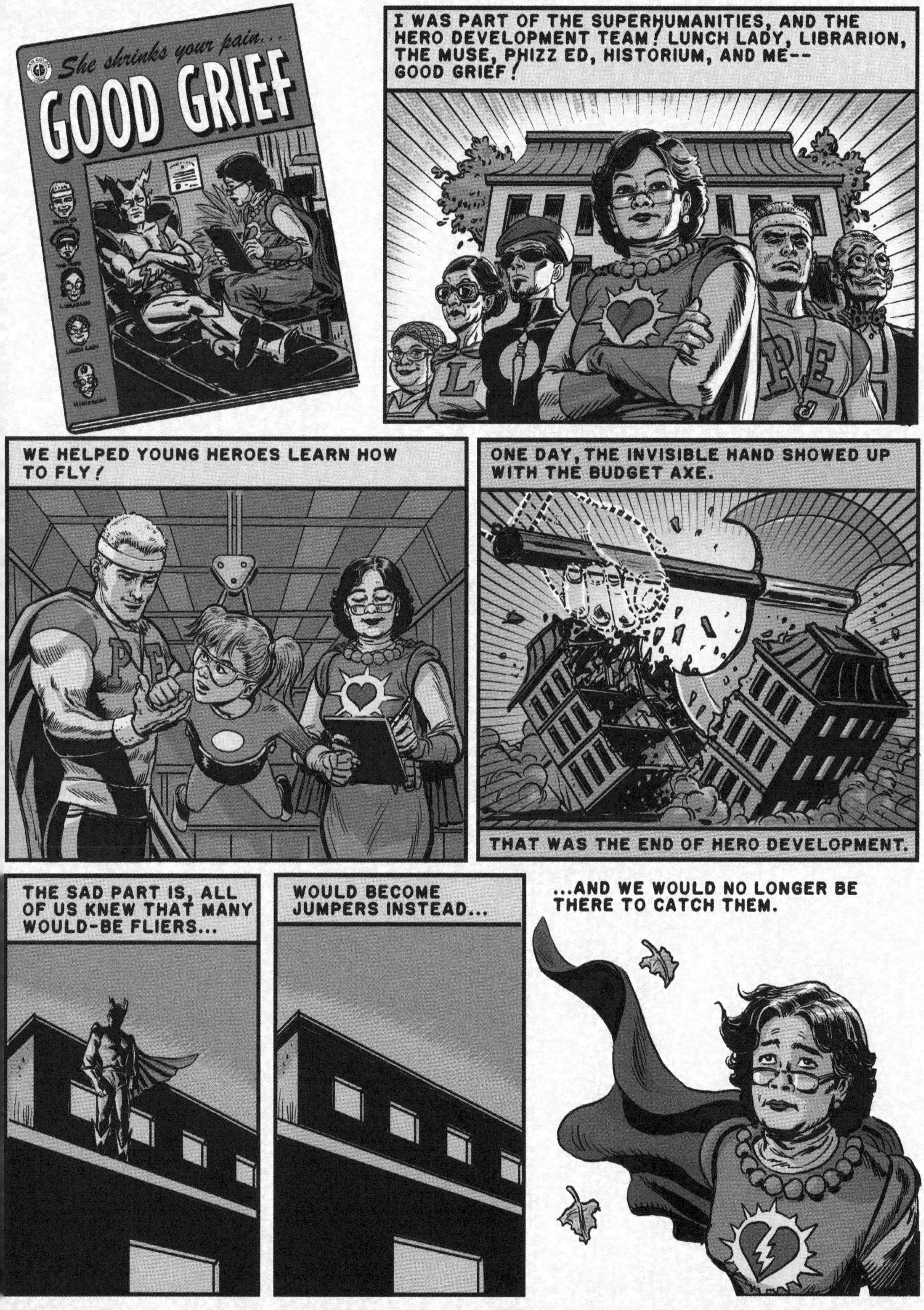
She shrinks your pain...
GOOD GRIEF
I WAS PART OF THE SUPERHUMANITIES, AND THE HERO DEVELOPMENT TEAM! LUNCH LADY, LIBRARION, THE MUSE, PHIZZ ED, HISTORIUM, AND ME-- GOOD GRIEF!
WE HELPED YOUNG HEROES LEARN HOW TO FLY!
ONE DAY, THE INVISIBLE HAND SHOWED UP WITH THE BUDGET AXE.
THAT WAS THE END OF HERO DEVELOPMENT.
THE SAD PART IS, ALL OF US KNEW THAT MANY WOULD-BE FLIERS...
WOULD BECOME JUMPERS INSTEAD...
...AND WE WOULD NO LONGER BE THERE TO CATCH THEM.

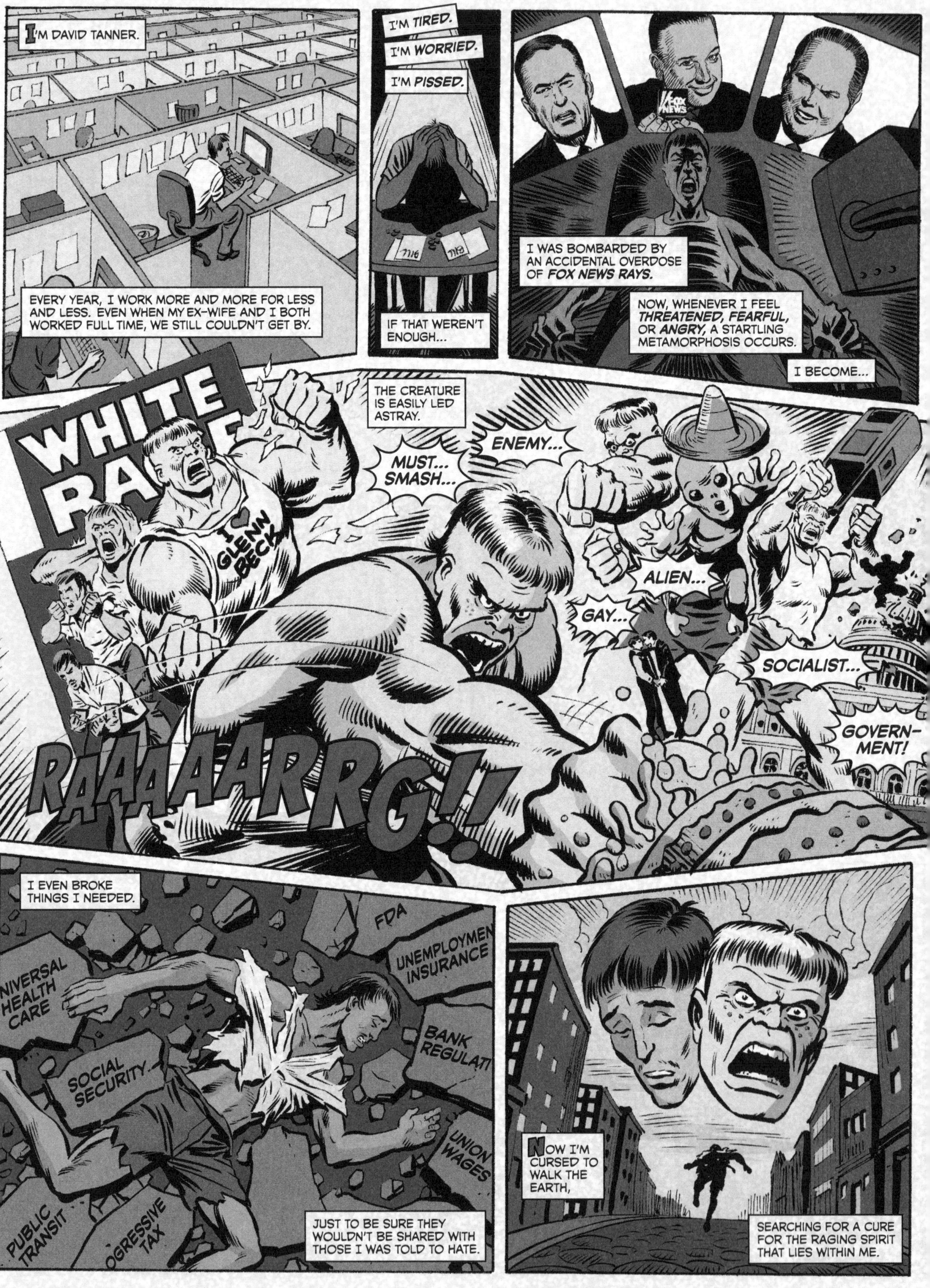
I'M DAVID TANNER.
EVERY YEAR, I WORK MORE AND MORE FOR LESS AND LESS. EVEN WHEN MY EX-WIFE AND I BOTH WORKED FULL TIME, WE STILL COULDN'T GET BY.
I'M TIRED.
I'M WORRIED.
I'M PISSED.
BILL
BILL
IF THAT WEREN'T ENOUGH...
FOX NEWS
I WAS BOMBARDED BY AN ACCIDENTAL OVERDOSE OF FOX NEWS RAYS.
NOW, WHENEVER I FEEL THREATENED, FEARFUL, OR ANGRY, A STARTLING METAMORPHOSIS OCCURS.
I BECOME...
WHITE RAGE
THE CREATURE IS EASILY LED ASTRAY.
I ♥ GLENN BECK
MUST... SMASH...
ENEMY...
ALIEN...
GAY...
SOCIALIST...
GOVERN-MENT!
RAAAAARRG!!
I EVEN BROKE THINGS I NEEDED.
FDA
UNEMPLOYMEN INSURANCE
NIVERSAL HEALTH CARE
BANK REGULATI
SOCIAL SECURITY
UNION WAGES
PUBLIC TRANSIT
OGRESSIVE TAX
JUST TO BE SURE THEY WOULDN'T BE SHARED WITH THOSE I WAS TOLD TO HATE.
NOW I'M CURSED TO WALK THE EARTH,
SEARCHING FOR A CURE FOR THE RAGING SPIRIT THAT LIES WITHIN ME.

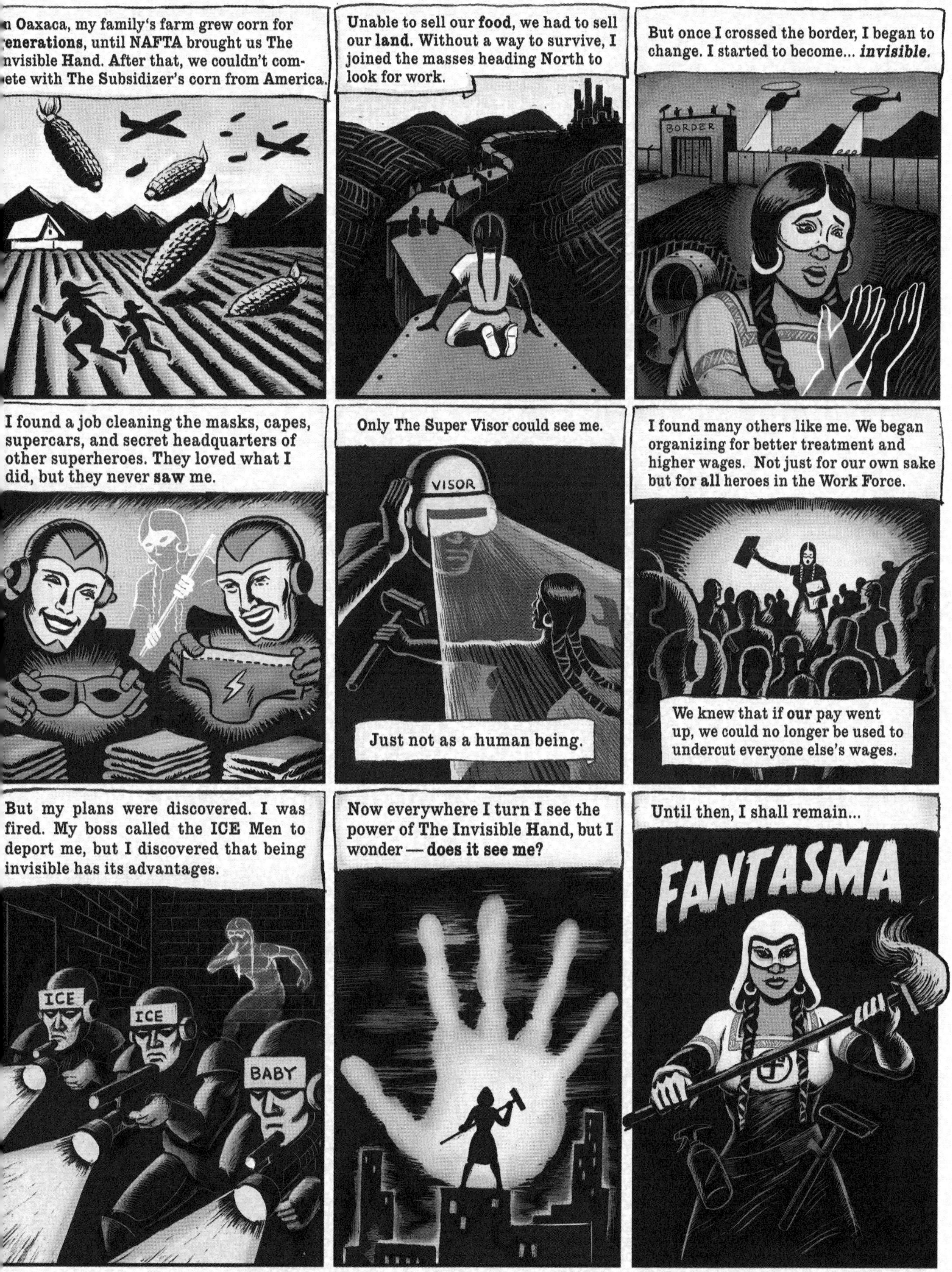
n Oaxaca, my family's farm grew corn for
enerations, until NAFTA brought us The
nvisible Hand. After that, we couldn't com-
ete with The Subsidizer's corn from America.
Unable to sell our food, we had to sell our land. Without a way to survive, I joined the masses heading North to look for work.
But once I crossed the border, I began to change. I started to become... *invisible.*
BORDER
I found a job cleaning the masks, capes, supercars, and secret headquarters of other superheroes. They loved what I did, but they never saw me.
Only The Super Visor could see me.
VISOR
Just not as a human being.
I found many others like me. We began organizing for better treatment and higher wages. Not just for our own sake but for all heroes in the Work Force.
We knew that if our pay went up, we could no longer be used to undercut everyone else's wages.
But my plans were discovered. I was fired. My boss called the ICE Men to deport me, but I discovered that being invisible has its advantages.
ICE
ICE
BABY
Now everywhere I turn I see the power of The Invisible Hand, but I wonder — does it see me?
Until then, I shall remain...
FANTASMA

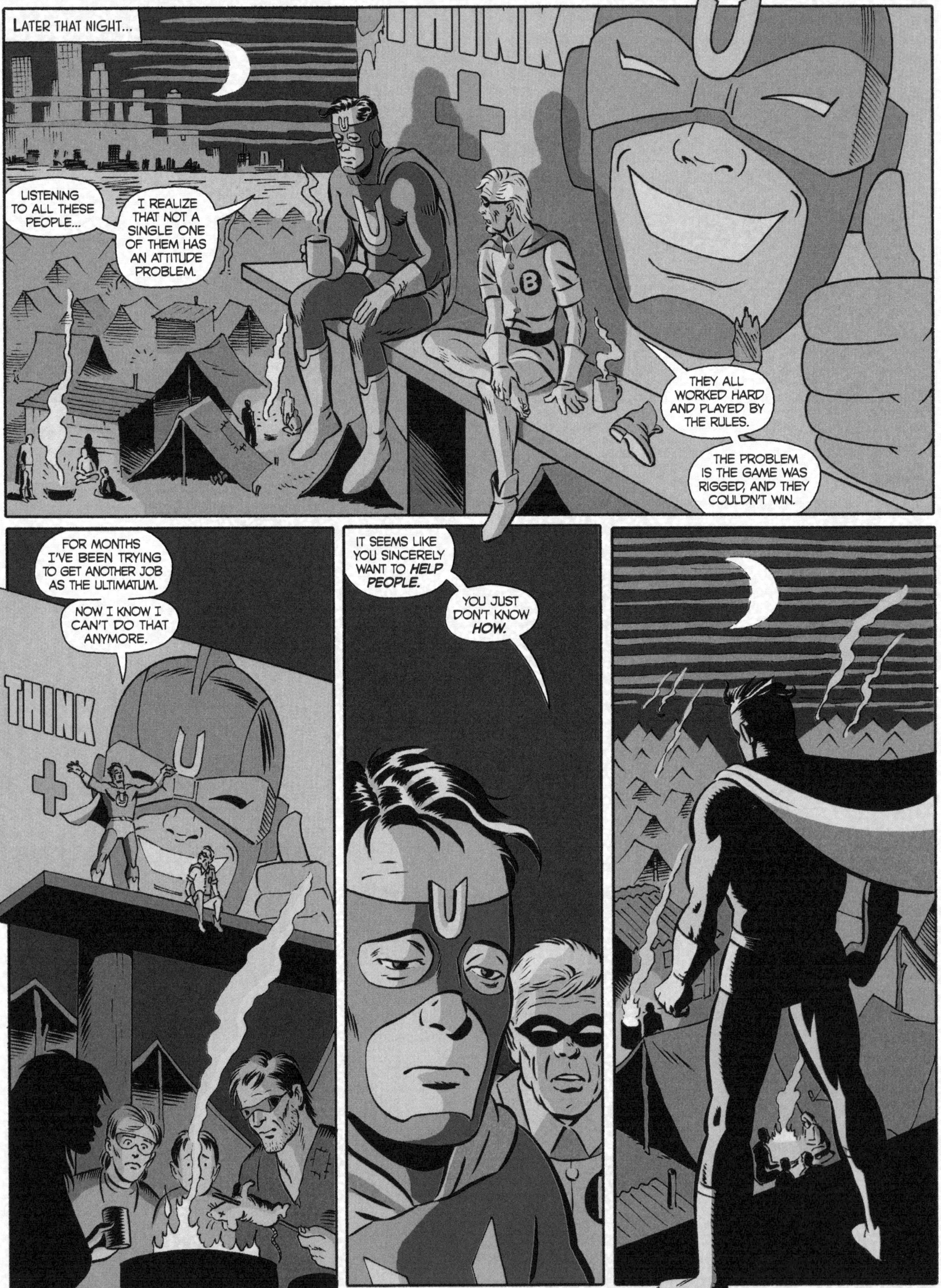
LATER THAT NIGHT...
LISTENING TO ALL THESE PEOPLE...
I REALIZE THAT NOT A SINGLE ONE OF THEM HAS AN ATTITUDE PROBLEM.
THINK
THEY ALL WORKED HARD AND PLAYED BY THE RULES.
THE PROBLEM IS THE GAME WAS RIGGED, AND THEY COULDN'T WIN.
FOR MONTHS I'VE BEEN TRYING TO GET ANOTHER JOB AS THE ULTIMATUM.
NOW I KNOW I CAN'T DO THAT ANYMORE.
THINK
IT SEEMS LIKE YOU SINCERELY WANT TO *HELP PEOPLE.*
YOU JUST DON'T KNOW *HOW.*

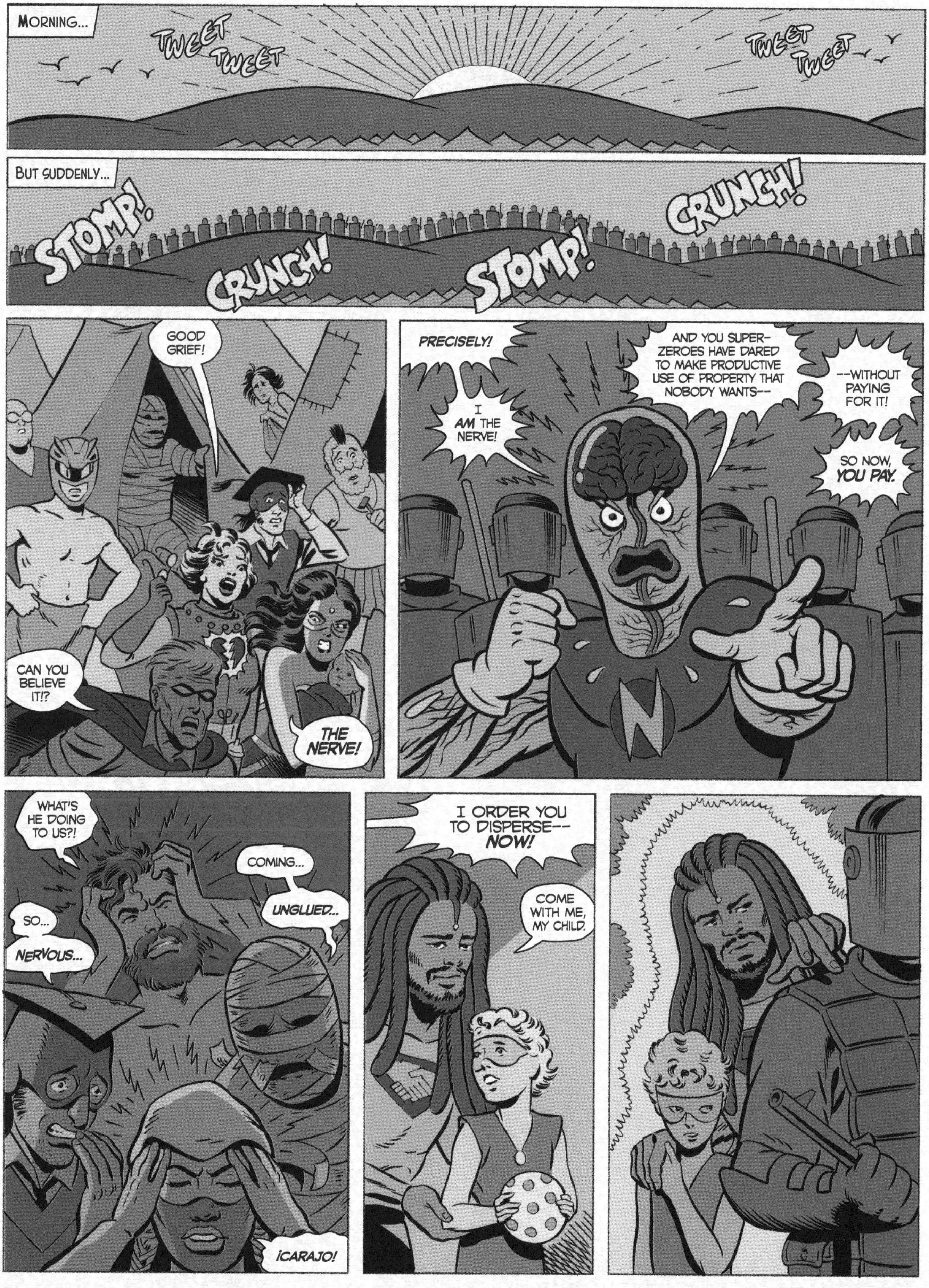
MORNING...
TWEET TWEET
TWEET TWEET
BUT SUDDENLY...
STOMP!
CRUNCH!
STOMP!
CRUNCH!
GOOD GRIEF!
CAN YOU BELIEVE IT!?
THE NERVE!
PRECISELY!
I AM THE NERVE!
AND YOU SUPER-ZEROES HAVE DARED TO MAKE PRODUCTIVE USE OF PROPERTY THAT NOBODY WANTS--
--WITHOUT PAYING FOR IT!
SO NOW, YOU PAY.
WHAT'S HE DOING TO US?!
COMING...
UNGLUED...
SO...
NERVOUS...
¡CARAJO!
I ORDER YOU TO DISPERSE--NOW!
COME WITH ME, MY CHILD.

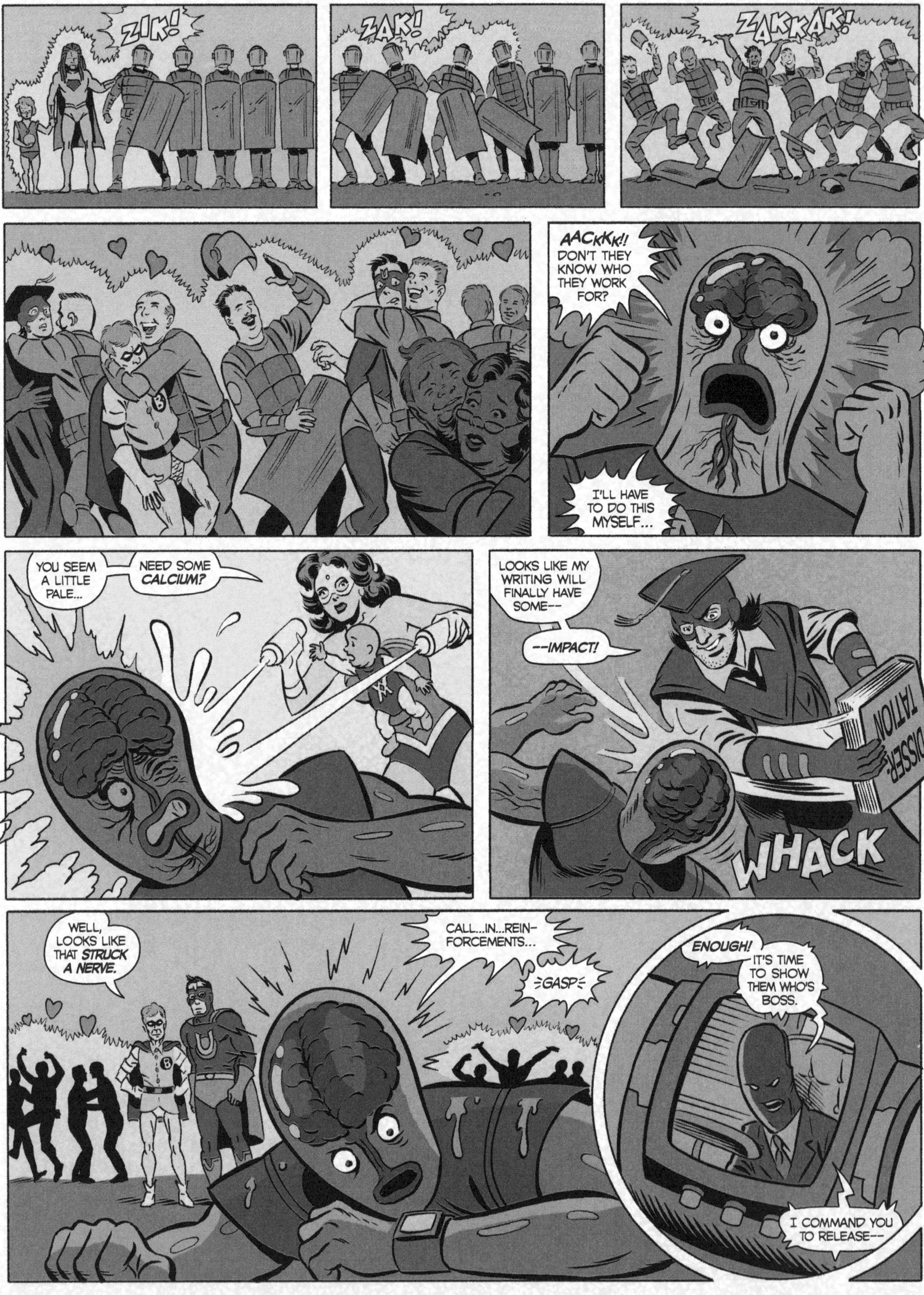
ZIK!
ZAK!
ZAKKAK!
AACKKK!! DON'T THEY KNOW WHO THEY WORK FOR?
I'LL HAVE TO DO THIS MYSELF...
YOU SEEM A LITTLE PALE...
NEED SOME CALCIUM?
LOOKS LIKE MY WRITING WILL FINALLY HAVE SOME--
--IMPACT!
DISSER-TATION
WHACK
WELL, LOOKS LIKE THAT STRUCK A NERVE.
CALL...IN...REIN-FORCEMENTS...
GASP
ENOUGH!
IT'S TIME TO SHOW THEM WHO'S BOSS.
I COMMAND YOU TO RELEASE--

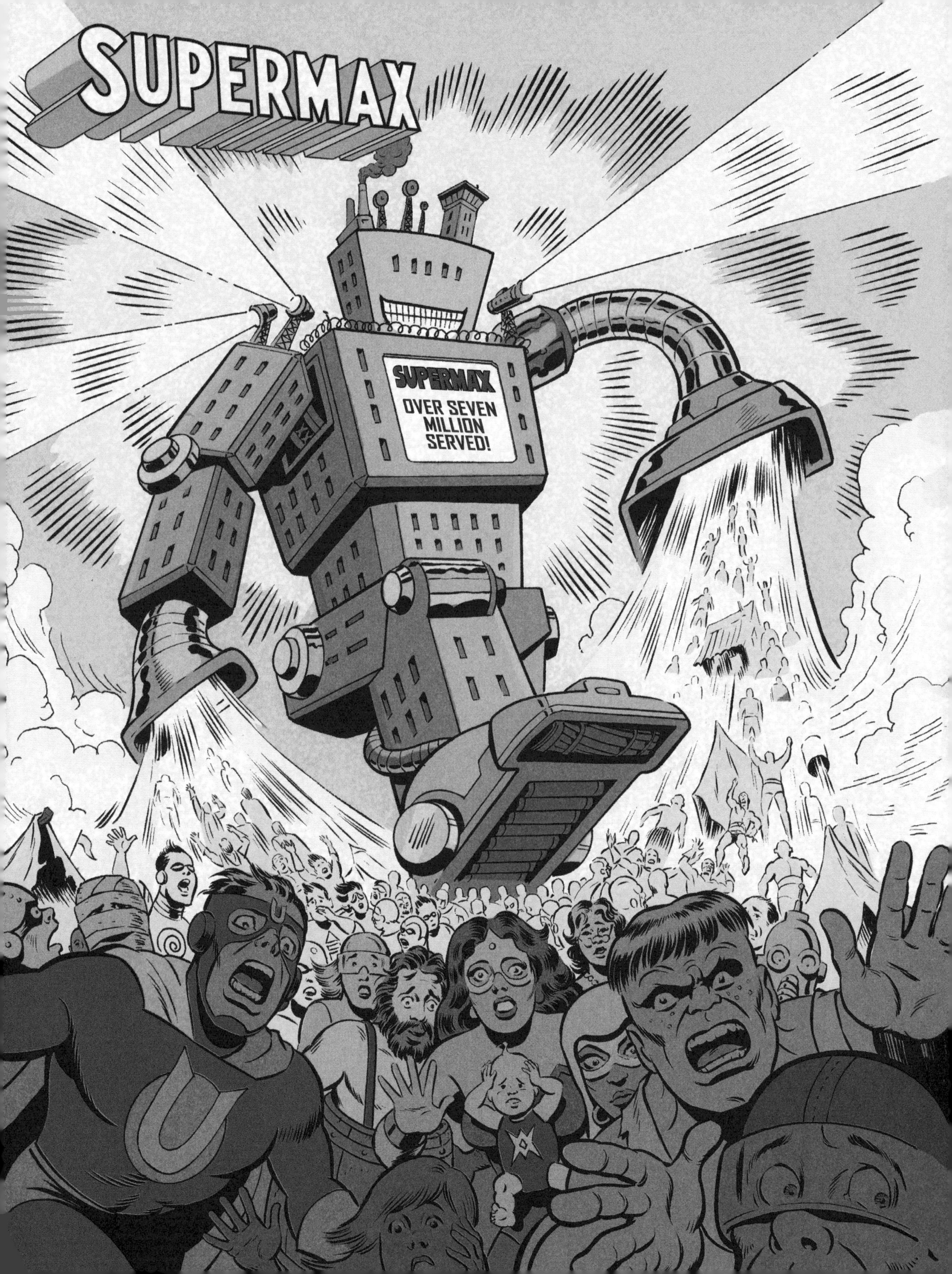
SUPERMAX
SUPERMAX
OVER SEVEN MILLION SERVED!

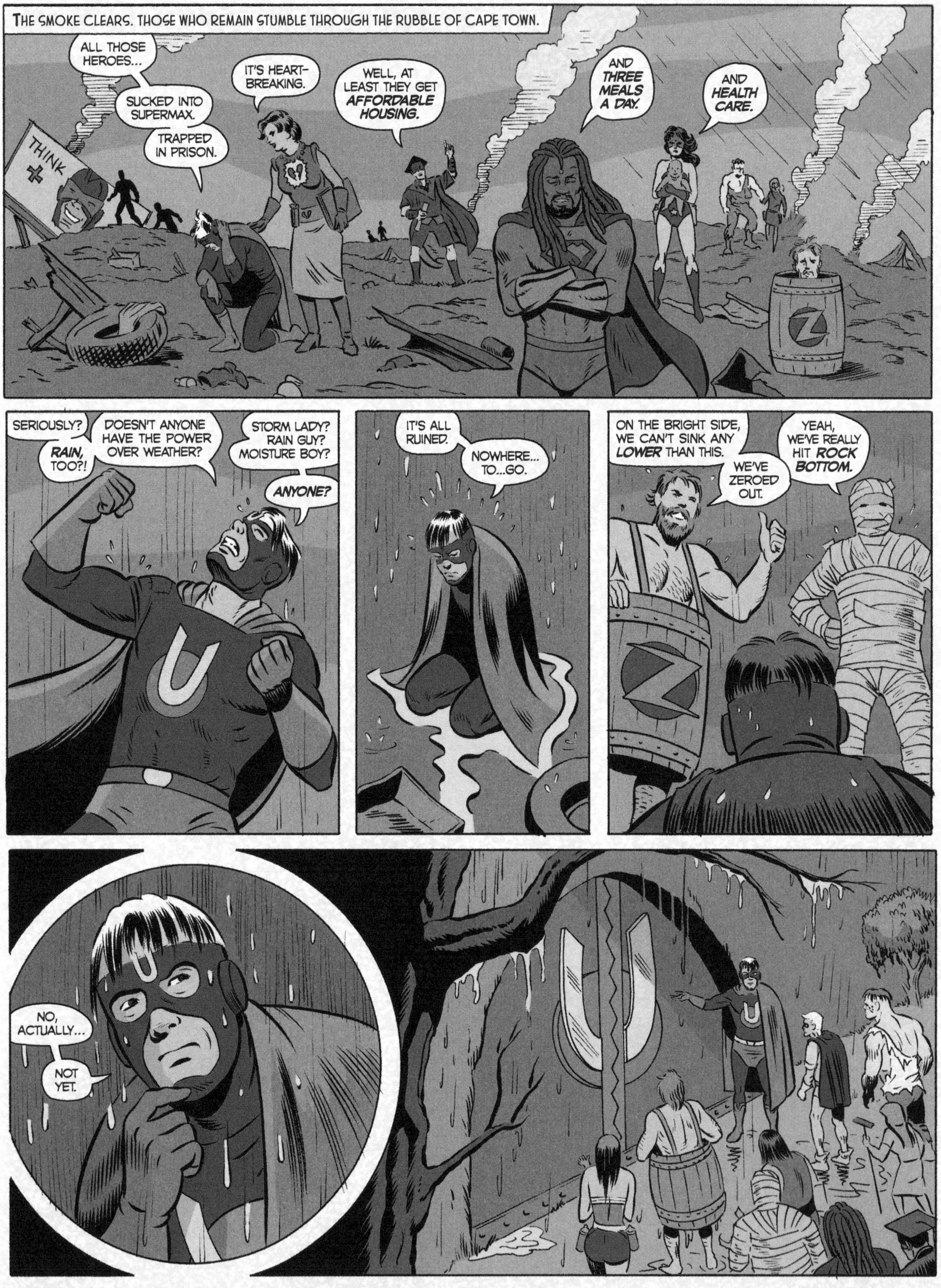

THE SMOKE CLEARS. THOSE WHO REMAIN STUMBLE THROUGH THE RUBBLE OF CAPE TOWN.
ALL THOSE HEROES...
SUCKED INTO SUPERMAX.
TRAPPED IN PRISON.
IT'S HEART-BREAKING.
WELL, AT LEAST THEY GET AFFORDABLE HOUSING.
AND THREE MEALS A DAY.
AND HEALTH CARE.
THINK
SERIOUSLY? RAIN, TOO?!
DOESN'T ANYONE HAVE THE POWER OVER WEATHER?
STORM LADY? RAIN GUY? MOISTURE BOY?
ANYONE?
IT'S ALL RUINED.
NOWHERE... TO...GO.
ON THE BRIGHT SIDE, WE CAN'T SINK ANY LOWER THAN THIS.
WE'VE ZEROED OUT.
YEAH, WE'VE REALLY HIT ROCK BOTTOM.
NO, ACTUALLY...
NOT YET.

TIME FOR MORE FANTASTIC FACTS

Because There's No Such Things As TOO MUCH INFORMATION!

WE'RE NUMBER ONE!

AMONG THE DEVELOPED NATIONS OF EARTH, THE *USA* HAS THE *HIGHEST PERCENTAGE OF CITIZENS IN PRISON* -- 700 PER 100,000. IN COMPARISON, CHINA HAS 110, FRANCE 80, AND SAUDI ARABIA 45 PER 100,000. SUCK IT, TOTALITARIAN REGIMES, YOU LOSE!

WE'RE NUMBER ONE!

AMERICA IS NOT ONLY THE RICHEST NATION IN HISTORY, WE ALSO HAVE THE *HIGHEST POVERTY RATE* IN THE INDUSTRIALIZED WORLD! A STUNNING 50% OF *U.S.* CHILDREN WILL USE FOOD STAMPS AT SOME POINT IN THEIR CHILDHOODS, AND 60% OF AMERICANS LIVE PAYCHECK TO PAYCHECK.

I BELIEVE I CAN FLY!

EVEN BEFORE THE *GREAT RECESSION*, 4.5 MILLION YOUNG HEROES AGES 18-24 HAD NOT GRADUATED HIGH SCHOOL, NOR HAD FOUND JOBS. NOT TO WORRY, THEY'LL FIND WORK IN PRISON! SINCE 1980, EXPENDITURES ON *INCARCERATION* HAVE INCREASED BY ROUGHLY 1000%, ABOUT 2.5 TIMES THE SPENDING INCREASE ON ALL LEVELS OF *EDUCATION*.

LAST, BUT NOT LEAST!

MORE THAN 160 NATIONS ON EARTH GUARANTEE *PAID MATERNITY LEAVE* -- BUT NOT THE GOOD OL' *US OF A!* THE ONLY OTHER NATIONS THAT DON'T ARE PAPUA NEW GUINEA, SWAZILAND, AND LESOTHO. AND PAID FAMILY LEAVE HAS BEEN SHOWN TO REDUCE INFANT MORTALITY BY AS MUCH AS 20%. THE *USA* CURRENTLY RANKS 37TH IN INFANT MORTALITY. HEY, WE MADE THE TOP 100!

AN INGENIOUS ECONOMIC INVENTION!

"INVISIBLE HELMET"

LOOK AWAY

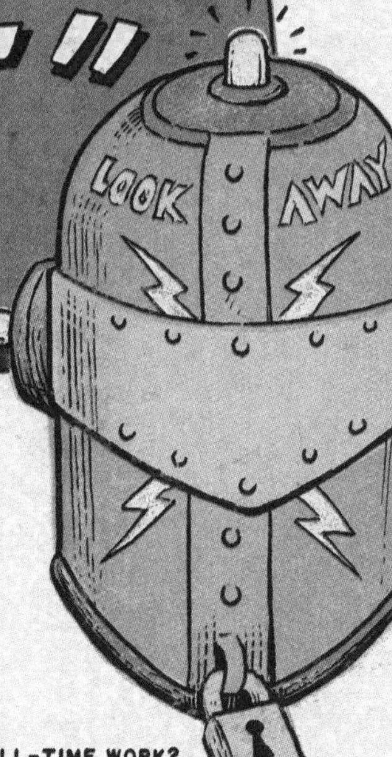

INCLUDES LATENT INDICATOR LIGHTS. & CHILD PROOF LOCK.

ALL YOU HAVE TO DO IS...

PUT IT ON...

NOW -- YOU CAN'T SEE PEOPLE -- THEY CAN'T SEE YOU!

PROBLEM SOLVED!

"THE ECONOMY IS PEOPLE." US. SO, HOW WELL ARE *WE* DOING?

WELL, A LOT BETTER WHEN CERTAIN PEOPLE BECOME -- *INVISIBLE!*

WHICH IS WHERE *YOU* COME IN.
- ARE YOU WORKING PART TIME BECAUSE YOU CAN'T FIND FULL-TIME WORK?
- HAVE YOU BEEN LOOKING FOR WORK TOO LONG?
- HAVE YOU STOPPED LOOKING FOR WORK?
- DO YOU CONSUME FOOD, ENERGY, OR OTHER THINGS NOT INCLUDED IN THE OFFICIAL MEASURE OF INFLATION?

IF SO, THEN THE INVISIBLE HELMET IS FOR YOU!

SOME MIGHT CALL IT CREATIVE ACCOUNTING, BUT YOU AND YOUR KIND WILL CALL IT RELIEF! NO LONGER WILL YOU BE EMBARRASSED BY YOUR SITUATION. INSTEAD, YOU WILL SIMPLY *DISAPPEAR!*

MADE IN AMERICA BY *LOOKAWAY*. A DIVISION OF THE INVISIBLE HAND.

WARNING: DOES NOT ACTUALLY MAKE YOU OR YOUR MISERY INVISIBLE.

FOR ECONOMIC NOVELTY USE ONLY.

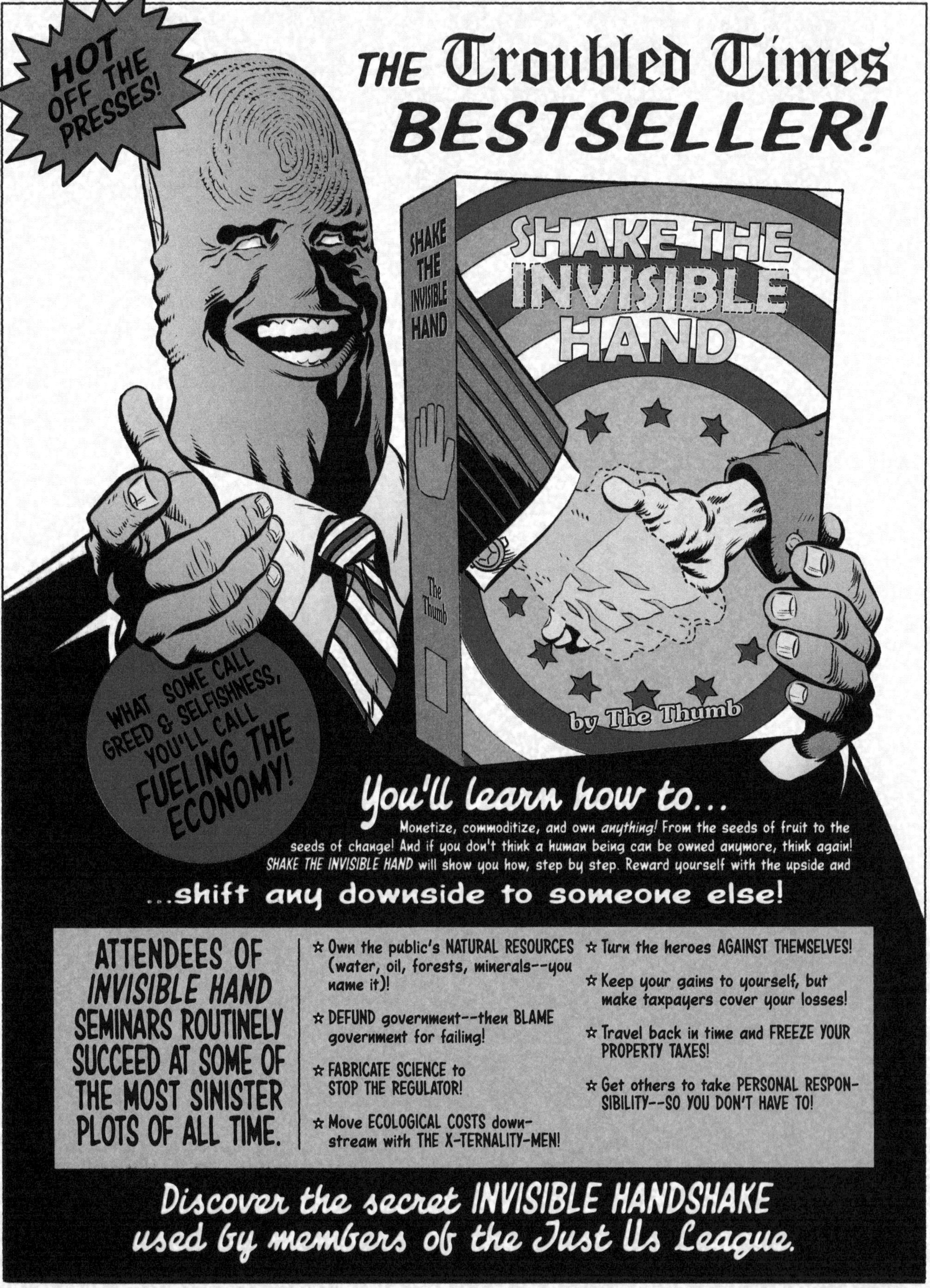

HOT OFF THE PRESSES!
THE Troubled Times BESTSELLER!
SHAKE THE INVISIBLE HAND
The Thumb
SHAKE THE INVISIBLE HAND
by The Thumb
WHAT SOME CALL GREED & SELFISHNESS, YOU'LL CALL FUELING THE ECONOMY!
You'll learn how to...
Monetize, commoditize, and own anything! From the seeds of fruit to the seeds of change! And if you don't think a human being can be owned anymore, think again! SHAKE THE INVISIBLE HAND will show you how, step by step. Reward yourself with the upside and
...shift any downside to someone else!
ATTENDEES OF INVISIBLE HAND SEMINARS ROUTINELY SUCCEED AT SOME OF THE MOST SINISTER PLOTS OF ALL TIME.
☆ Own the public's NATURAL RESOURCES (water, oil, forests, minerals--you name it)!
☆ DEFUND government--then BLAME government for failing!
☆ FABRICATE SCIENCE to STOP THE REGULATOR!
☆ Move ECOLOGICAL COSTS downstream with THE X-TERNALITY-MEN!
☆ Turn the heroes AGAINST THEMSELVES!
☆ Keep your gains to yourself, but make taxpayers cover your losses!
☆ Travel back in time and FREEZE YOUR PROPERTY TAXES!
☆ Get others to take PERSONAL RESPONSIBILITY--SO YOU DON'T HAVE TO!
Discover the secret INVISIBLE HANDSHAKE used by members of the Just Us League.

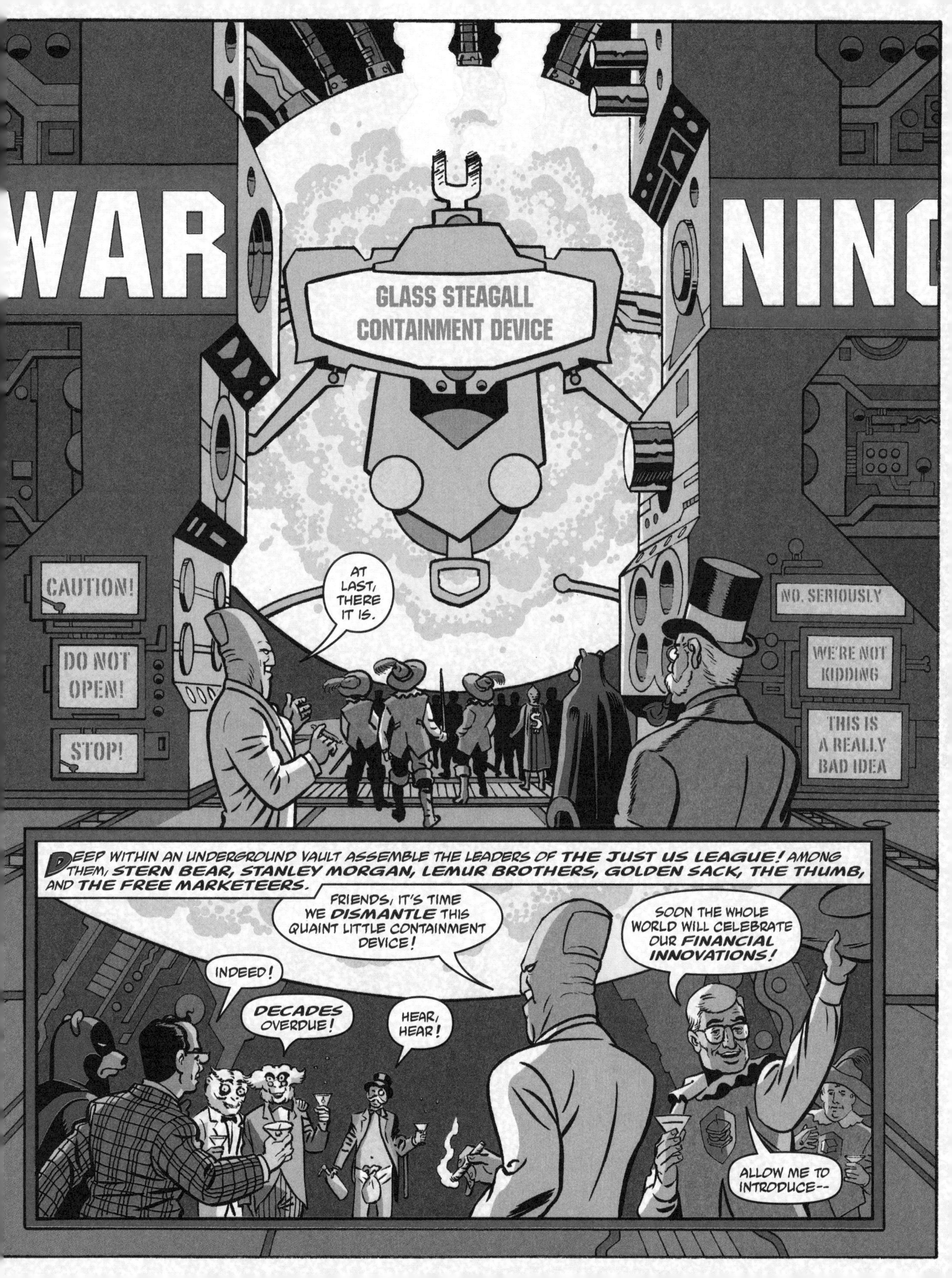
WAR
NING
GLASS STEAGALL CONTAINMENT DEVICE
CAUTION!
DO NOT OPEN!
STOP!
AT LAST, THERE IT IS.
NO. SERIOUSLY
WE'RE NOT KIDDING
THIS IS A REALLY BAD IDEA
DEEP WITHIN AN UNDERGROUND VAULT ASSEMBLE THE LEADERS OF THE JUST US LEAGUE! AMONG THEM, STERN BEAR, STANLEY MORGAN, LEMUR BROTHERS, GOLDEN SACK, THE THUMB, AND THE FREE MARKETEERS.
FRIENDS, IT'S TIME WE DISMANTLE THIS QUAINT LITTLE CONTAINMENT DEVICE!
SOON THE WHOLE WORLD WILL CELEBRATE OUR FINANCIAL INNOVATIONS!
INDEED!
DECADES OVERDUE!
HEAR, HEAR!
ALLOW ME TO INTRODUCE--

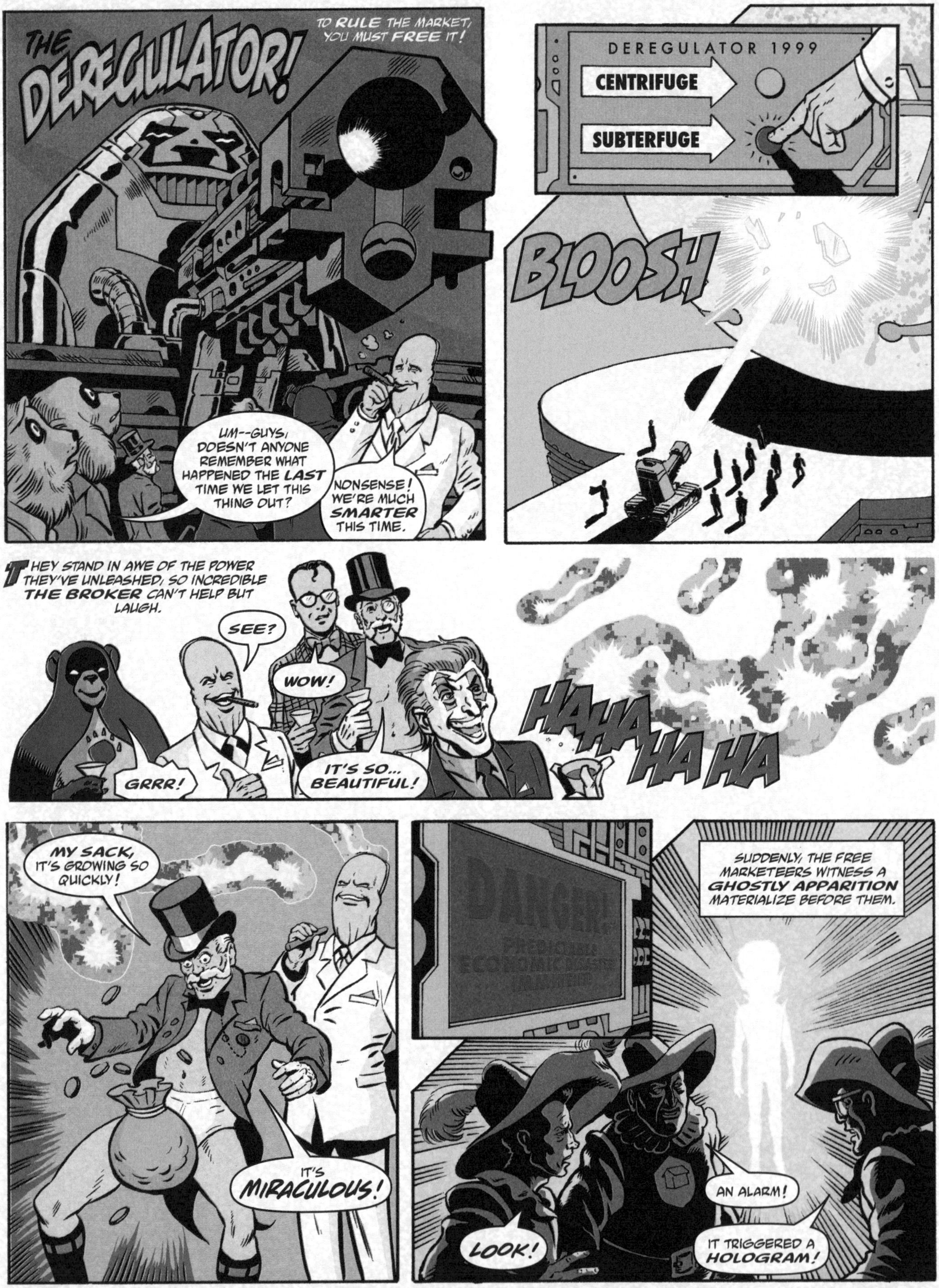
THE DEREGULATOR!
TO RULE THE MARKET, YOU MUST FREE IT!
UM--GUYS, DOESN'T ANYONE REMEMBER WHAT HAPPENED THE LAST TIME WE LET THIS THING OUT?
NONSENSE! WE'RE MUCH SMARTER THIS TIME.
DEREGULATOR 1999
CENTRIFUGE
SUBTERFUGE
BLOOSH
THEY STAND IN AWE OF THE POWER THEY'VE UNLEASHED, SO INCREDIBLE THE BROKER CAN'T HELP BUT LAUGH.
SEE?
WOW!
GRRR!
IT'S SO... BEAUTIFUL!
HAHAHAHAHA
MY SACK, IT'S GROWING SO QUICKLY!
IT'S MIRACULOUS!
SUDDENLY, THE FREE MARKETEERS WITNESS A GHOSTLY APPARITION MATERIALIZE BEFORE THEM.
DANGER!
AN ALARM!
LOOK!
IT TRIGGERED A HOLOGRAM!

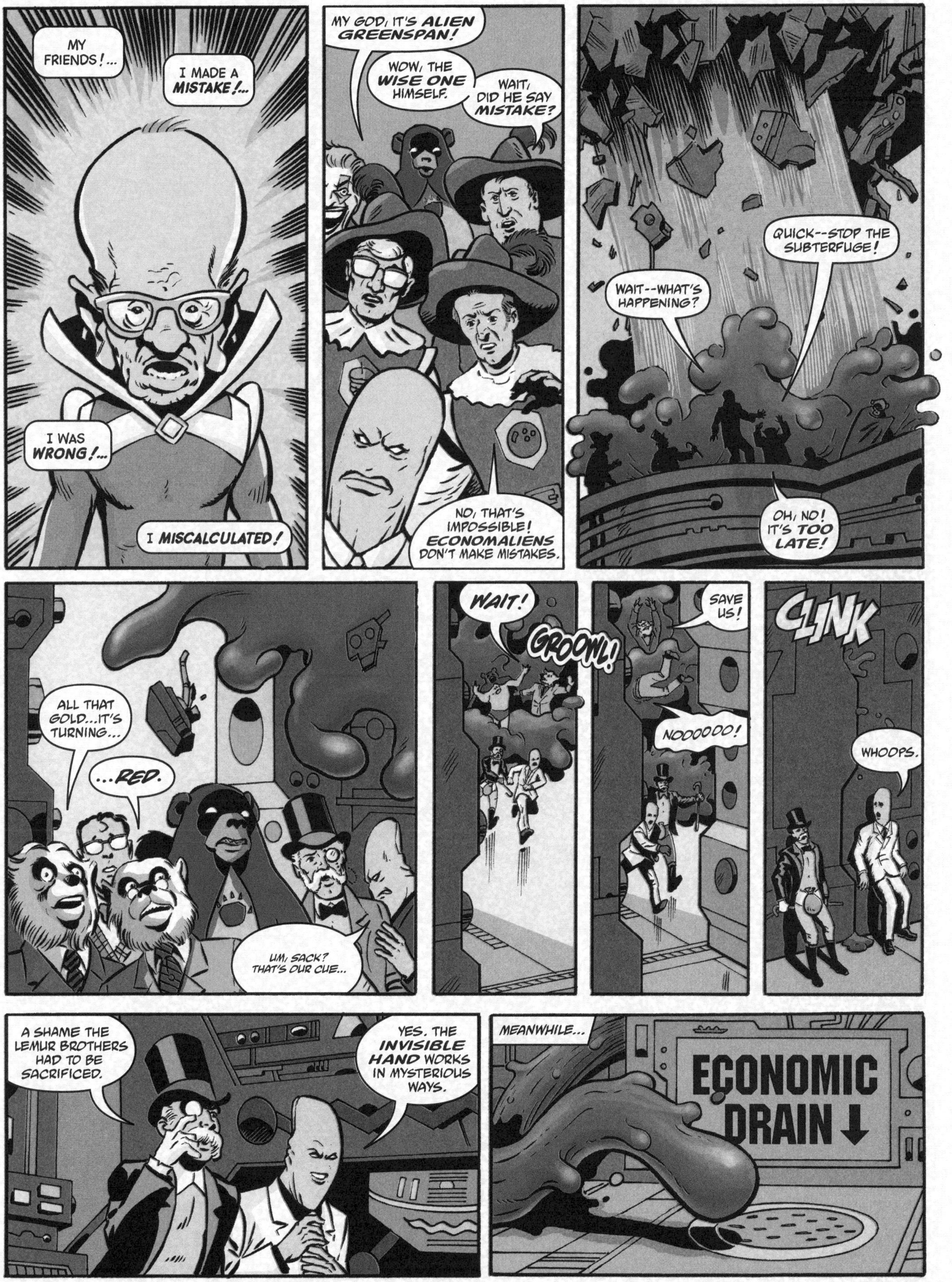
MY FRIENDS!...
I MADE A MISTAKE!...
I WAS WRONG!...
I MISCALCULATED!
MY GOD, IT'S ALIEN GREENSPAN!
WOW, THE WISE ONE HIMSELF.
WAIT, DID HE SAY MISTAKE?
NO, THAT'S IMPOSSIBLE! ECONOMALIENS DON'T MAKE MISTAKES.
QUICK--STOP THE SUBTERFUGE!
WAIT--WHAT'S HAPPENING?
OH, NO! IT'S TOO LATE!
ALL THAT GOLD...IT'S TURNING...
...RED.
UM, SACK? THAT'S OUR CUE...
WAIT!
GROOWL!
SAVE US!
NOOOOOO!
CLINK
WHOOPS.
A SHAME THE LEMUR BROTHERS HAD TO BE SACRIFICED.
YES. THE INVISIBLE HAND WORKS IN MYSTERIOUS WAYS.
MEANWHILE...
ECONOMIC DRAIN

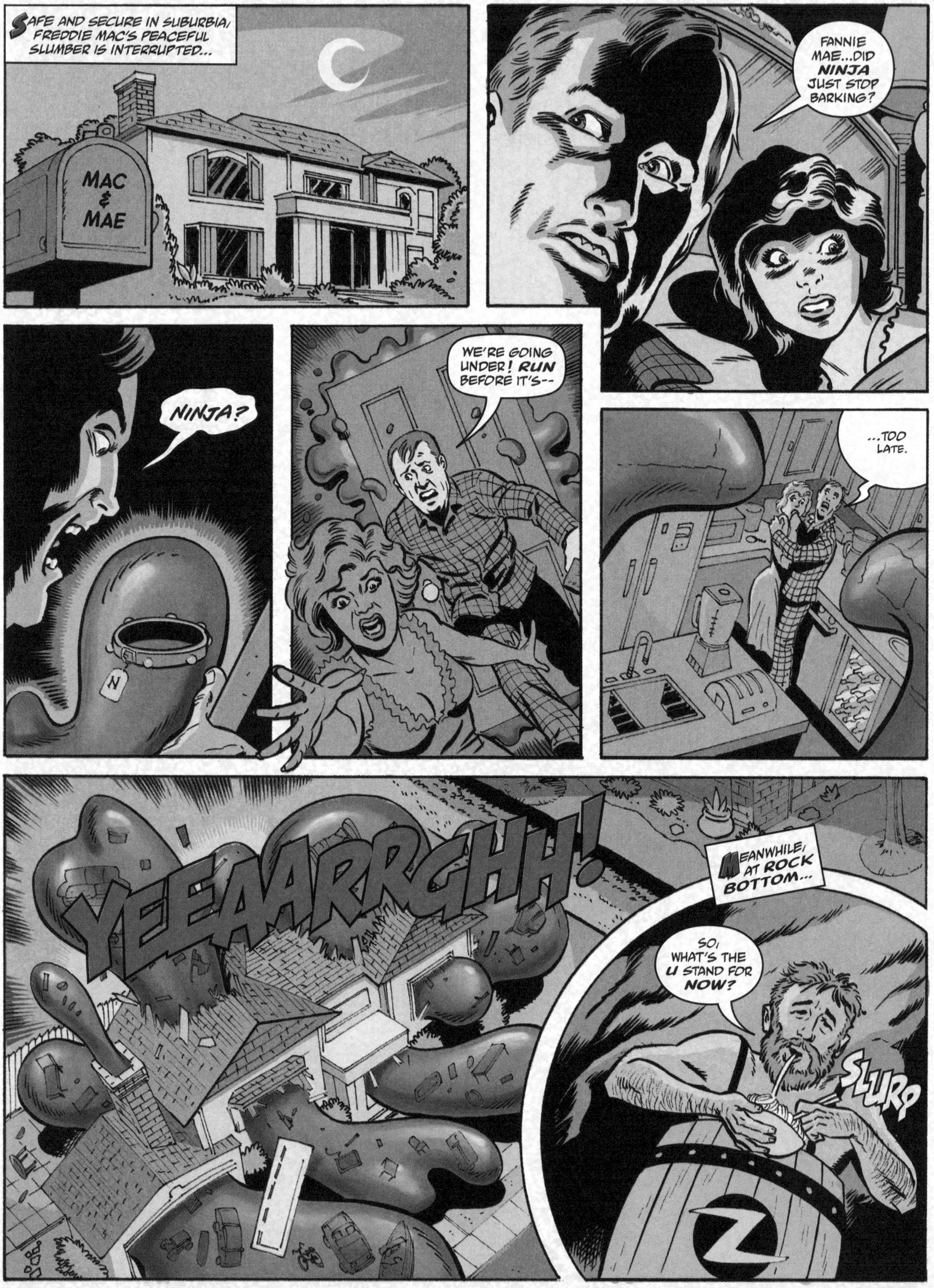
SAFE AND SECURE IN SUBURBIA, FREDDIE MAC'S PEACEFUL SLUMBER IS INTERRUPTED...
MAC & MAE
FANNIE MAE...DID NINJA JUST STOP BARKING?
NINJA?
N
WE'RE GOING UNDER! RUN BEFORE IT'S--
...TOO LATE.
YEEAARRGHH!
MEANWHILE, AT ROCK BOTTOM...
SO, WHAT'S THE U STAND FOR NOW?
SLURP

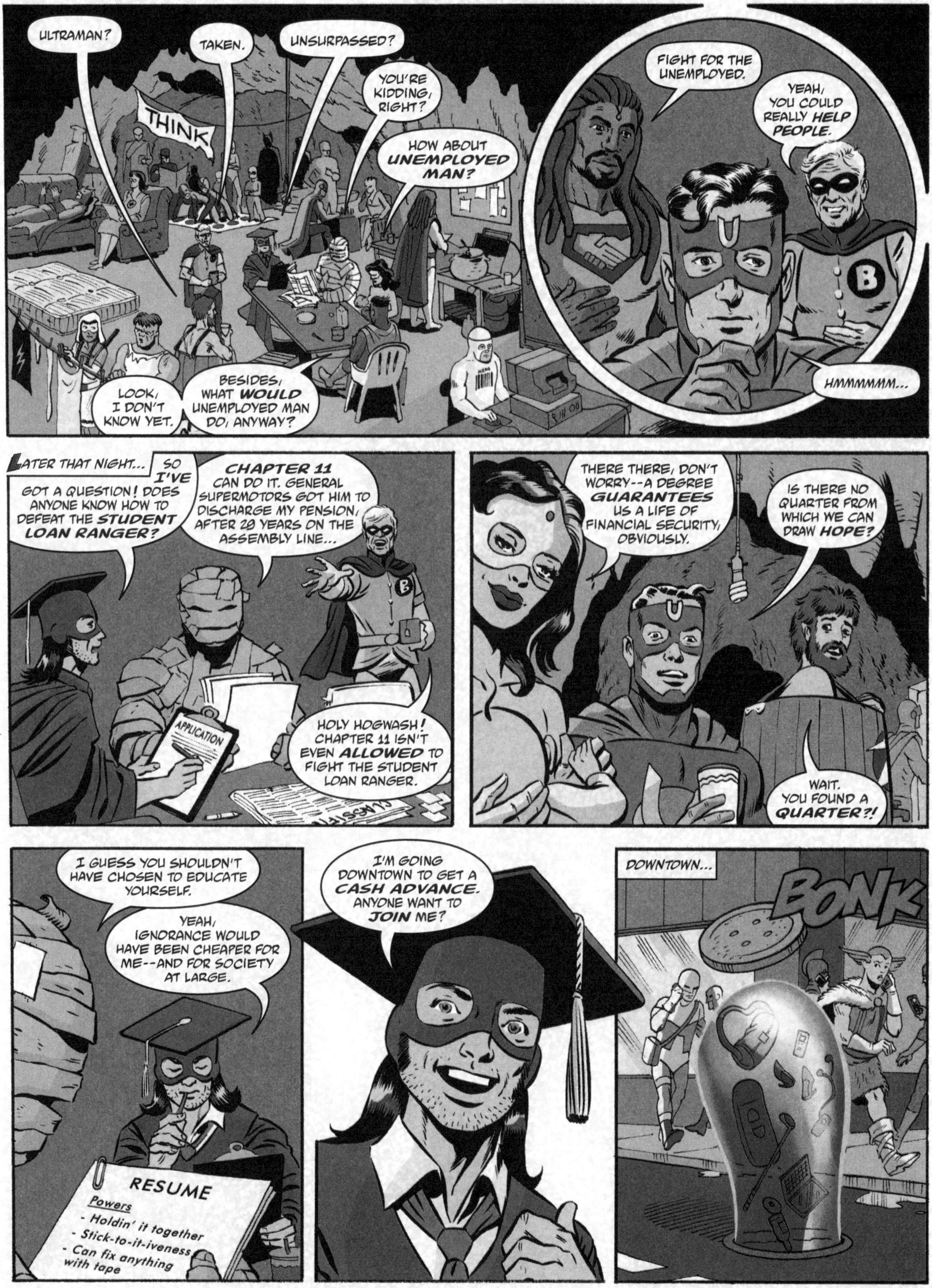
ULTRAMAN?
TAKEN.
UNSURPASSED?
YOU'RE KIDDING, RIGHT?
HOW ABOUT UNEMPLOYED MAN?
THINK
LOOK, I DON'T KNOW YET.
BESIDES, WHAT WOULD UNEMPLOYED MAN DO, ANYWAY?
FIGHT FOR THE UNEMPLOYED.
YEAH, YOU COULD REALLY HELP PEOPLE.
HMMMMMM...
LATER THAT NIGHT...
SO I'VE GOT A QUESTION! DOES ANYONE KNOW HOW TO DEFEAT THE STUDENT LOAN RANGER?
CHAPTER 11 CAN DO IT. GENERAL SUPERMOTORS GOT HIM TO DISCHARGE MY PENSION, AFTER 20 YEARS ON THE ASSEMBLY LINE...
HOLY HOGWASH! CHAPTER 11 ISN'T EVEN ALLOWED TO FIGHT THE STUDENT LOAN RANGER.
APPLICATION
THERE THERE, DON'T WORRY--A DEGREE GUARANTEES US A LIFE OF FINANCIAL SECURITY, OBVIOUSLY.
IS THERE NO QUARTER FROM WHICH WE CAN DRAW HOPE?
WAIT. YOU FOUND A QUARTER?!
I GUESS YOU SHOULDN'T HAVE CHOSEN TO EDUCATE YOURSELF.
YEAH, IGNORANCE WOULD HAVE BEEN CHEAPER FOR ME--AND FOR SOCIETY AT LARGE.
RESUME
Powers
- Holdin' it together
- Stick-to-it-iveness
- Can fix anything with tape
I'M GOING DOWNTOWN TO GET A CASH ADVANCE. ANYONE WANT TO JOIN ME?
DOWNTOWN...
BONK

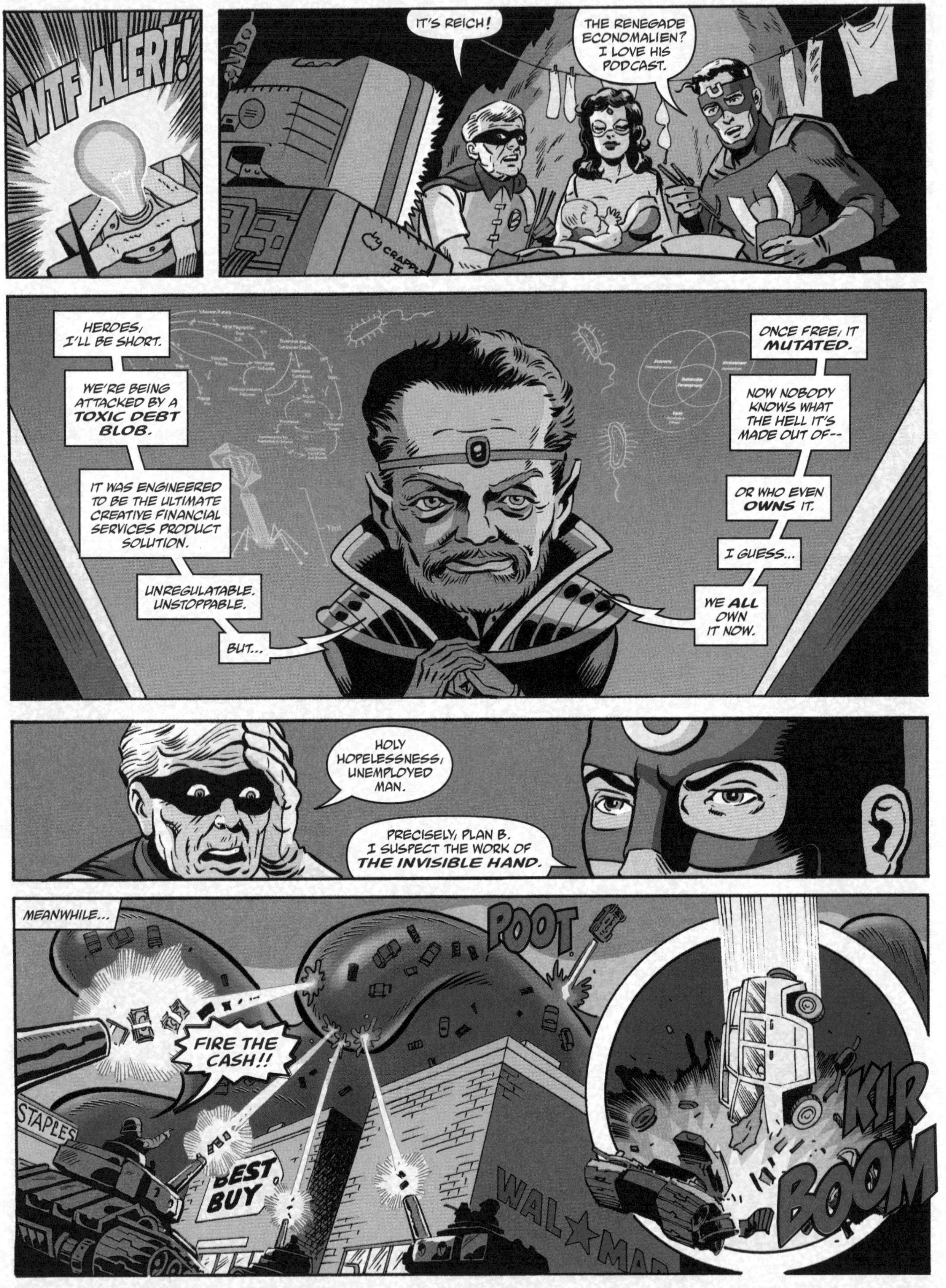
WTF ALERT!
IT'S REICH!
THE RENEGADE ECONOMALIEN? I LOVE HIS PODCAST.
CRAPPLE II
HEROES, I'LL BE SHORT.
WE'RE BEING ATTACKED BY A TOXIC DEBT BLOB.
IT WAS ENGINEERED TO BE THE ULTIMATE CREATIVE FINANCIAL SERVICES PRODUCT SOLUTION.
UNREGULATABLE. UNSTOPPABLE.
BUT...
ONCE FREE, IT MUTATED.
NOW NOBODY KNOWS WHAT THE HELL IT'S MADE OUT OF--
OR WHO EVEN OWNS IT.
I GUESS...
WE ALL OWN IT NOW.
HOLY HOPELESSNESS, UNEMPLOYED MAN.
PRECISELY, PLAN B. I SUSPECT THE WORK OF THE INVISIBLE HAND.
MEANWHILE...
POOT
FIRE THE CASH!!
STAPLES
BEST BUY
WAL★MAR
KIR
BOOM

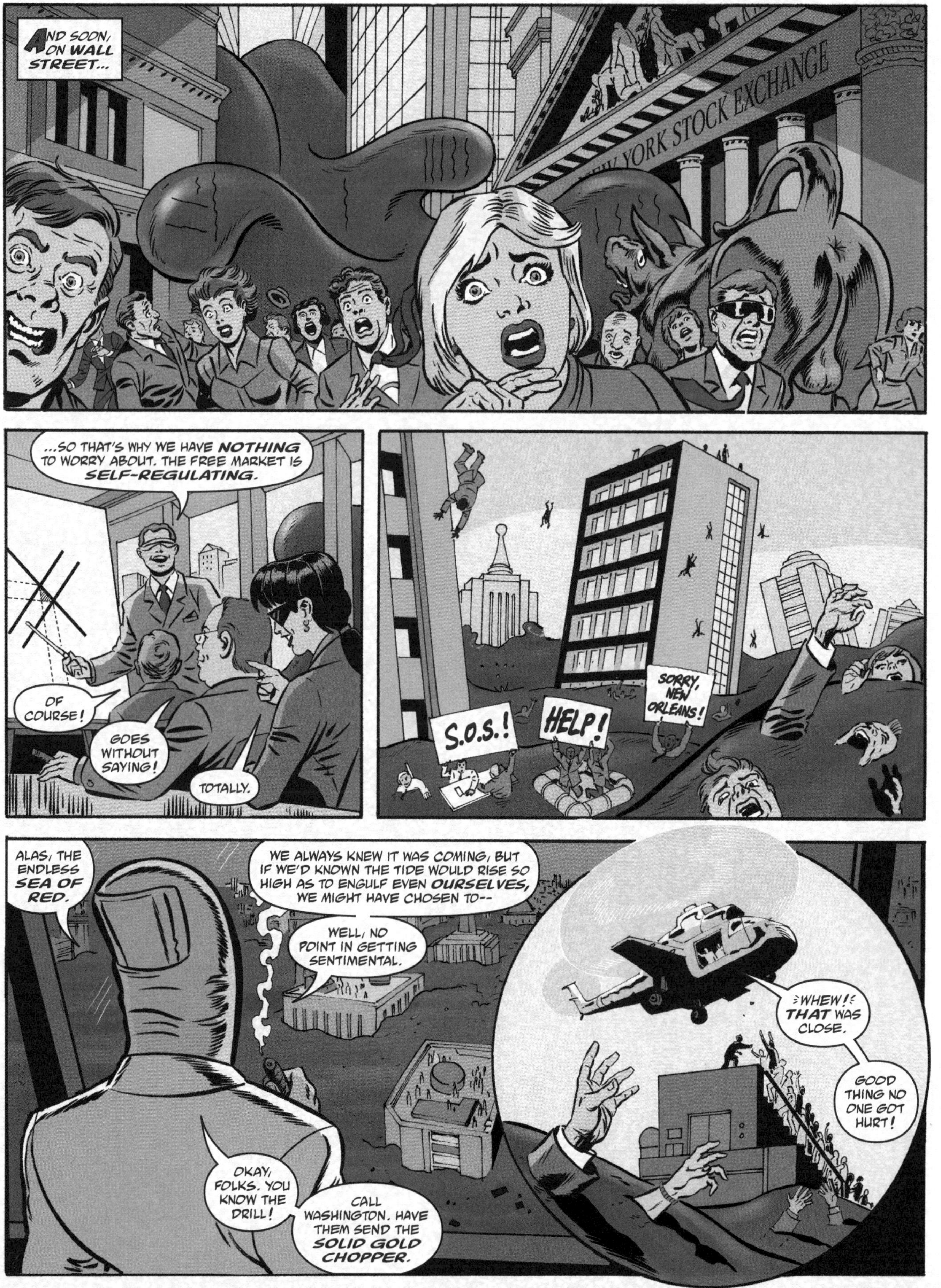

AND SOON, ON WALL STREET...
YORK STOCK EXCHANGE
...SO THAT'S WHY WE HAVE NOTHING TO WORRY ABOUT. THE FREE MARKET IS SELF-REGULATING.
OF COURSE!
GOES WITHOUT SAYING!
TOTALLY.
S.O.S.!
HELP!
SORRY, NEW ORLEANS!
ALAS, THE ENDLESS SEA OF RED.
WE ALWAYS KNEW IT WAS COMING, BUT IF WE'D KNOWN THE TIDE WOULD RISE SO HIGH AS TO ENGULF EVEN OURSELVES, WE MIGHT HAVE CHOSEN TO--
WELL, NO POINT IN GETTING SENTIMENTAL.
OKAY, FOLKS. YOU KNOW THE DRILL!
CALL WASHINGTON. HAVE THEM SEND THE SOLID GOLD CHOPPER.
WHEW! THAT WAS CLOSE.
GOOD THING NO ONE GOT HURT!

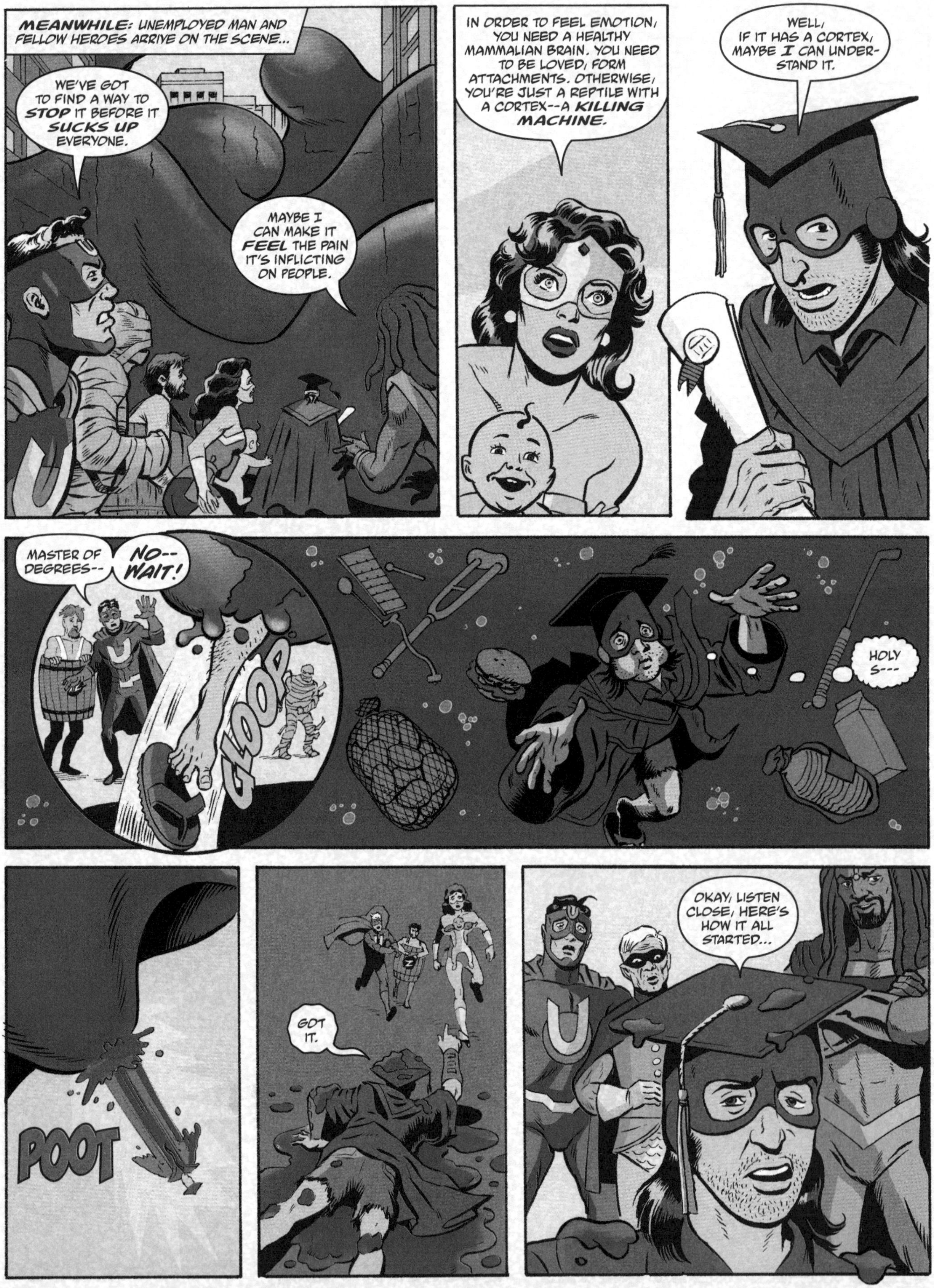
MEANWHILE: UNEMPLOYED MAN AND FELLOW HEROES ARRIVE ON THE SCENE...
WE'VE GOT TO FIND A WAY TO STOP IT BEFORE IT SUCKS UP EVERYONE.
MAYBE I CAN MAKE IT FEEL THE PAIN IT'S INFLICTING ON PEOPLE.
IN ORDER TO FEEL EMOTION, YOU NEED A HEALTHY MAMMALIAN BRAIN. YOU NEED TO BE LOVED, FORM ATTACHMENTS. OTHERWISE, YOU'RE JUST A REPTILE WITH A CORTEX--A KILLING MACHINE.
WELL, IF IT HAS A CORTEX, MAYBE I CAN UNDERSTAND IT.
MASTER OF DEGREES--
NO-- WAIT!
GLOOP
HOLY S---
POOT
GOT IT.
OKAY, LISTEN CLOSE, HERE'S HOW IT ALL STARTED...

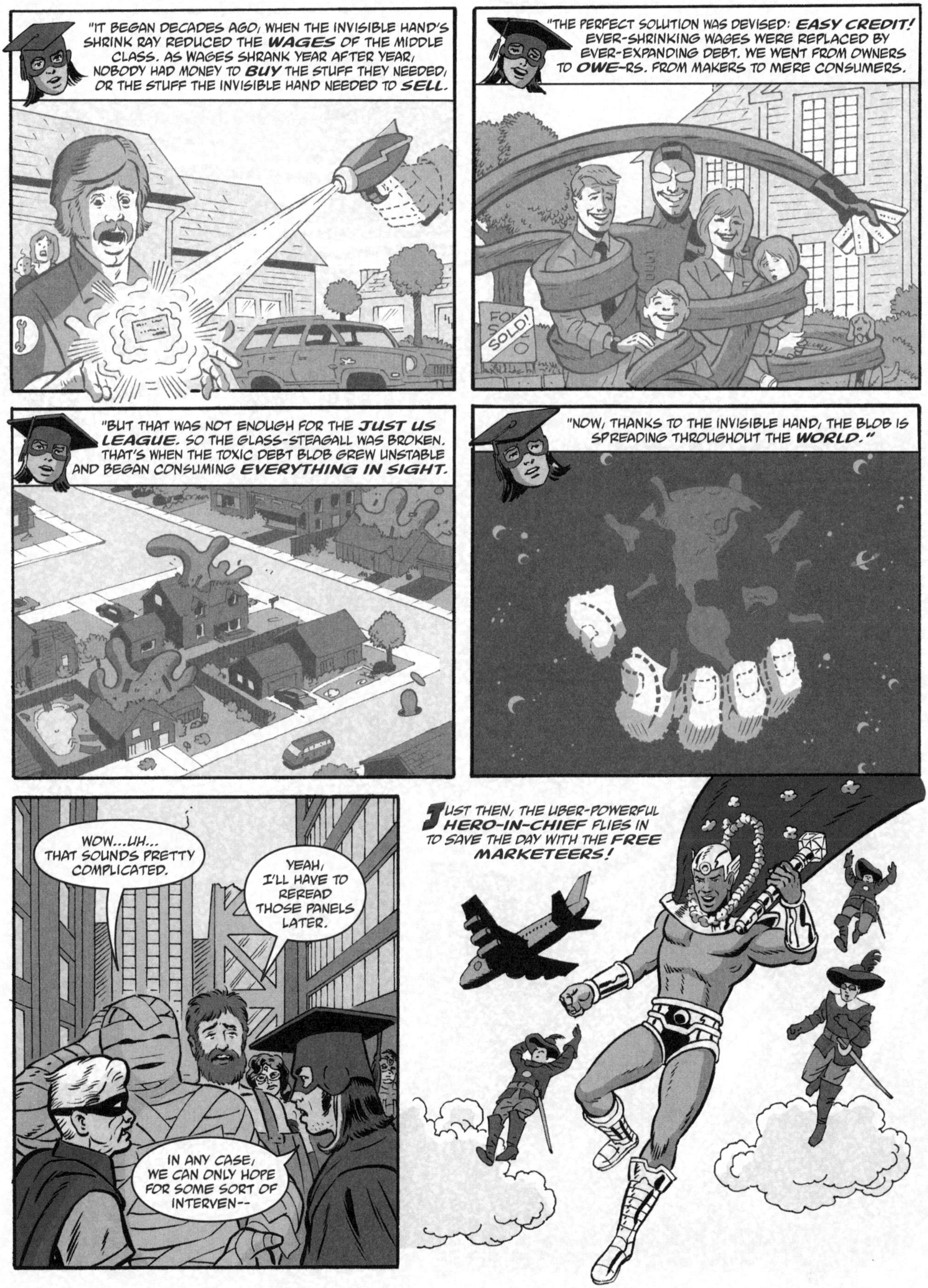
"IT BEGAN DECADES AGO, WHEN THE INVISIBLE HAND'S SHRINK RAY REDUCED THE WAGES OF THE MIDDLE CLASS. AS WAGES SHRANK YEAR AFTER YEAR, NOBODY HAD MONEY TO BUY THE STUFF THEY NEEDED, OR THE STUFF THE INVISIBLE HAND NEEDED TO SELL.
"THE PERFECT SOLUTION WAS DEVISED: EASY CREDIT! EVER-SHRINKING WAGES WERE REPLACED BY EVER-EXPANDING DEBT. WE WENT FROM OWNERS TO OWE-RS. FROM MAKERS TO MERE CONSUMERS.
SOLD!
"BUT THAT WAS NOT ENOUGH FOR THE JUST US LEAGUE. SO THE GLASS-STEAGALL WAS BROKEN. THAT'S WHEN THE TOXIC DEBT BLOB GREW UNSTABLE AND BEGAN CONSUMING EVERYTHING IN SIGHT.
"NOW, THANKS TO THE INVISIBLE HAND, THE BLOB IS SPREADING THROUGHOUT THE WORLD."
WOW...UH... THAT SOUNDS PRETTY COMPLICATED.
YEAH, I'LL HAVE TO REREAD THOSE PANELS LATER.
IN ANY CASE, WE CAN ONLY HOPE FOR SOME SORT OF INTERVEN--
JUST THEN, THE UBER-POWERFUL HERO-IN-CHIEF FLIES IN TO SAVE THE DAY WITH THE FREE MARKETEERS!

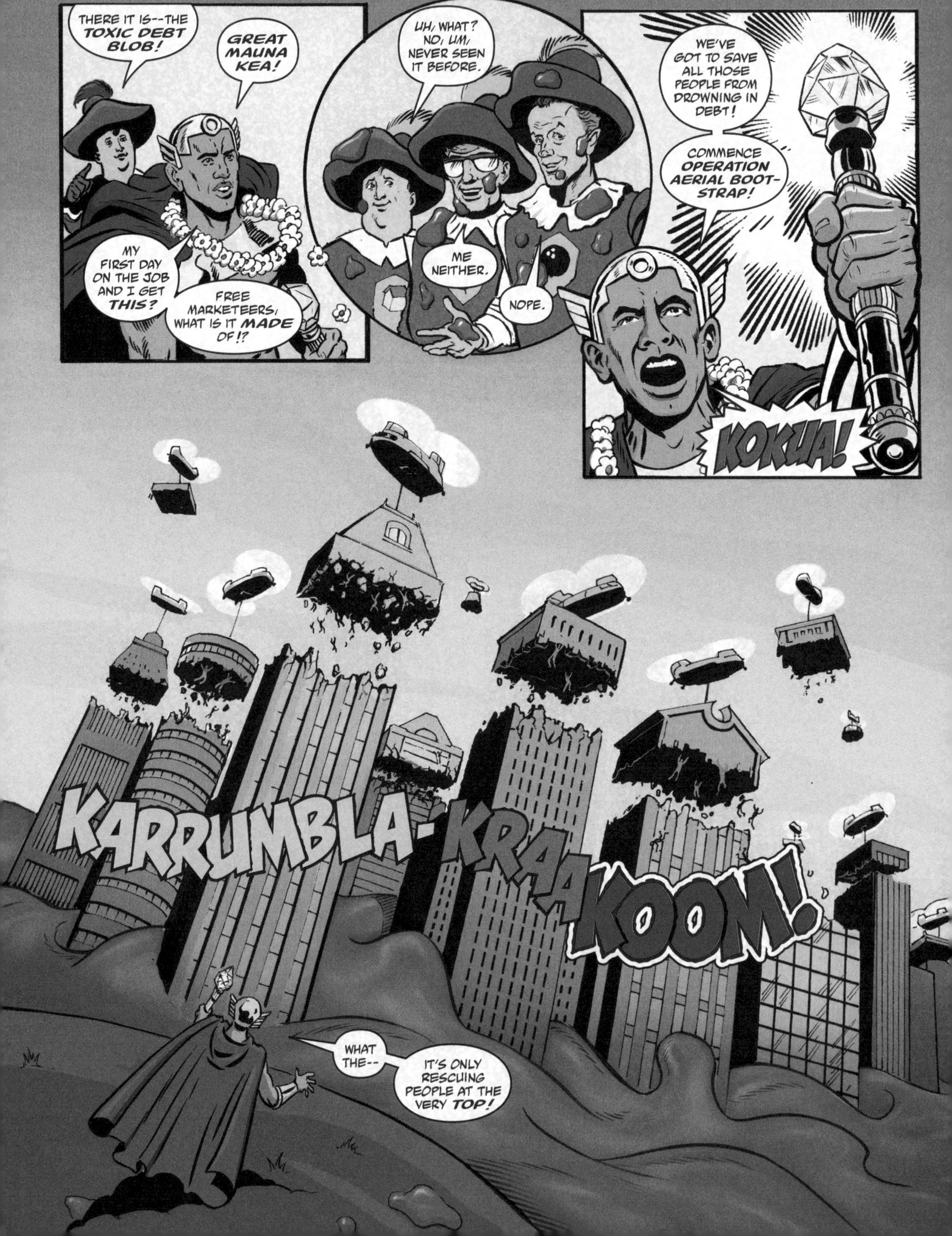
THERE IT IS--THE TOXIC DEBT BLOB!
GREAT MAUNA KEA!
MY FIRST DAY ON THE JOB AND I GET THIS?
FREE MARKETEERS, WHAT IS IT MADE OF!?
UH, WHAT? NO, UM, NEVER SEEN IT BEFORE.
ME NEITHER.
NOPE.
WE'VE GOT TO SAVE ALL THOSE PEOPLE FROM DROWNING IN DEBT!
COMMENCE OPERATION AERIAL BOOT-STRAP!
KOKUA!
KARRUMBLA-KRAAKOOM!
WHAT THE--
IT'S ONLY RESCUING PEOPLE AT THE VERY TOP!

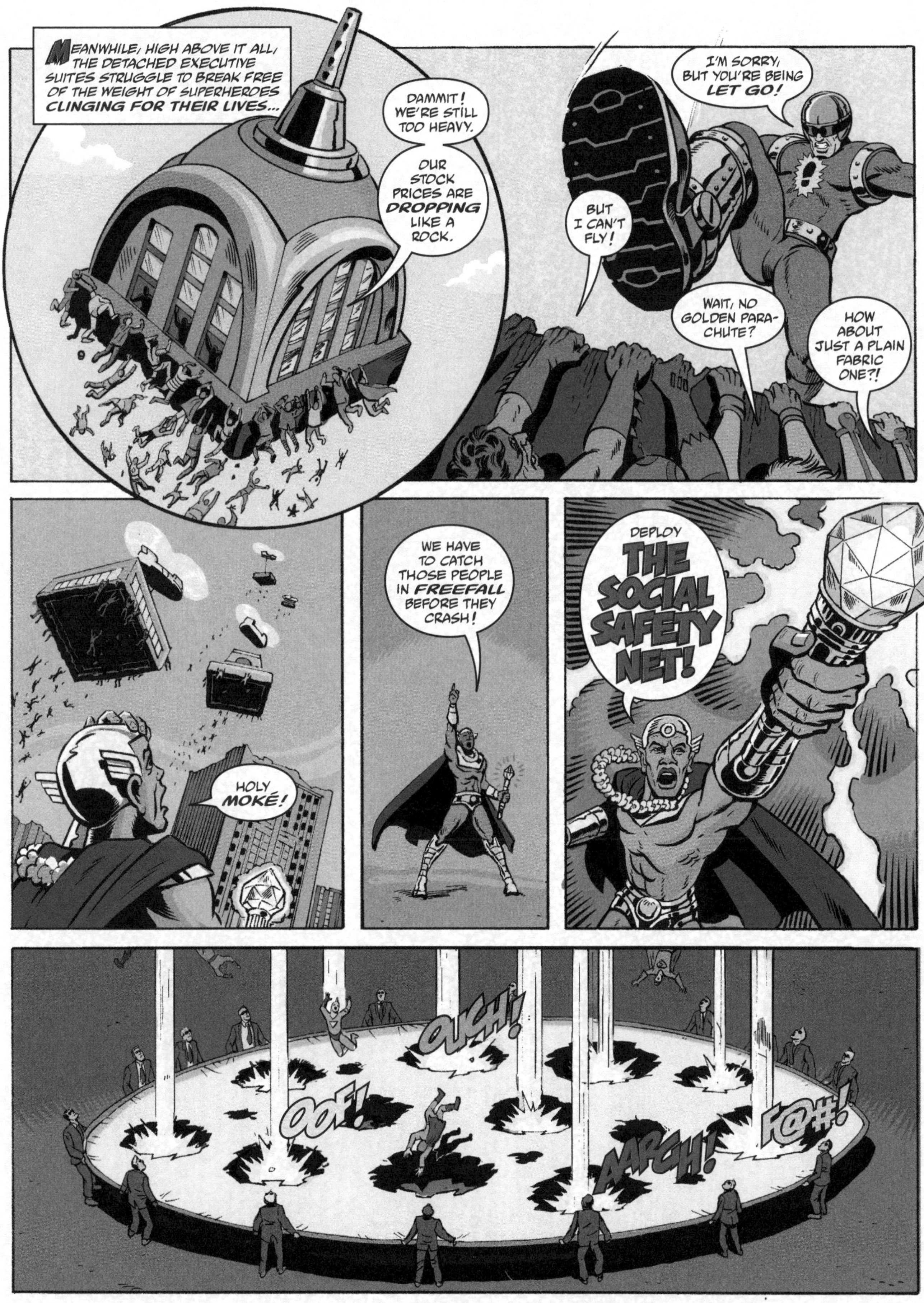
MEANWHILE, HIGH ABOVE IT ALL, THE DETACHED EXECUTIVE SUITES STRUGGLE TO BREAK FREE OF THE WEIGHT OF SUPERHEROES CLINGING FOR THEIR LIVES...
DAMMIT! WE'RE STILL TOO HEAVY.
OUR STOCK PRICES ARE DROPPING LIKE A ROCK.
I'M SORRY, BUT YOU'RE BEING LET GO!
BUT I CAN'T FLY!
WAIT, NO GOLDEN PARA-CHUTE?
HOW ABOUT JUST A PLAIN FABRIC ONE?!
HOLY MOKÉ!
WE HAVE TO CATCH THOSE PEOPLE IN FREEFALL BEFORE THEY CRASH!
DEPLOY THE SOCIAL SAFETY NET!
OUCH!
OOF!
AARGH!
F@#!

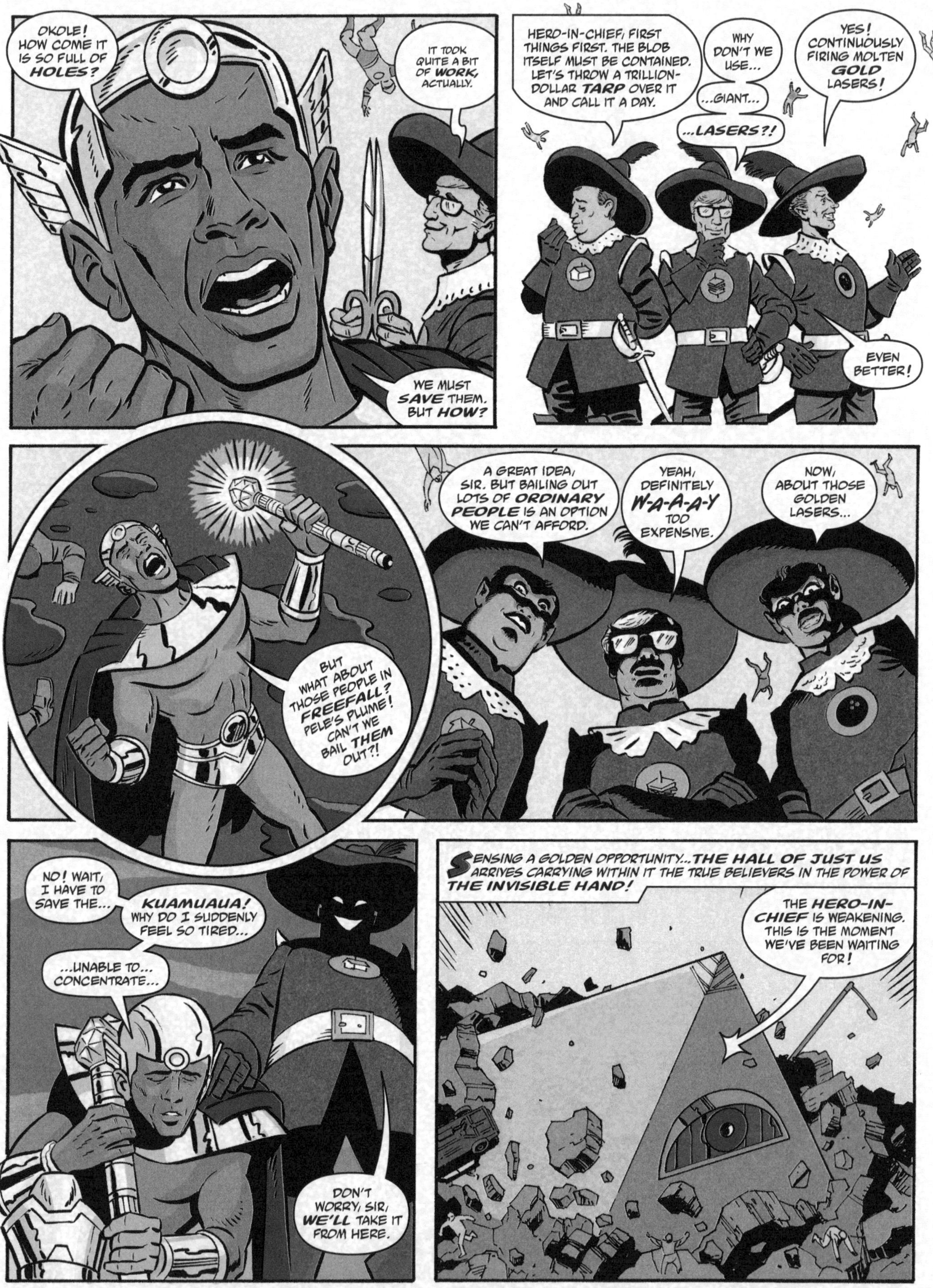
OKOLE! HOW COME IT IS SO FULL OF HOLES?
IT TOOK QUITE A BIT OF WORK, ACTUALLY.
WE MUST SAVE THEM. BUT HOW?
HERO-IN-CHIEF, FIRST THINGS FIRST. THE BLOB ITSELF MUST BE CONTAINED. LET'S THROW A TRILLION-DOLLAR TARP OVER IT AND CALL IT A DAY.
WHY DON'T WE USE...
...GIANT...
...LASERS?!
YES! CONTINUOUSLY FIRING MOLTEN GOLD LASERS!
EVEN BETTER!
BUT WHAT ABOUT THOSE PEOPLE IN FREEFALL? PELE'S PLUME! CAN'T WE BAIL THEM OUT?!
A GREAT IDEA, SIR. BUT BAILING OUT LOTS OF ORDINARY PEOPLE IS AN OPTION WE CAN'T AFFORD.
YEAH, DEFINITELY W-A-A-A-Y TOO EXPENSIVE.
NOW, ABOUT THOSE GOLDEN LASERS...
NO! WAIT, I HAVE TO SAVE THE...
KUAMUAUA! WHY DO I SUDDENLY FEEL SO TIRED...
...UNABLE TO... CONCENTRATE...
DON'T WORRY, SIR, WE'LL TAKE IT FROM HERE.
SENSING A GOLDEN OPPORTUNITY... THE HALL OF JUST US ARRIVES CARRYING WITHIN IT THE TRUE BELIEVERS IN THE POWER OF THE INVISIBLE HAND!
THE HERO-IN-CHIEF IS WEAKENING. THIS IS THE MOMENT WE'VE BEEN WAITING FOR!

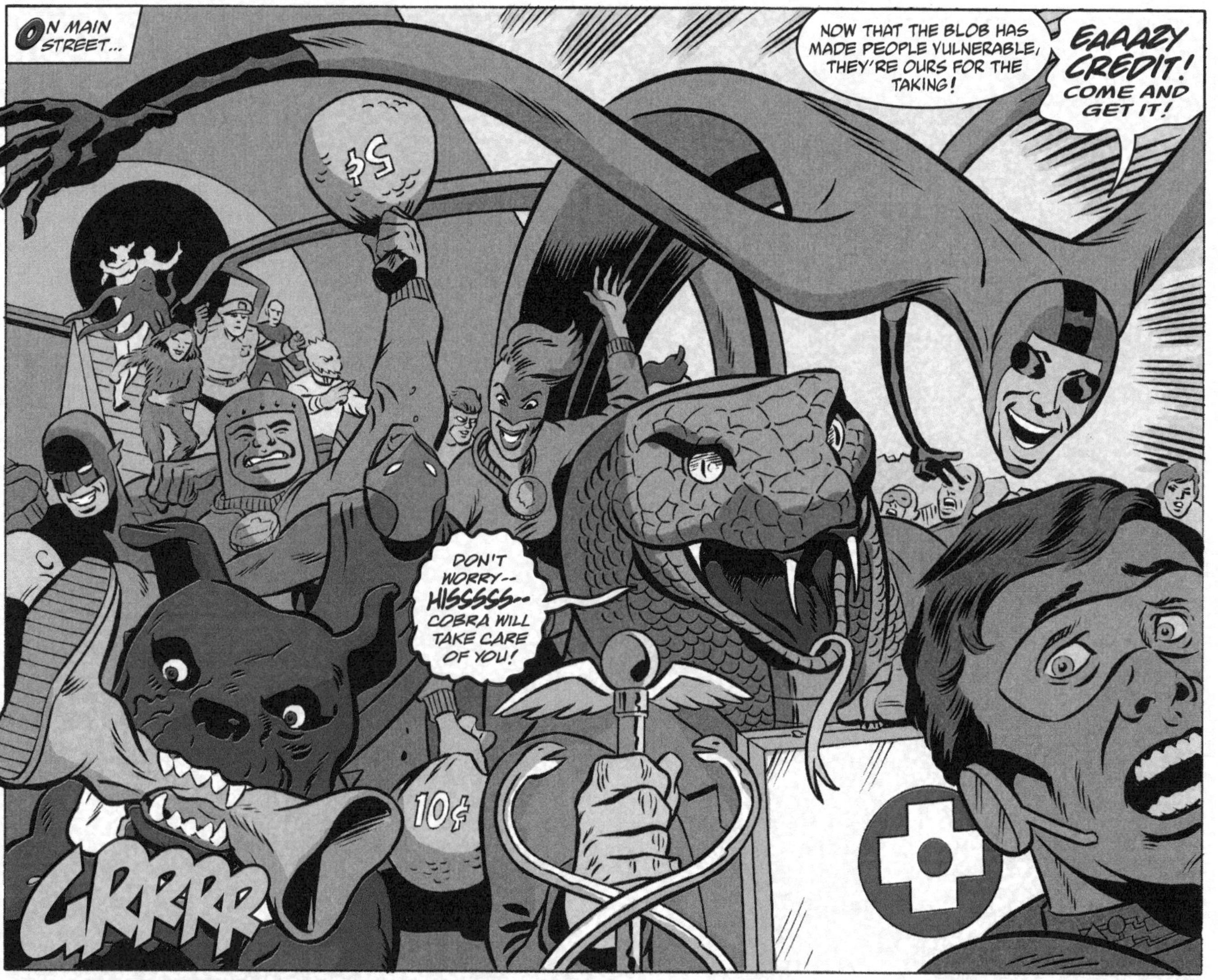
ON MAIN STREET...
NOW THAT THE BLOB HAS MADE PEOPLE VULNERABLE, THEY'RE OURS FOR THE TAKING!
EAAAZY CREDIT! COME AND GET IT!
DON'T WORRY-- HISSSSS-- COBRA WILL TAKE CARE OF YOU!
5¢
10¢
GRRRR

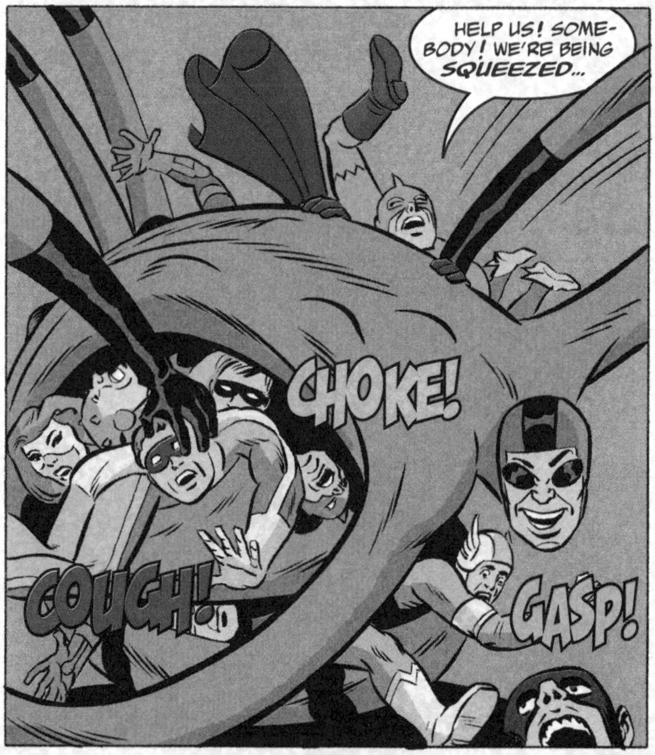
HELP US! SOMEBODY! WE'RE BEING SQUEEZED...
CHOKE!
COUGH!
GASP!

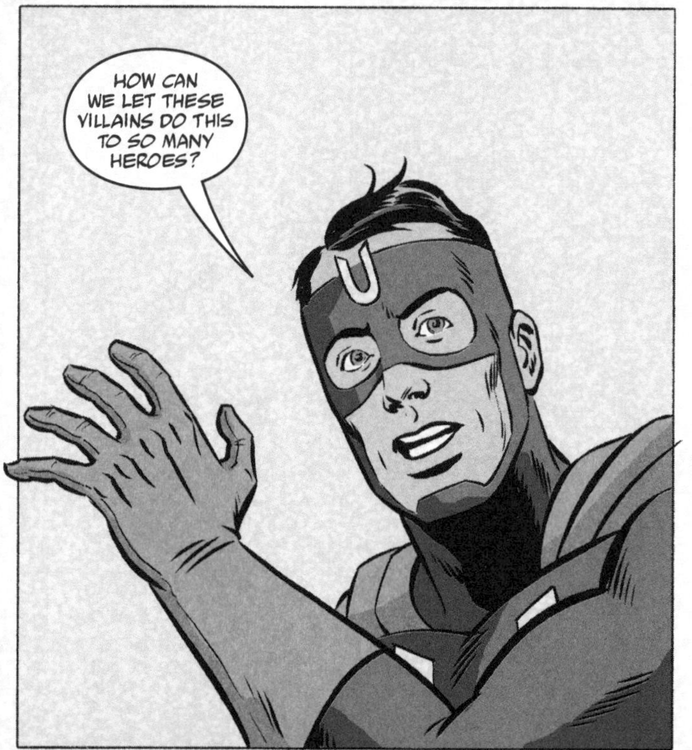
HOW CAN WE LET THESE VILLAINS DO THIS TO SO MANY HEROES?

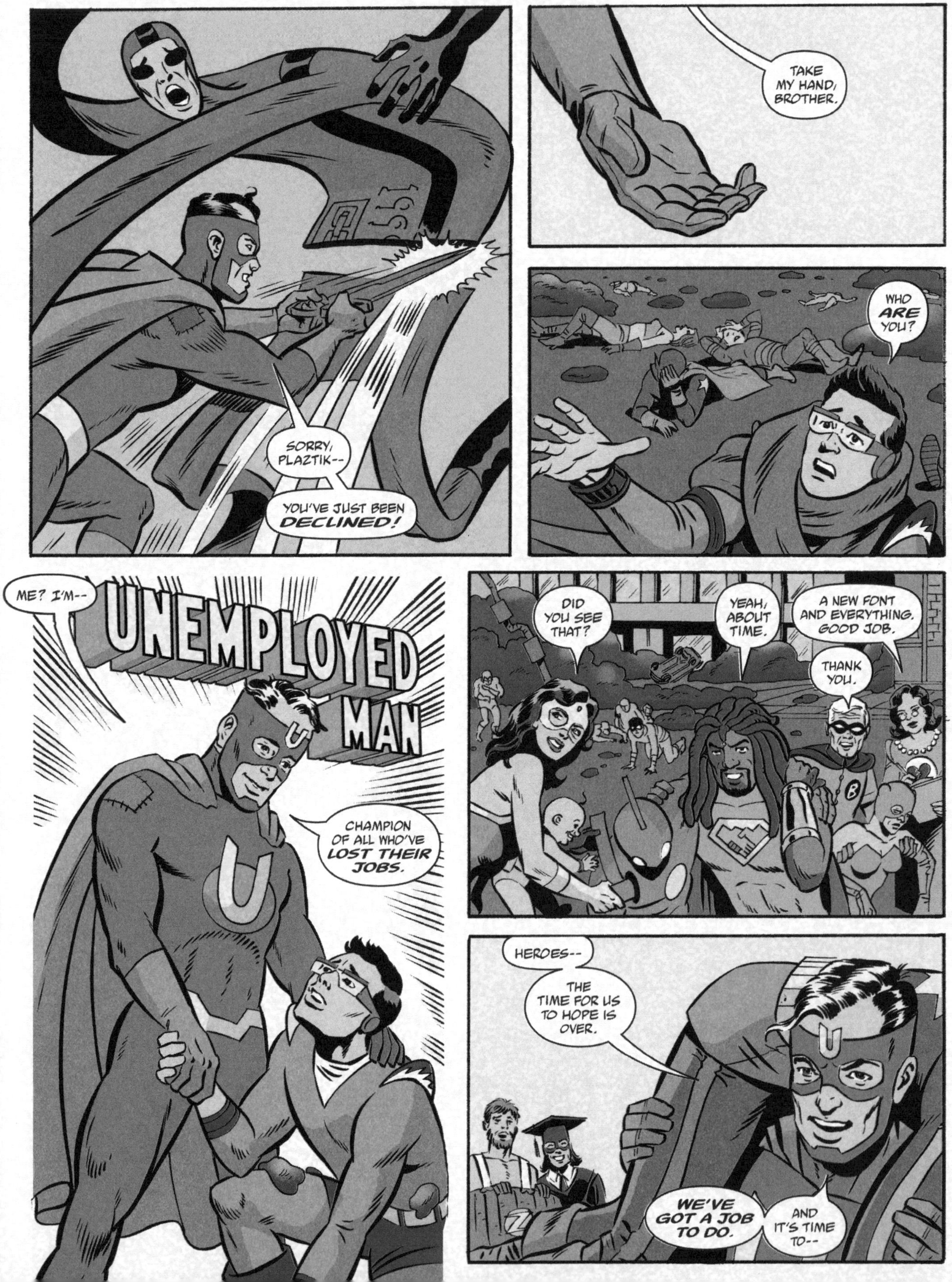

SORRY, PLAZTIK--
YOU'VE JUST BEEN DECLINED!
TAKE MY HAND, BROTHER.
WHO ARE YOU?
ME? I'M--
UNEMPLOYED MAN
CHAMPION OF ALL WHO'VE LOST THEIR JOBS.
DID YOU SEE THAT?
YEAH, ABOUT TIME.
A NEW FONT AND EVERYTHING. GOOD JOB.
THANK YOU.
HEROES--
THE TIME FOR US TO HOPE IS OVER.
WE'VE GOT A JOB TO DO.
AND IT'S TIME TO--

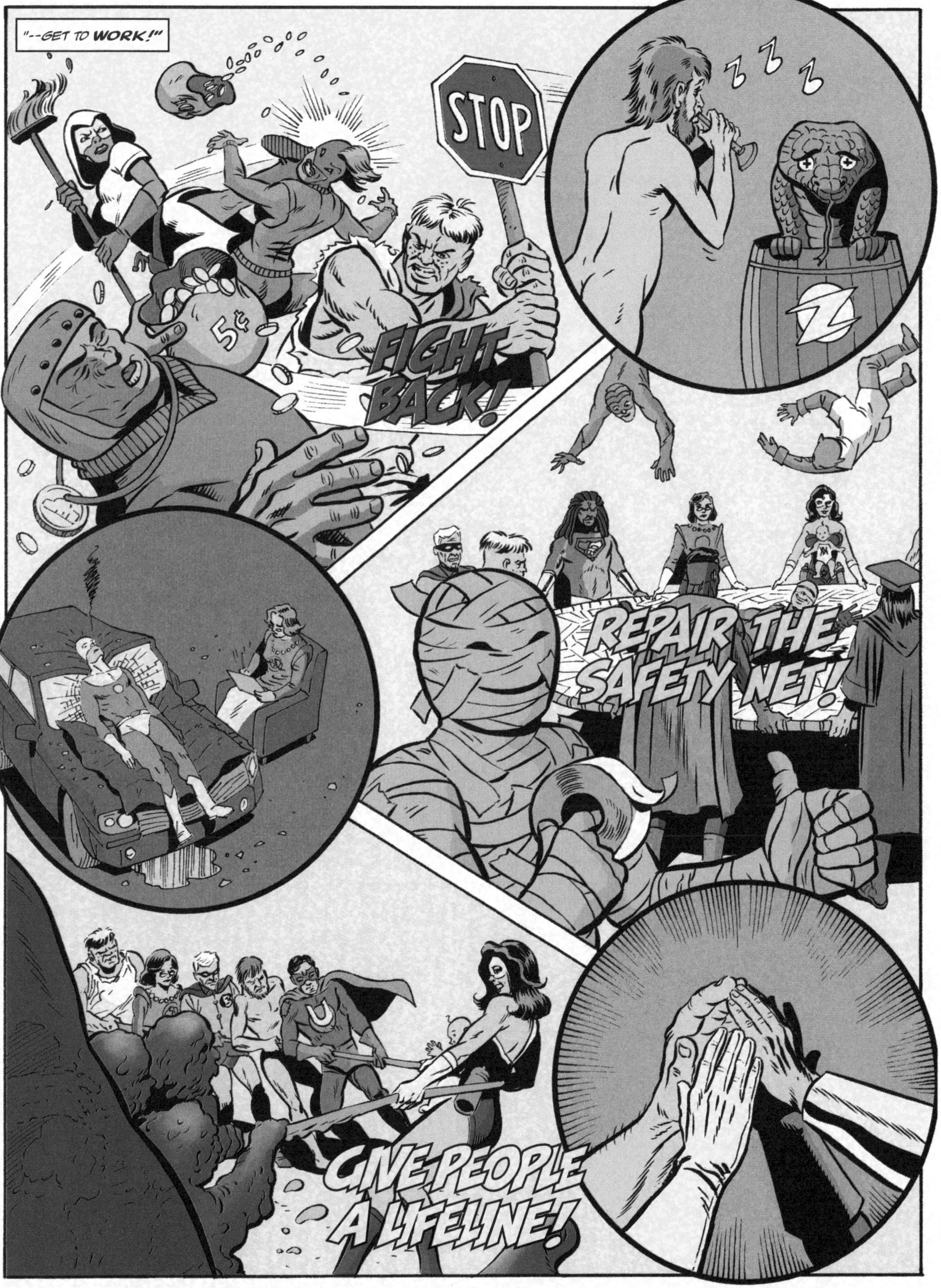
"--GET TO WORK!"
STOP
5¢
FIGHT BACK!
ZZZ
REPAIR THE SAFETY NET!
GIVE PEOPLE A LIFELINE!

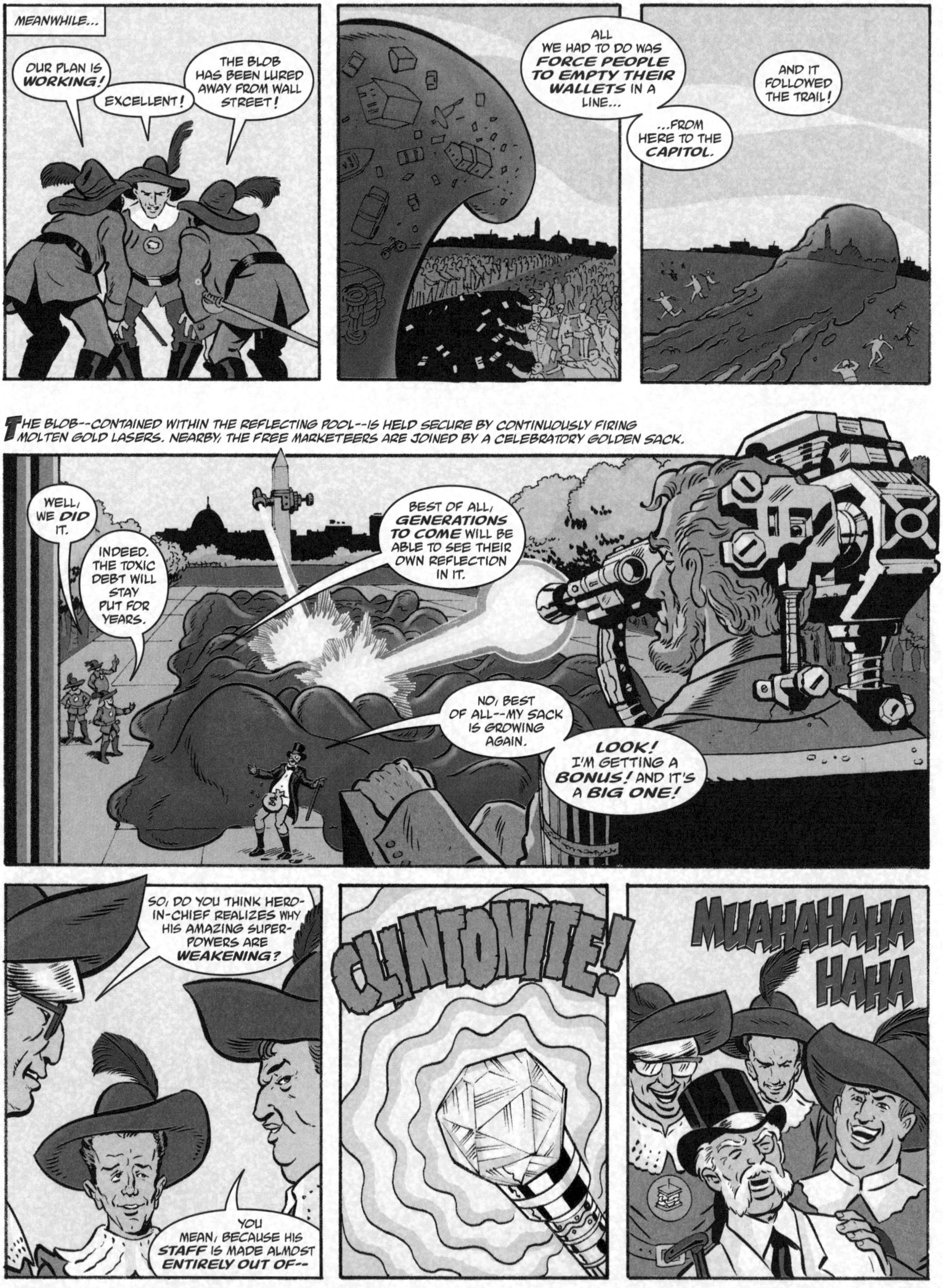

MEANWHILE...
OUR PLAN IS WORKING!
EXCELLENT!
THE BLOB HAS BEEN LURED AWAY FROM WALL STREET!
ALL WE HAD TO DO WAS FORCE PEOPLE TO EMPTY THEIR WALLETS IN A LINE...
...FROM HERE TO THE CAPITOL.
AND IT FOLLOWED THE TRAIL!
THE BLOB--CONTAINED WITHIN THE REFLECTING POOL--IS HELD SECURE BY CONTINUOUSLY FIRING MOLTEN GOLD LASERS. NEARBY, THE FREE MARKETEERS ARE JOINED BY A CELEBRATORY GOLDEN SACK.
WELL, WE DID IT.
INDEED. THE TOXIC DEBT WILL STAY PUT FOR YEARS.
BEST OF ALL, GENERATIONS TO COME WILL BE ABLE TO SEE THEIR OWN REFLECTION IN IT.
NO, BEST OF ALL--MY SACK IS GROWING AGAIN.
LOOK! I'M GETTING A BONUS! AND IT'S A BIG ONE!
SO, DO YOU THINK HERO-IN-CHIEF REALIZES WHY HIS AMAZING SUPER-POWERS ARE WEAKENING?
YOU MEAN, BECAUSE HIS STAFF IS MADE ALMOST ENTIRELY OUT OF--
CLINTONITE!
MUAHAHAHA HAHA

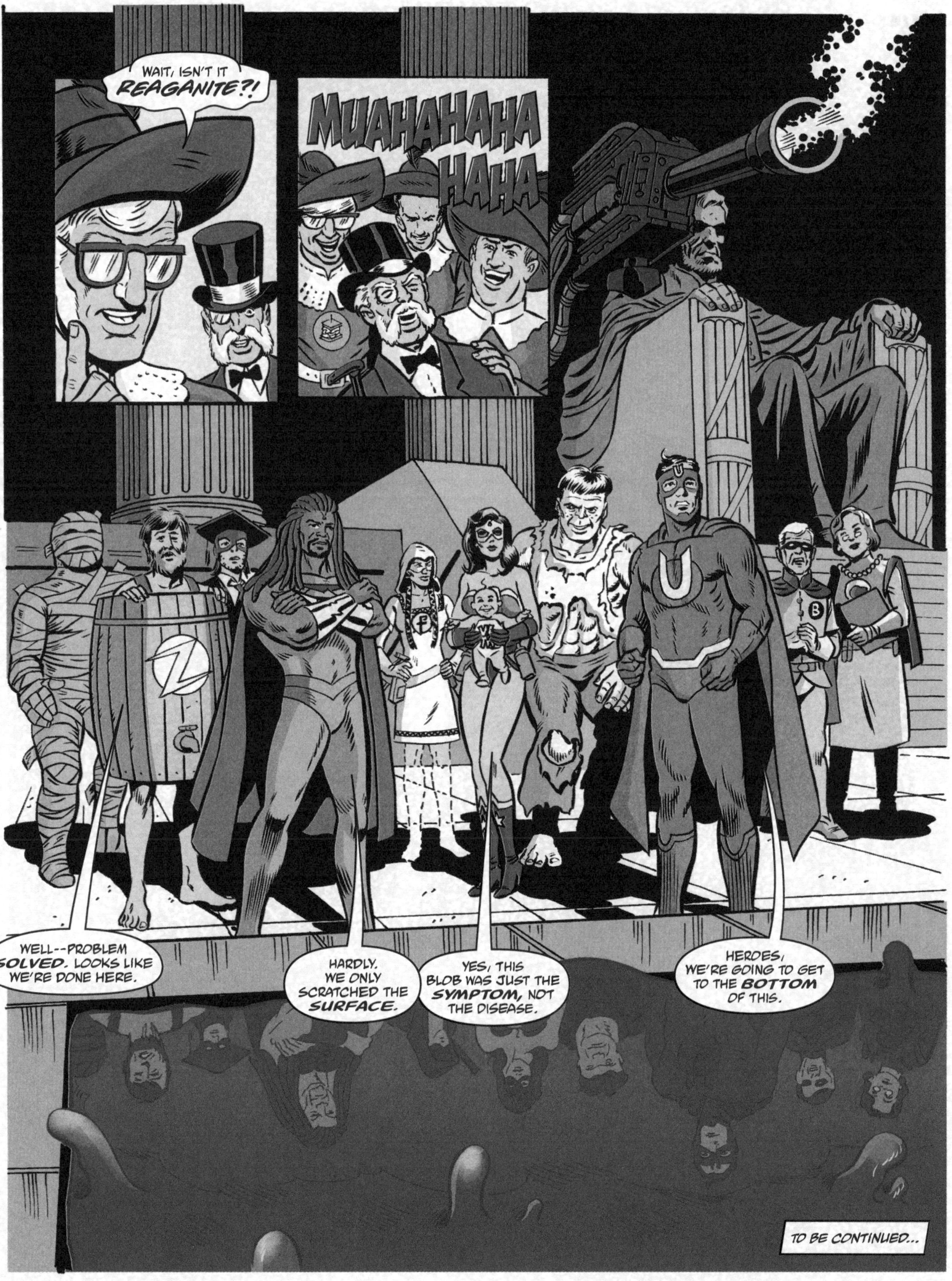
WAIT, ISN'T IT REAGANITE?!
MUAHAHAHA HAHA
WELL--PROBLEM SOLVED. LOOKS LIKE WE'RE DONE HERE.
HARDLY. WE ONLY SCRATCHED THE SURFACE.
YES, THIS BLOB WAS JUST THE SYMPTOM, NOT THE DISEASE.
HEROES, WE'RE GOING TO GET TO THE BOTTOM OF THIS.
TO BE CONTINUED...

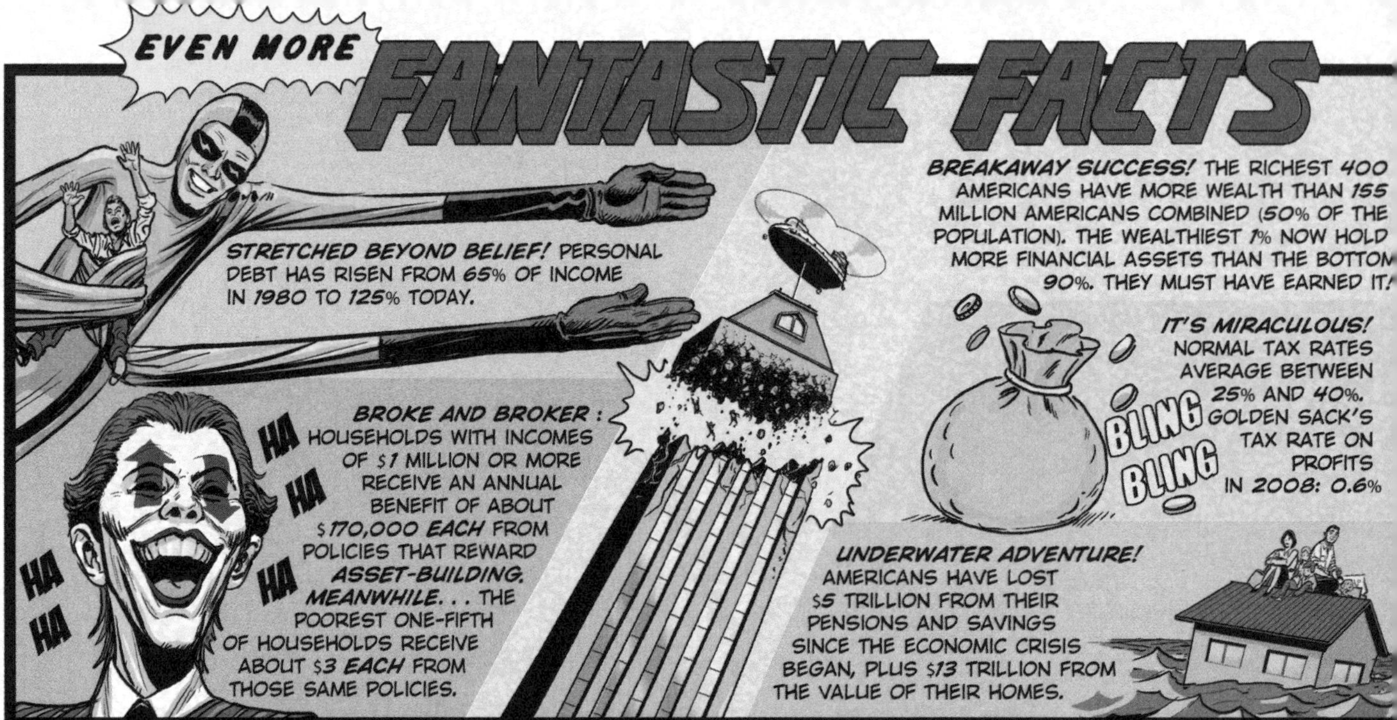
EVEN MORE
FANTASTIC FACTS
STRETCHED BEYOND BELIEF! PERSONAL DEBT HAS RISEN FROM 65% OF INCOME IN 1980 TO 125% TODAY.
BREAKAWAY SUCCESS! THE RICHEST 400 AMERICANS HAVE MORE WEALTH THAN 155 MILLION AMERICANS COMBINED (50% OF THE POPULATION). THE WEALTHIEST 1% NOW HOLD MORE FINANCIAL ASSETS THAN THE BOTTOM 90%. THEY MUST HAVE EARNED IT!
BROKE AND BROKER : HOUSEHOLDS WITH INCOMES OF $1 MILLION OR MORE RECEIVE AN ANNUAL BENEFIT OF ABOUT $170,000 EACH FROM POLICIES THAT REWARD ASSET-BUILDING. MEANWHILE. . . THE POOREST ONE-FIFTH OF HOUSEHOLDS RECEIVE ABOUT $3 EACH FROM THOSE SAME POLICIES.
HA HA HA HA HA HA
IT'S MIRACULOUS! NORMAL TAX RATES AVERAGE BETWEEN 25% AND 40%. GOLDEN SACK'S TAX RATE ON PROFITS IN 2008: 0.6%
BLING BLING BLING
UNDERWATER ADVENTURE! AMERICANS HAVE LOST $5 TRILLION FROM THEIR PENSIONS AND SAVINGS SINCE THE ECONOMIC CRISIS BEGAN, PLUS $13 TRILLION FROM THE VALUE OF THEIR HOMES.

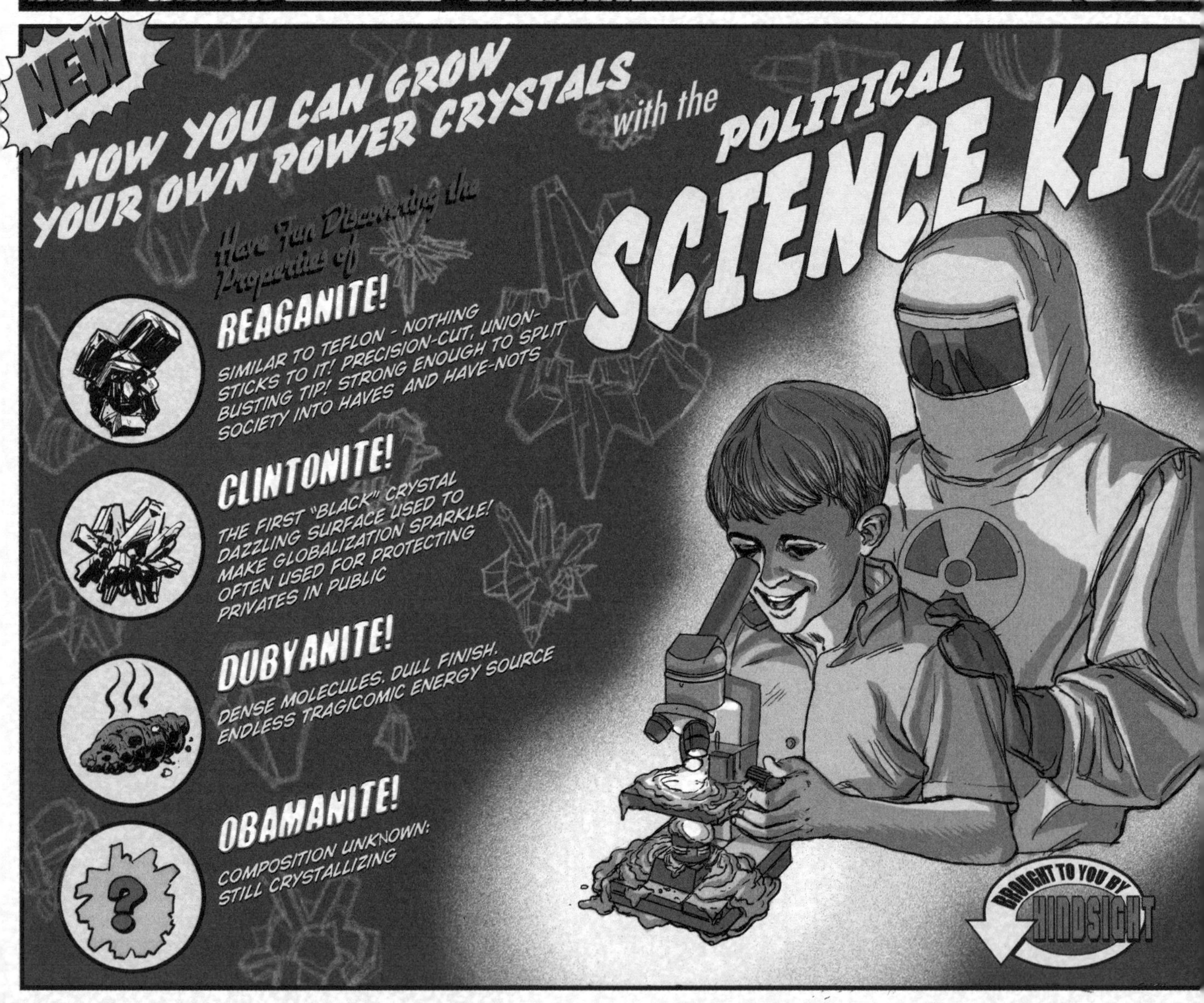
NEW
NOW YOU CAN GROW YOUR OWN POWER CRYSTALS with the POLITICAL SCIENCE KIT
Have Fun Discovering the Properties of
REAGANITE!
SIMILAR TO TEFLON - NOTHING STICKS TO IT! PRECISION-CUT, UNION-BUSTING TIP! STRONG ENOUGH TO SPLIT SOCIETY INTO HAVES AND HAVE-NOTS
CLINTONITE!
THE FIRST "BLACK" CRYSTAL DAZZLING SURFACE USED TO MAKE GLOBALIZATION SPARKLE! OFTEN USED FOR PROTECTING PRIVATES IN PUBLIC
DUBYANITE!
DENSE MOLECULES. DULL FINISH. ENDLESS TRAGICOMIC ENERGY SOURCE
OBAMANITE!
COMPOSITION UNKNOWN: STILL CRYSTALLIZING
?
BROUGHT TO YOU BY HINDSIGHT

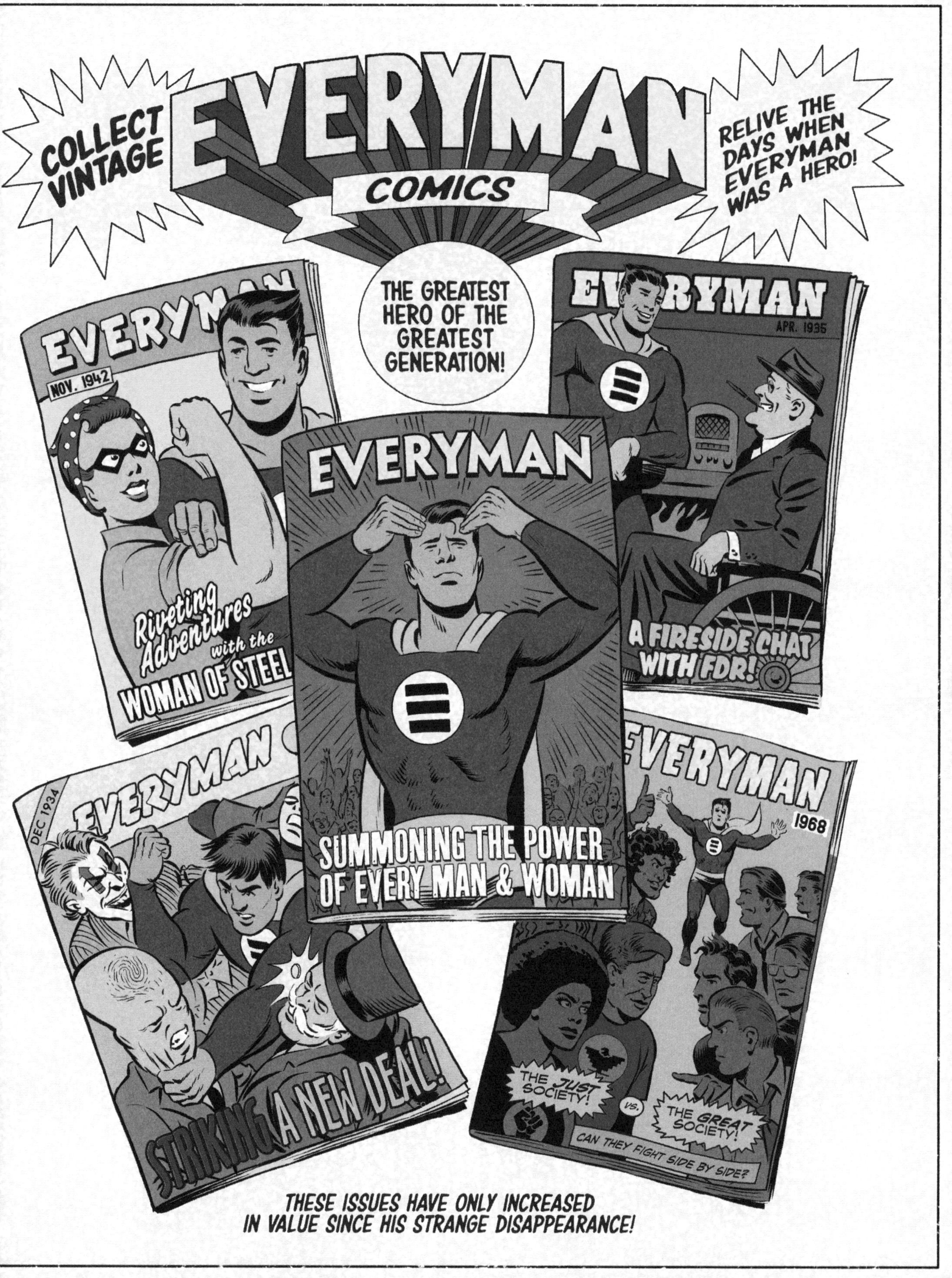
COLLECT VINTAGE
EVERYMAN
COMICS
RELIVE THE DAYS WHEN EVERYMAN WAS A HERO!
THE GREATEST HERO OF THE GREATEST GENERATION!
EVERYMAN
NOV. 1942
Riveting Adventures with the WOMAN OF STEEL
EVERYMAN
APR. 1935
A FIRESIDE CHAT WITH FDR!
EVERYMAN
SUMMONING THE POWER OF EVERY MAN & WOMAN
EVERYMAN
DEC 1934
STRIKING A NEW DEAL!
EVERYMAN
1968
THE JUST SOCIETY!
VS.
THE GREAT SOCIETY!
CAN THEY FIGHT SIDE BY SIDE?
THESE ISSUES HAVE ONLY INCREASED IN VALUE SINCE HIS STRANGE DISAPPEARANCE!

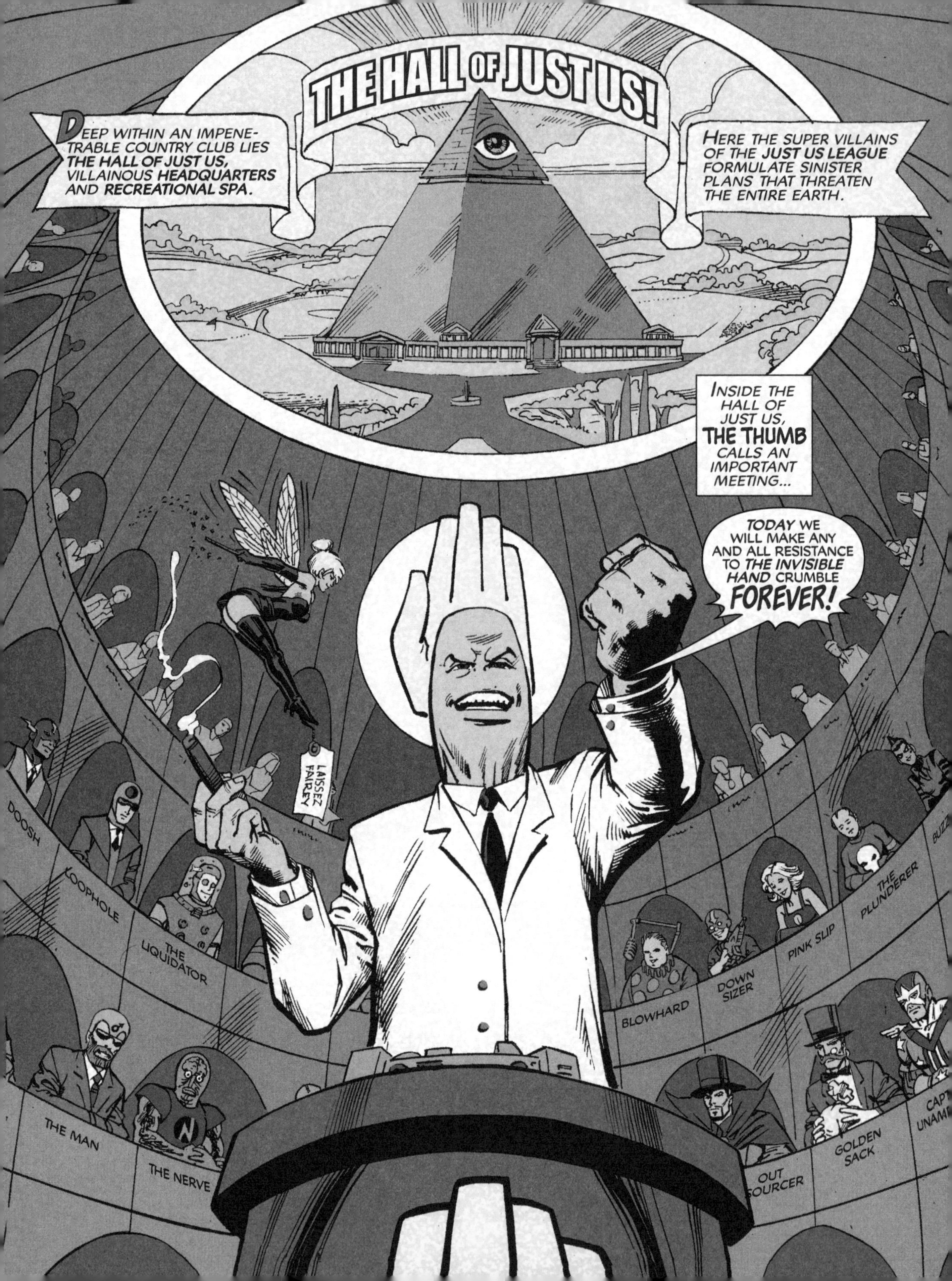
THE HALL OF JUST US!
DEEP WITHIN AN IMPENETRABLE COUNTRY CLUB LIES THE HALL OF JUST US, VILLAINOUS HEADQUARTERS AND RECREATIONAL SPA.
HERE THE SUPER VILLAINS OF THE JUST US LEAGUE FORMULATE SINISTER PLANS THAT THREATEN THE ENTIRE EARTH.
INSIDE THE HALL OF JUST US, THE THUMB CALLS AN IMPORTANT MEETING...
TODAY WE WILL MAKE ANY AND ALL RESISTANCE TO THE INVISIBLE HAND CRUMBLE FOREVER!
LAISSEZ FAIREY
DOOSH
LOOPHOLE
THE LIQUIDATOR
THE MAN
THE NERVE
BUZZ
THE PLUNDERER
PINK SLIP
DOWN SIZER
BLOWHARD
OUT SOURCER
GOLDEN SACK
CAPT UNAM

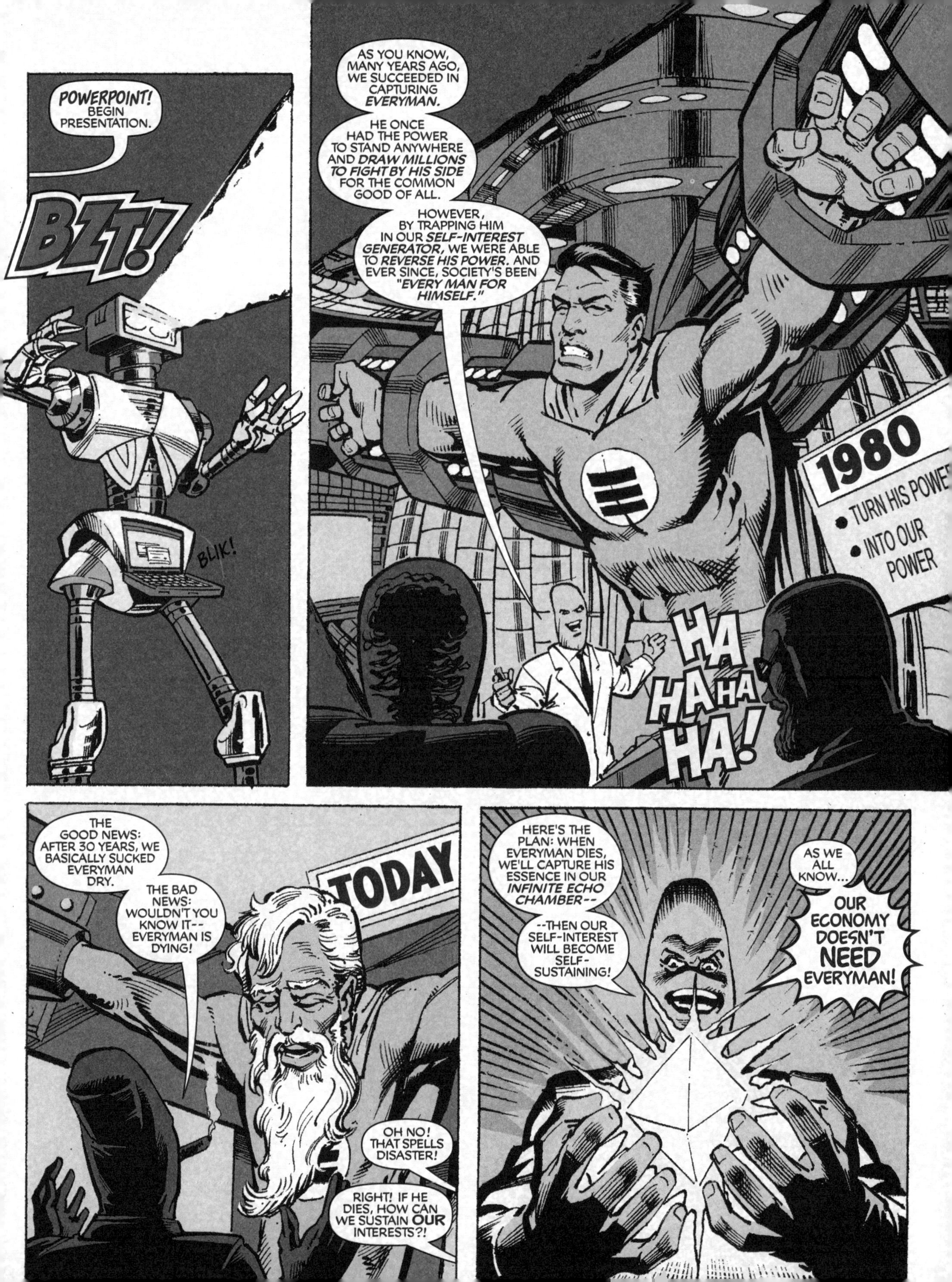
POWERPOINT! BEGIN PRESENTATION.
BZT!
BLIK!
AS YOU KNOW, MANY YEARS AGO, WE SUCCEEDED IN CAPTURING EVERYMAN.
HE ONCE HAD THE POWER TO STAND ANYWHERE AND DRAW MILLIONS TO FIGHT BY HIS SIDE FOR THE COMMON GOOD OF ALL.
HOWEVER, BY TRAPPING HIM IN OUR SELF-INTEREST GENERATOR, WE WERE ABLE TO REVERSE HIS POWER. AND EVER SINCE, SOCIETY'S BEEN "EVERY MAN FOR HIMSELF."
1980
• TURN HIS POWE
• INTO OUR POWER
HA HA HA HA HA!
THE GOOD NEWS: AFTER 30 YEARS, WE BASICALLY SUCKED EVERYMAN DRY.
TODAY
THE BAD NEWS: WOULDN'T YOU KNOW IT-- EVERYMAN IS DYING!
OH NO! THAT SPELLS DISASTER!
RIGHT! IF HE DIES, HOW CAN WE SUSTAIN OUR INTERESTS?!
HERE'S THE PLAN: WHEN EVERYMAN DIES, WE'LL CAPTURE HIS ESSENCE IN OUR INFINITE ECHO CHAMBER--
--THEN OUR SELF-INTEREST WILL BECOME SELF-SUSTAINING!
AS WE ALL KNOW...
OUR ECONOMY DOESN'T NEED EVERYMAN!

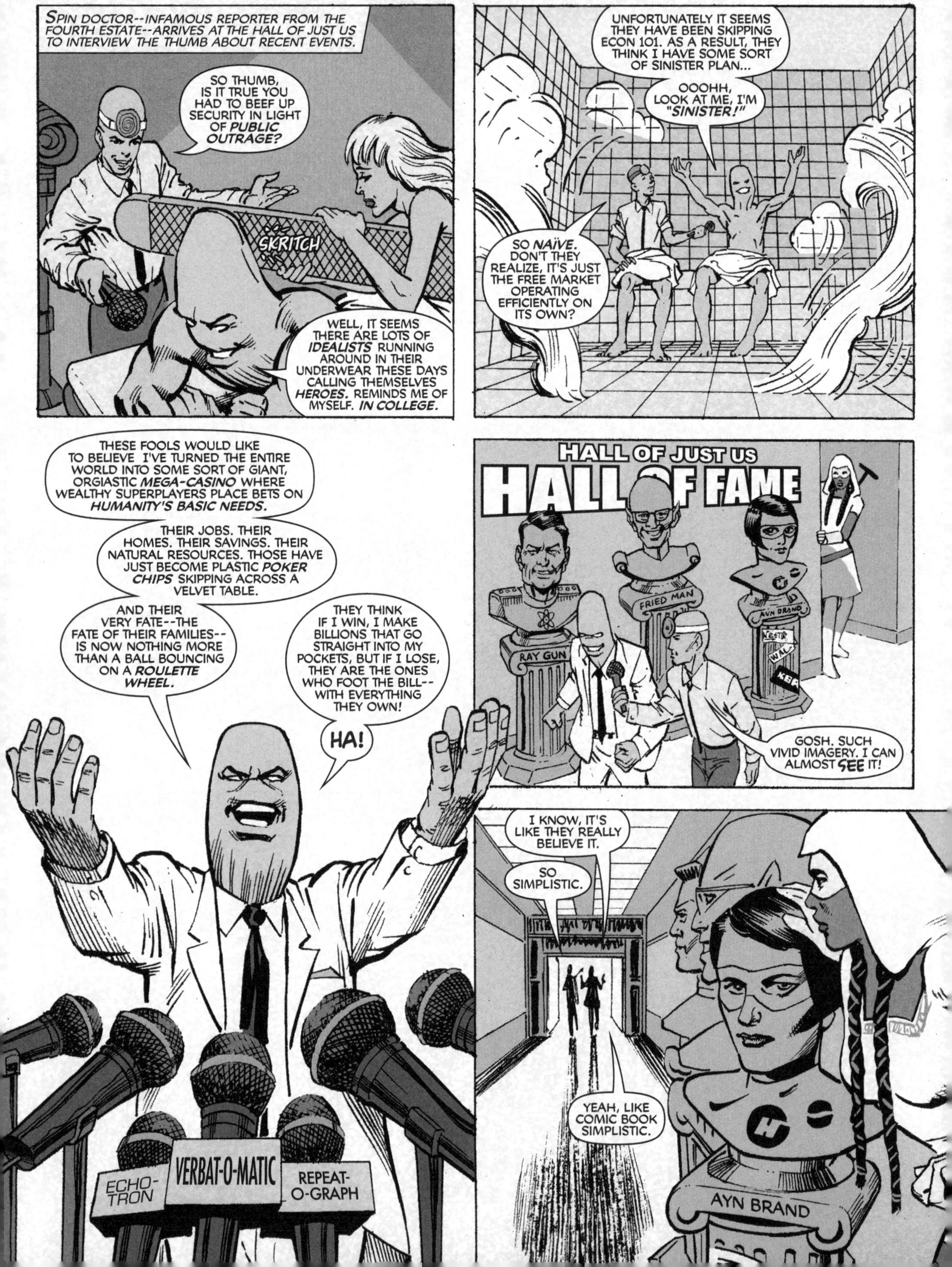
SPIN DOCTOR--INFAMOUS REPORTER FROM THE FOURTH ESTATE--ARRIVES AT THE HALL OF JUST US TO INTERVIEW THE THUMB ABOUT RECENT EVENTS.
SO THUMB, IS IT TRUE YOU HAD TO BEEF UP SECURITY IN LIGHT OF PUBLIC OUTRAGE?
SKRITCH
WELL, IT SEEMS THERE ARE LOTS OF IDEALISTS RUNNING AROUND IN THEIR UNDERWEAR THESE DAYS CALLING THEMSELVES HEROES. REMINDS ME OF MYSELF. IN COLLEGE.
UNFORTUNATELY IT SEEMS THEY HAVE BEEN SKIPPING ECON 101. AS A RESULT, THEY THINK I HAVE SOME SORT OF SINISTER PLAN...
OOOHH, LOOK AT ME, I'M "SINISTER!"
SO NAÏVE. DON'T THEY REALIZE, IT'S JUST THE FREE MARKET OPERATING EFFICIENTLY ON ITS OWN?
THESE FOOLS WOULD LIKE TO BELIEVE I'VE TURNED THE ENTIRE WORLD INTO SOME SORT OF GIANT, ORGIASTIC MEGA-CASINO WHERE WEALTHY SUPERPLAYERS PLACE BETS ON HUMANITY'S BASIC NEEDS.
THEIR JOBS. THEIR HOMES. THEIR SAVINGS. THEIR NATURAL RESOURCES. THOSE HAVE JUST BECOME PLASTIC POKER CHIPS SKIPPING ACROSS A VELVET TABLE.
AND THEIR VERY FATE--THE FATE OF THEIR FAMILIES--IS NOW NOTHING MORE THAN A BALL BOUNCING ON A ROULETTE WHEEL.
THEY THINK IF I WIN, I MAKE BILLIONS THAT GO STRAIGHT INTO MY POCKETS, BUT IF I LOSE, THEY ARE THE ONES WHO FOOT THE BILL--WITH EVERYTHING THEY OWN!
HA!
ECHO-TRON
VERBAT-O-MATIC
REPEAT-O-GRAPH
HALL OF JUST US
HALL OF FAME
RAY GUN
FRIED MAN
AYN BRAND
GOSH. SUCH VIVID IMAGERY. I CAN ALMOST SEE IT!
I KNOW, IT'S LIKE THEY REALLY BELIEVE IT.
SO SIMPLISTIC.
YEAH, LIKE COMIC BOOK SIMPLISTIC.
AYN BRAND

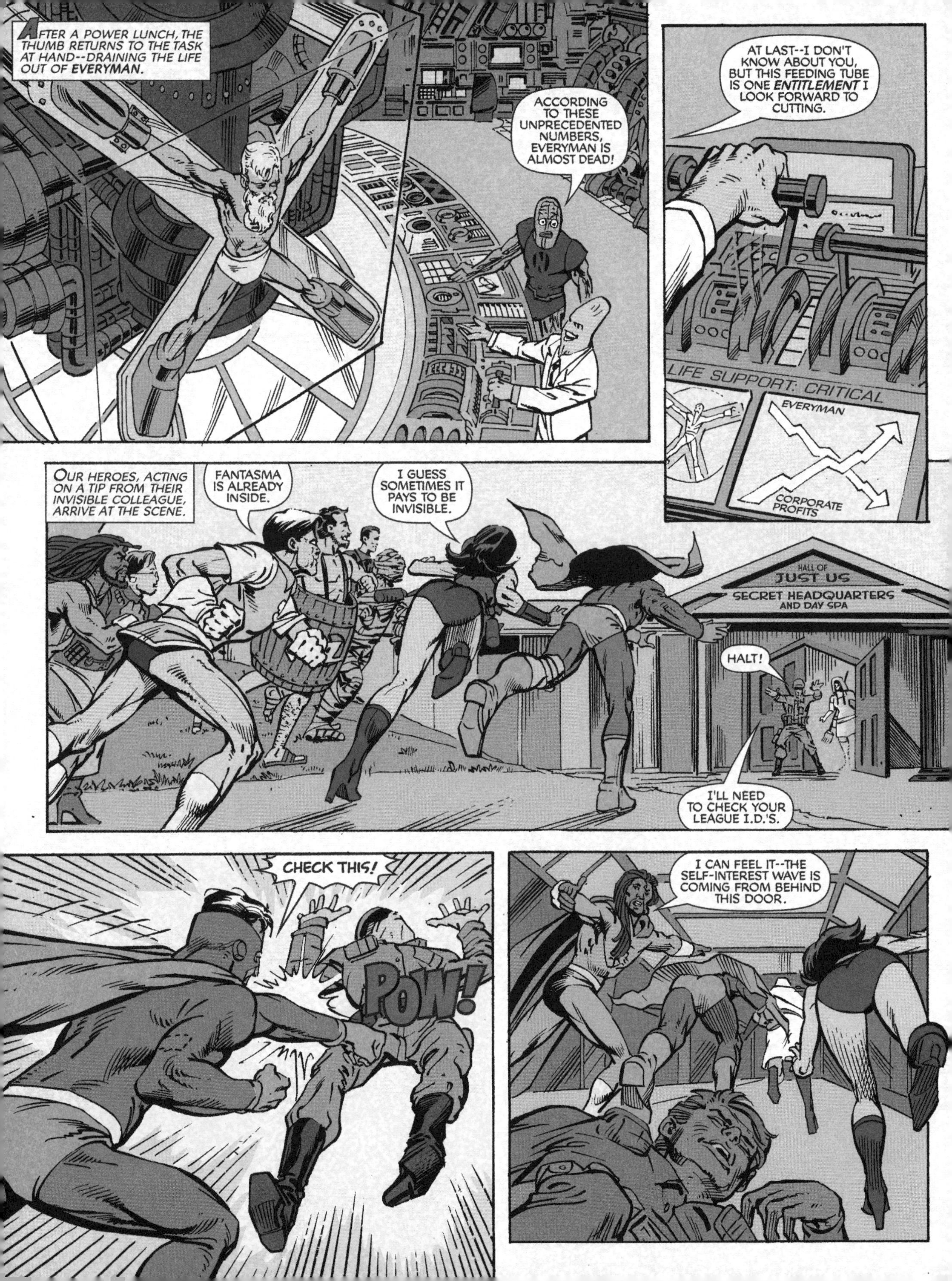
AFTER A POWER LUNCH, THE THUMB RETURNS TO THE TASK AT HAND--DRAINING THE LIFE OUT OF EVERYMAN.
ACCORDING TO THESE UNPRECEDENTED NUMBERS, EVERYMAN IS ALMOST DEAD!
AT LAST--I DON'T KNOW ABOUT YOU, BUT THIS FEEDING TUBE IS ONE ENTITLEMENT I LOOK FORWARD TO CUTTING.
LIFE SUPPORT: CRITICAL
EVERYMAN
CORPORATE PROFITS
OUR HEROES, ACTING ON A TIP FROM THEIR INVISIBLE COLLEAGUE, ARRIVE AT THE SCENE.
FANTASMA IS ALREADY INSIDE.
I GUESS SOMETIMES IT PAYS TO BE INVISIBLE.
HALL OF JUST US
SECRET HEADQUARTERS AND DAY SPA
HALT!
I'LL NEED TO CHECK YOUR LEAGUE I.D.'S.
CHECK THIS!
POW!
I CAN FEEL IT--THE SELF-INTEREST WAVE IS COMING FROM BEHIND THIS DOOR.

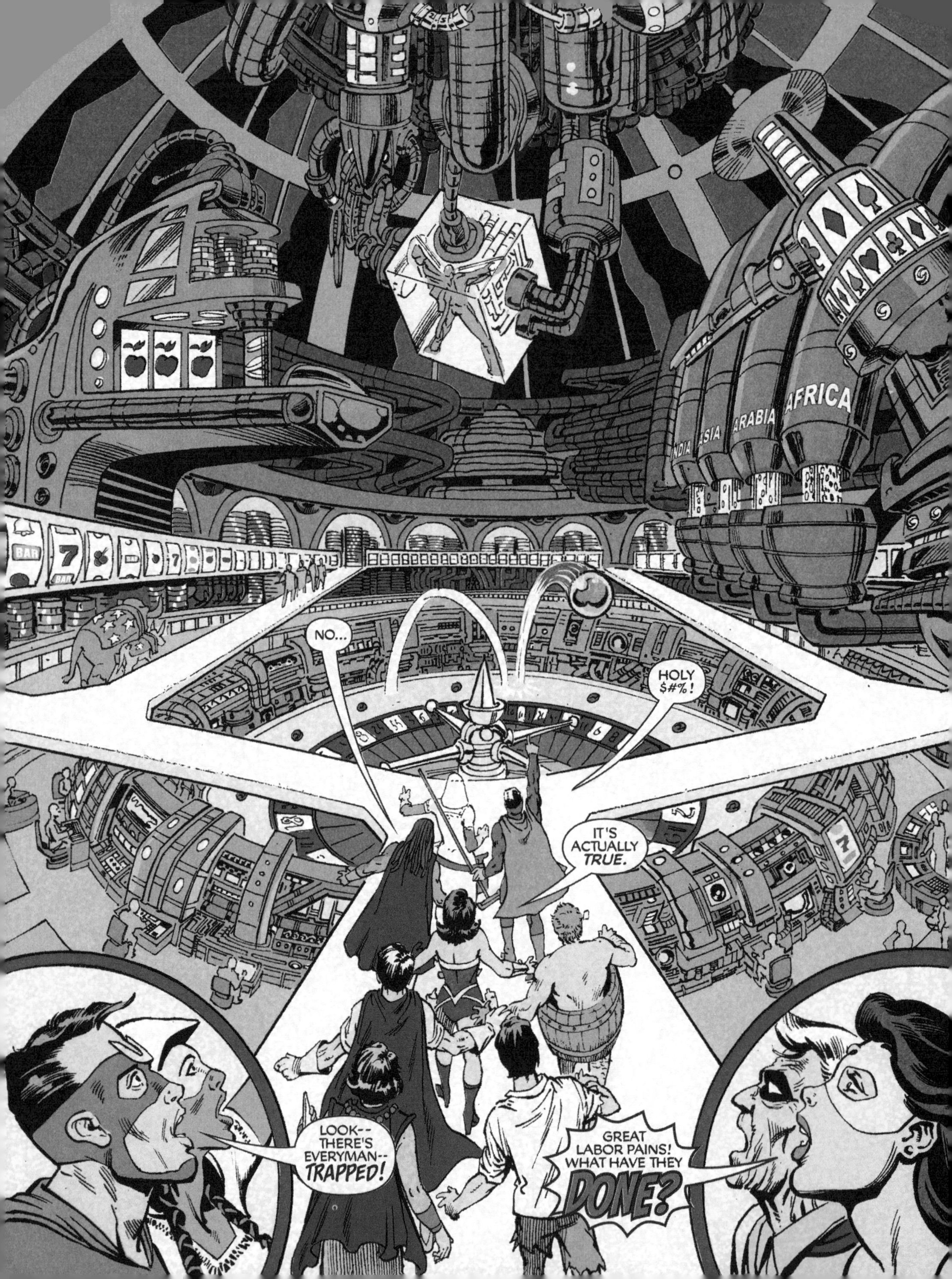

NO...
HOLY $#%!
IT'S ACTUALLY TRUE.
LOOK--THERE'S EVERYMAN--TRAPPED!
GREAT LABOR PAINS! WHAT HAVE THEY DONE?
INDIA
ASIA
ARABIA
AFRICA
BAR
7

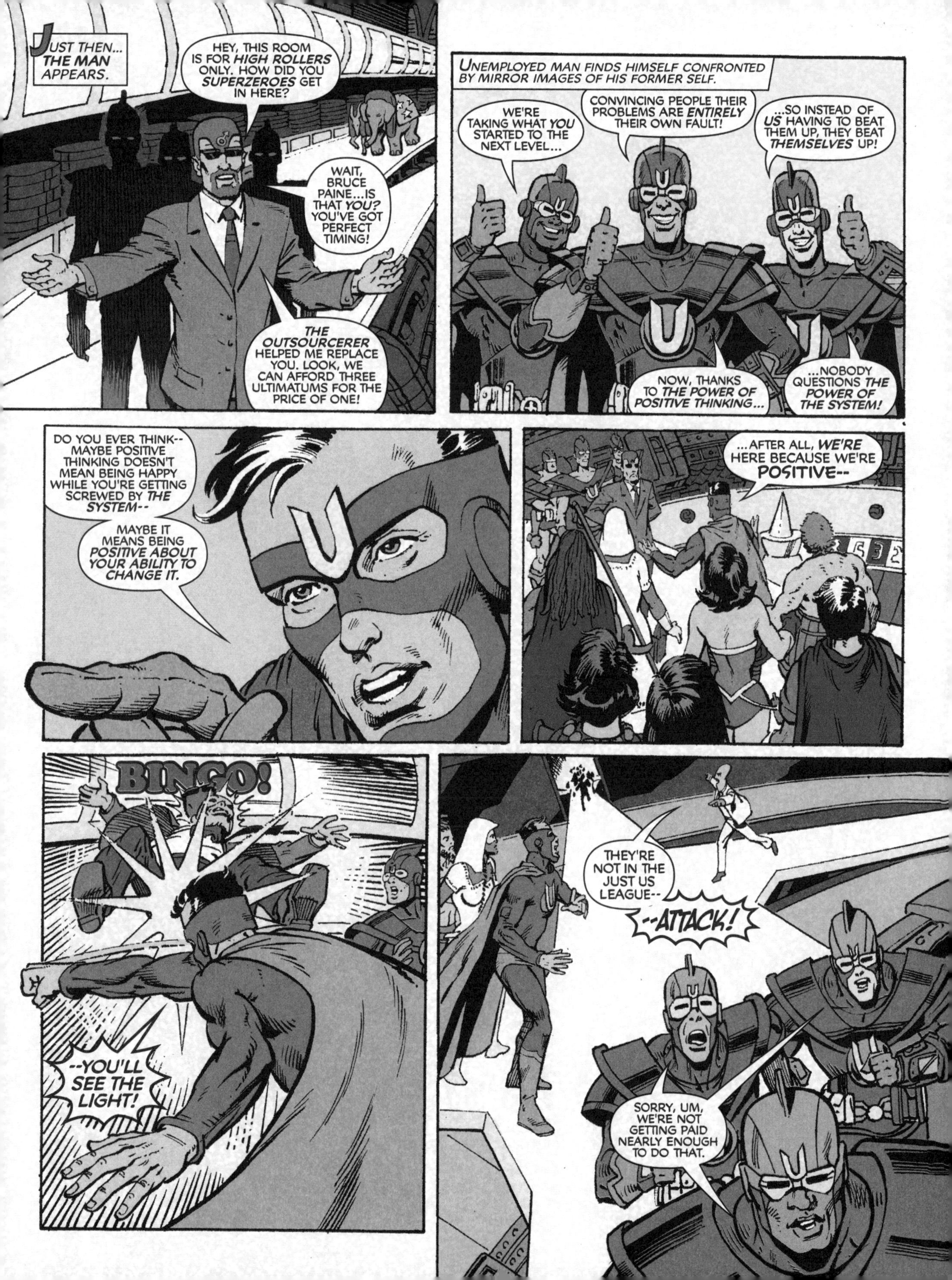
JUST THEN... THE MAN APPEARS.
HEY, THIS ROOM IS FOR HIGH ROLLERS ONLY. HOW DID YOU SUPERZEROES GET IN HERE?
WAIT, BRUCE PAINE...IS THAT YOU? YOU'VE GOT PERFECT TIMING!
THE OUTSOURCERER HELPED ME REPLACE YOU. LOOK, WE CAN AFFORD THREE ULTIMATUMS FOR THE PRICE OF ONE!
UNEMPLOYED MAN FINDS HIMSELF CONFRONTED BY MIRROR IMAGES OF HIS FORMER SELF.
WE'RE TAKING WHAT YOU STARTED TO THE NEXT LEVEL...
CONVINCING PEOPLE THEIR PROBLEMS ARE ENTIRELY THEIR OWN FAULT!
...SO INSTEAD OF US HAVING TO BEAT THEM UP, THEY BEAT THEMSELVES UP!
NOW, THANKS TO THE POWER OF POSITIVE THINKING...
...NOBODY QUESTIONS THE POWER OF THE SYSTEM!
DO YOU EVER THINK-- MAYBE POSITIVE THINKING DOESN'T MEAN BEING HAPPY WHILE YOU'RE GETTING SCREWED BY THE SYSTEM--
MAYBE IT MEANS BEING POSITIVE ABOUT YOUR ABILITY TO CHANGE IT.
...AFTER ALL, WE'RE HERE BECAUSE WE'RE POSITIVE--
BINGO!
--YOU'LL SEE THE LIGHT!
THEY'RE NOT IN THE JUST US LEAGUE--
--ATTACK!
SORRY, UM, WE'RE NOT GETTING PAID NEARLY ENOUGH TO DO THAT.

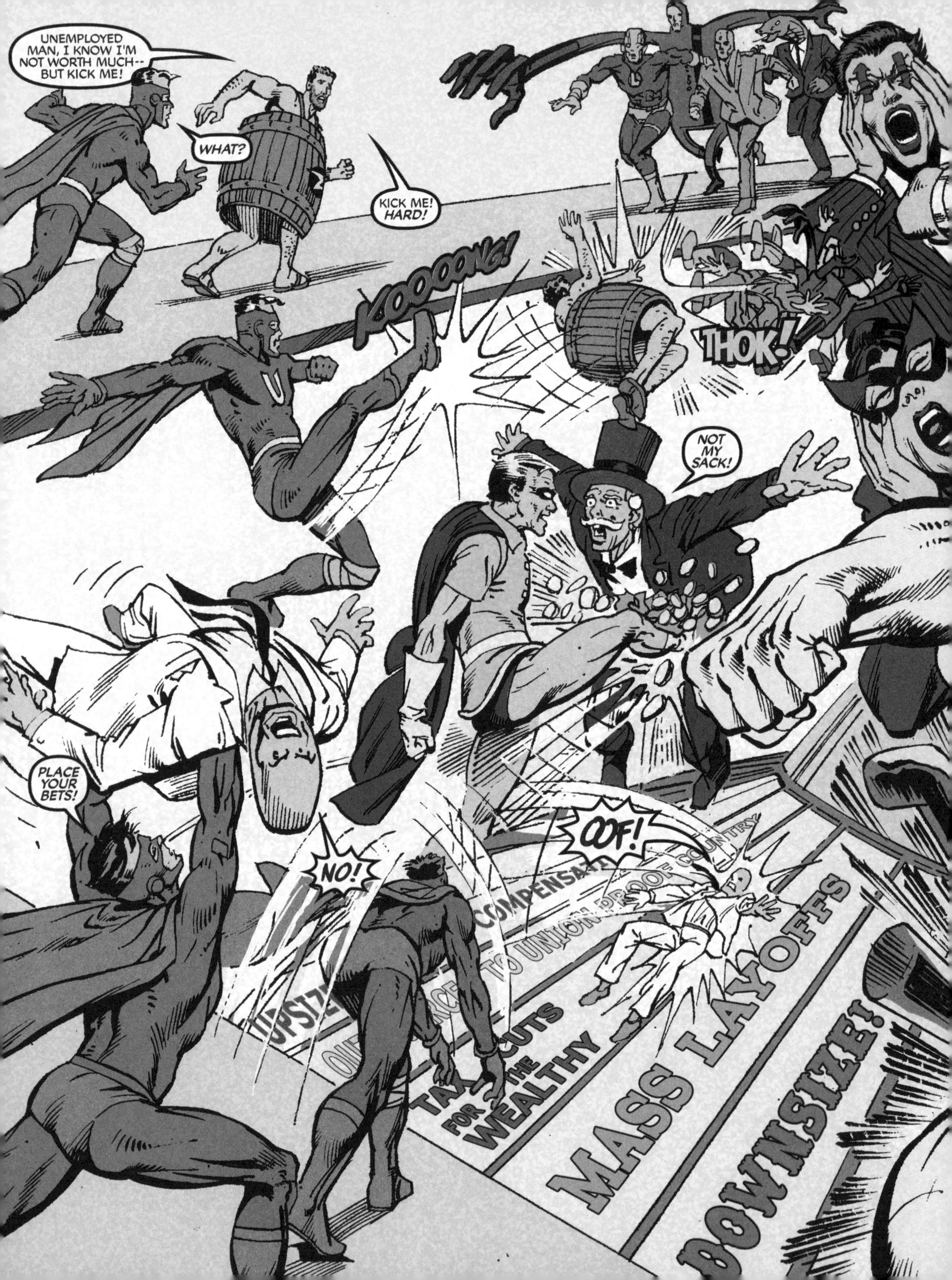
UNEMPLOYED MAN, I KNOW I'M NOT WORTH MUCH-- BUT KICK ME!
WHAT?
KICK ME! HARD!
KOOOONG!
THOK!
NOT MY SACK!
PLACE YOUR BETS!
NO!
OOF!
FOR THE WEALTHY
MASS LAYOFFS
DOWNSIZE!

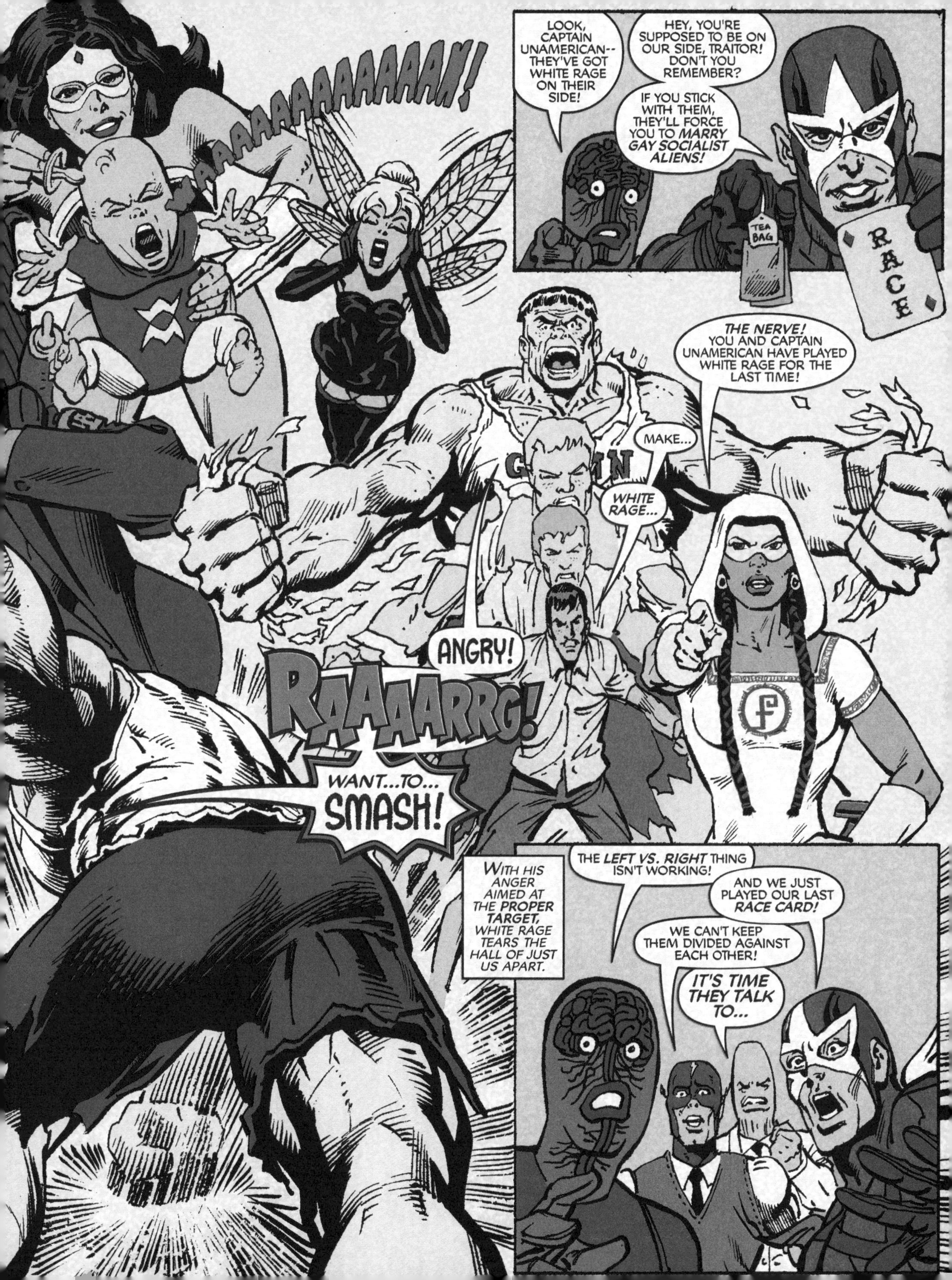
AAAAAAAAAAAAAAAAAAAAAAAAH!
LOOK, CAPTAIN UNAMERICAN-- THEY'VE GOT WHITE RAGE ON THEIR SIDE!
HEY, YOU'RE SUPPOSED TO BE ON OUR SIDE, TRAITOR! DON'T YOU REMEMBER?
IF YOU STICK WITH THEM, THEY'LL FORCE YOU TO MARRY GAY SOCIALIST ALIENS!
TEA BAG
RACE
THE NERVE! YOU AND CAPTAIN UNAMERICAN HAVE PLAYED WHITE RAGE FOR THE LAST TIME!
MAKE...
WHITE RAGE...
ANGRY!
RAAAAARRG!
WANT...TO... SMASH!
WITH HIS ANGER AIMED AT THE PROPER TARGET, WHITE RAGE TEARS THE HALL OF JUST US APART.
THE LEFT VS. RIGHT THING ISN'T WORKING!
AND WE JUST PLAYED OUR LAST RACE CARD!
WE CAN'T KEEP THEM DIVIDED AGAINST EACH OTHER!
IT'S TIME THEY TALK TO...

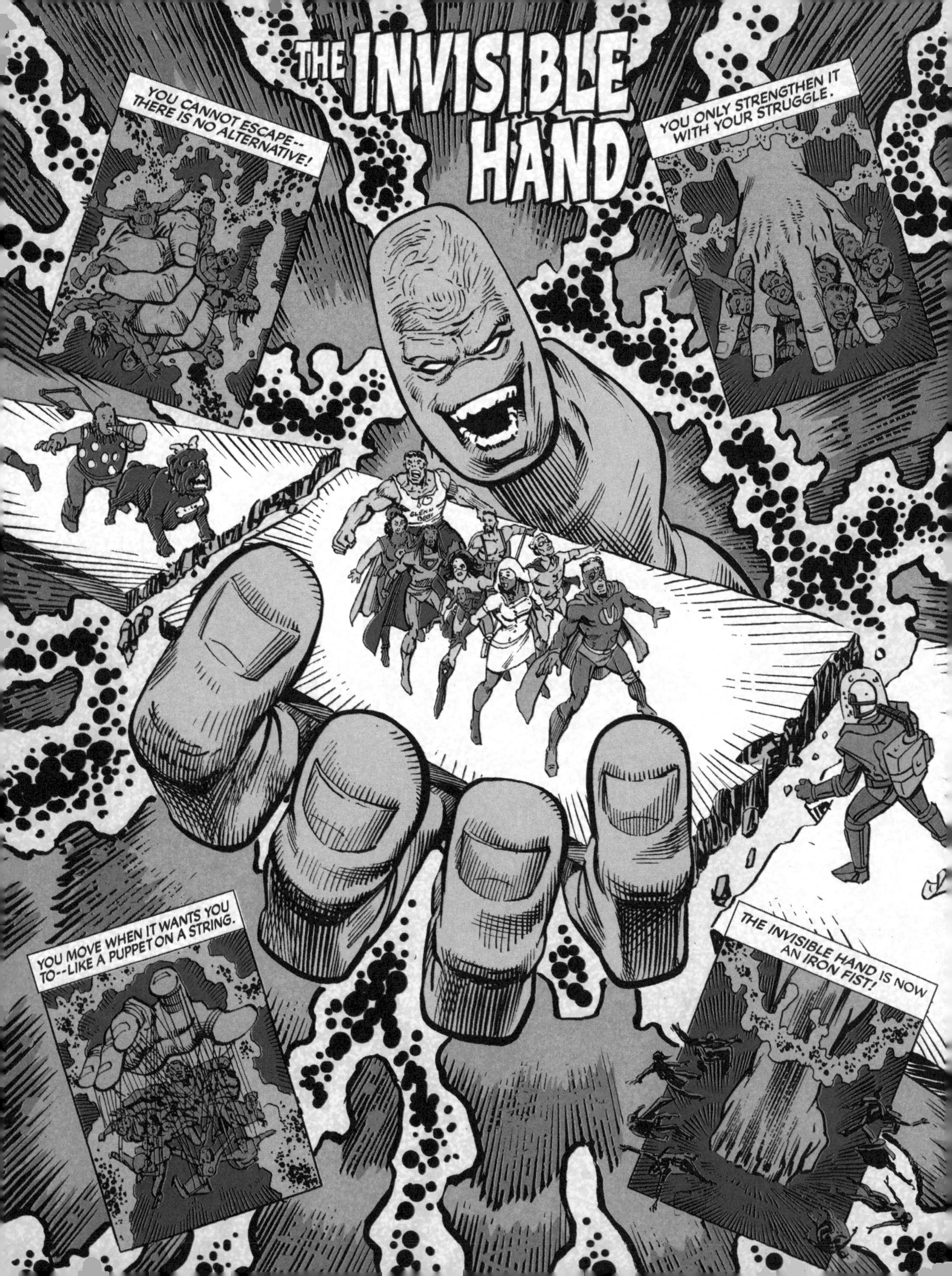
THE INVISIBLE HAND
YOU CANNOT ESCAPE-- THERE IS NO ALTERNATIVE!
YOU ONLY STRENGTHEN IT WITH YOUR STRUGGLE.
YOU MOVE WHEN IT WANTS YOU TO--LIKE A PUPPET ON A STRING.
THE INVISIBLE HAND IS NOW AN IRON FIST!

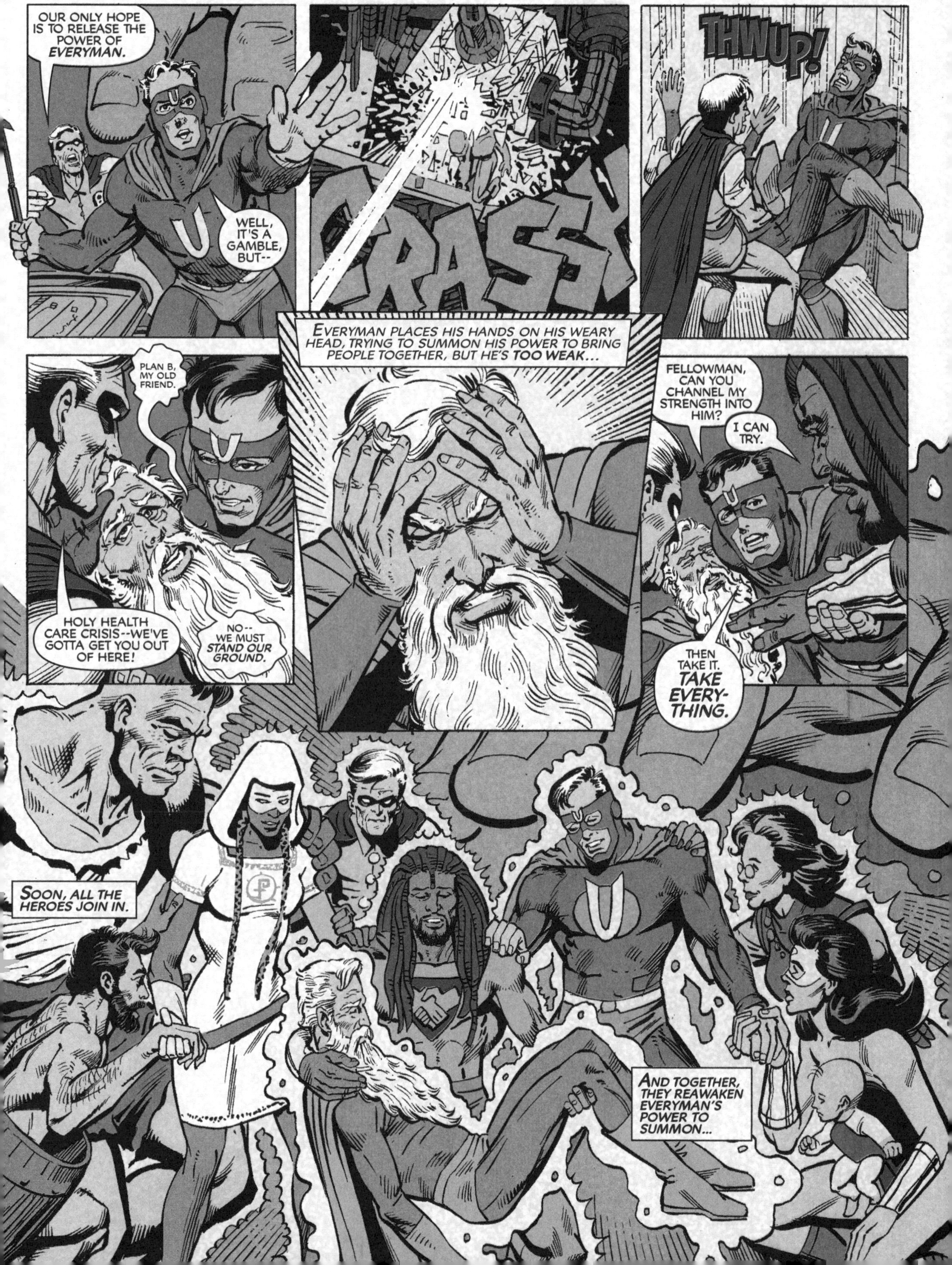

OUR ONLY HOPE IS TO RELEASE THE POWER OF *EVERYMAN.*
WELL, IT'S A GAMBLE, BUT--
CRASS
THWUP!
PLAN B, MY OLD FRIEND.
HOLY HEALTH CARE CRISIS--WE'VE GOTTA GET YOU OUT OF HERE!
NO-- WE MUST *STAND OUR GROUND.*
EVERYMAN PLACES HIS HANDS ON HIS WEARY HEAD, TRYING TO SUMMON HIS POWER TO BRING PEOPLE TOGETHER, BUT HE'S ***TOO WEAK...***
FELLOWMAN, CAN YOU CHANNEL MY STRENGTH INTO HIM?
I CAN TRY.
THEN TAKE IT. ***TAKE EVERY-THING.***
SOON, ALL THE HEROES JOIN IN.
AND TOGETHER, THEY REAWAKEN EVERYMAN'S POWER TO SUMMON...

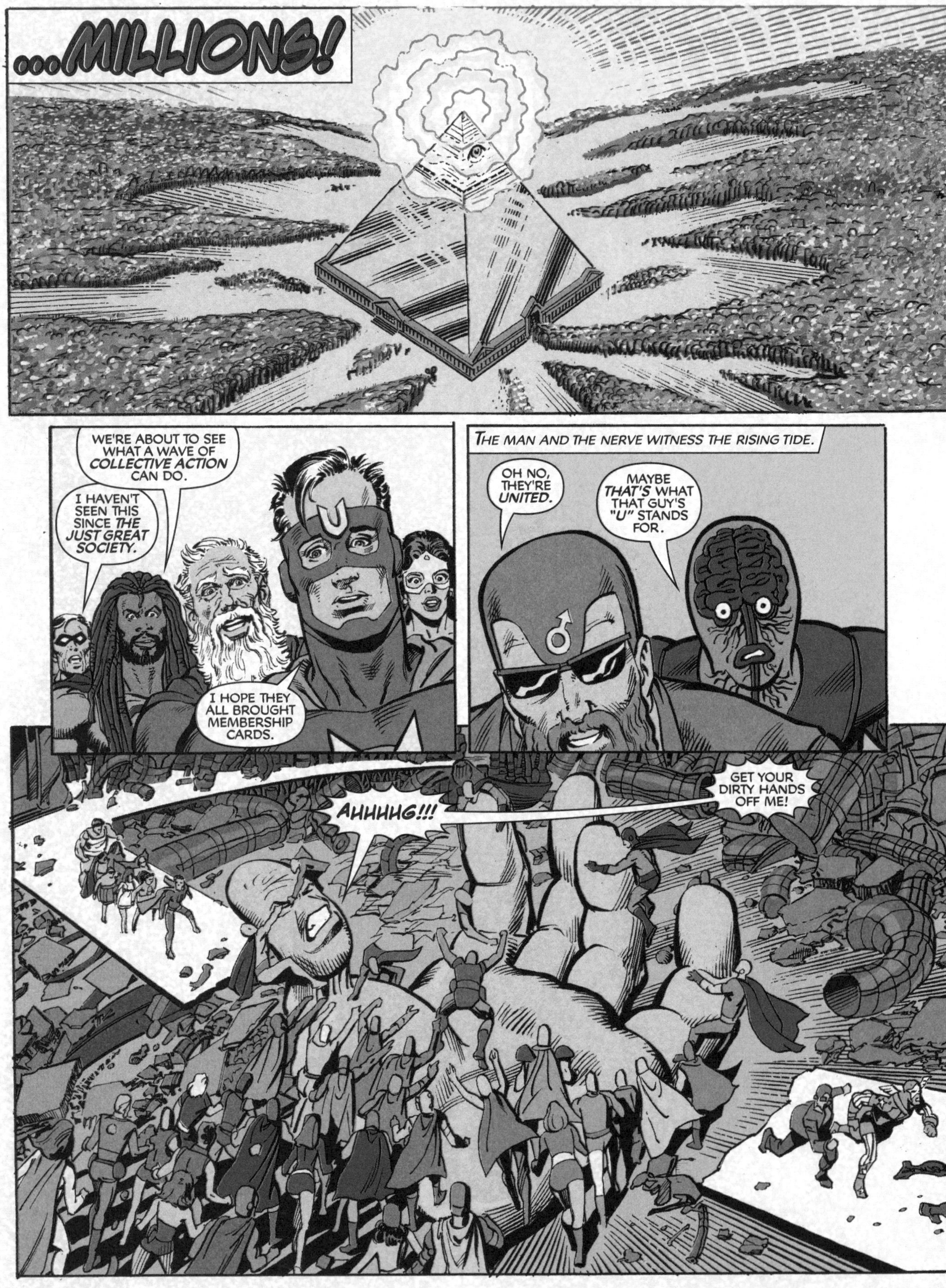
...MILLIONS!
WE'RE ABOUT TO SEE WHAT A WAVE OF COLLECTIVE ACTION CAN DO.
I HAVEN'T SEEN THIS SINCE THE JUST GREAT SOCIETY.
I HOPE THEY ALL BROUGHT MEMBERSHIP CARDS.
THE MAN AND THE NERVE WITNESS THE RISING TIDE.
OH NO, THEY'RE UNITED.
MAYBE THAT'S WHAT THAT GUY'S "U" STANDS FOR.
GET YOUR DIRTY HANDS OFF ME!
AHHHHG!!!

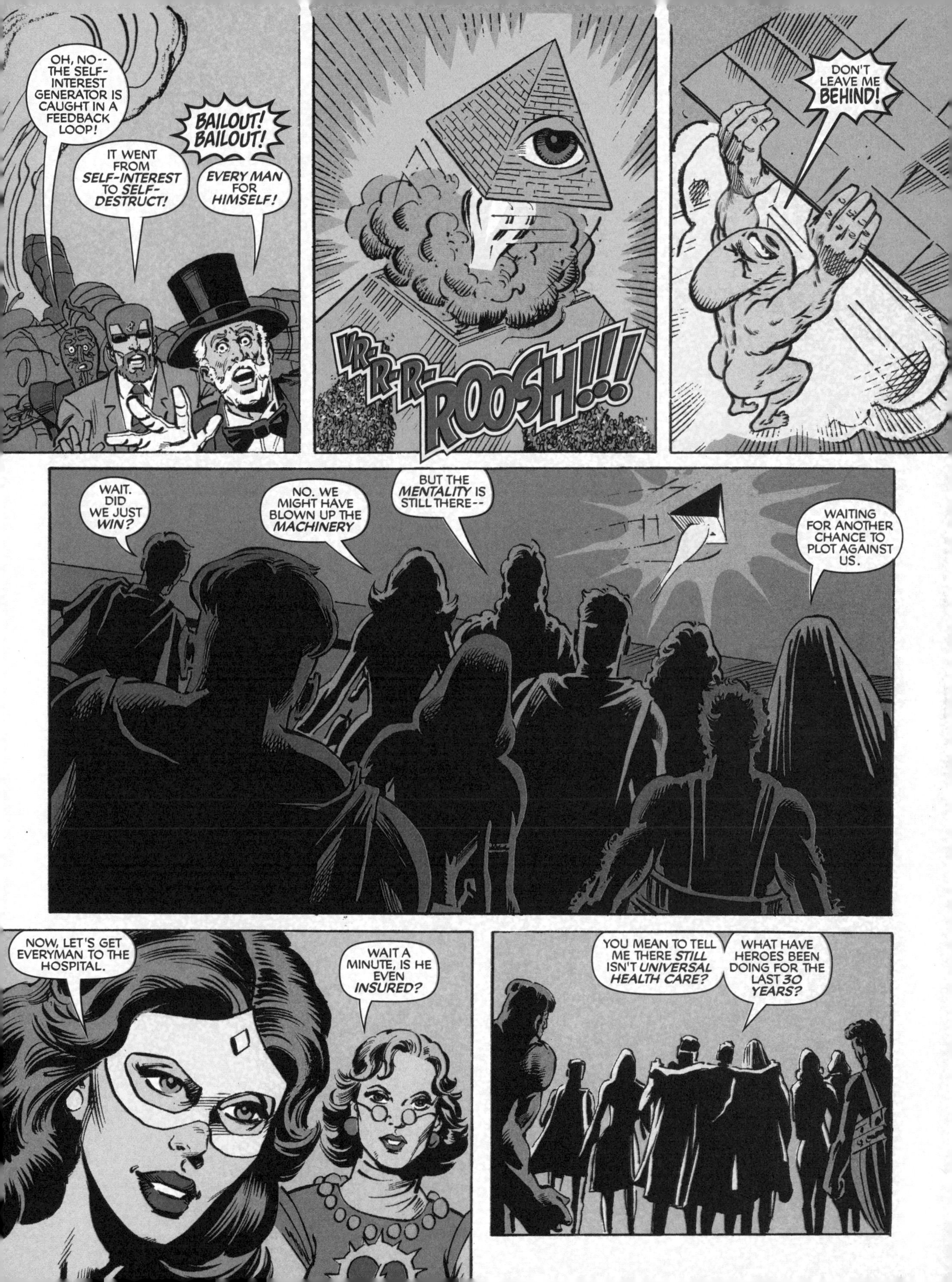
OH, NO-- THE SELF-INTEREST GENERATOR IS CAUGHT IN A FEEDBACK LOOP!
IT WENT FROM SELF-INTEREST TO SELF-DESTRUCT!
BAILOUT! BAILOUT!
EVERY MAN FOR HIMSELF!
VR-R-R-ROOSH!!!
DON'T LEAVE ME BEHIND!
WAIT. DID WE JUST WIN?
NO. WE MIGHT HAVE BLOWN UP THE MACHINERY
BUT THE MENTALITY IS STILL THERE--
WAITING FOR ANOTHER CHANCE TO PLOT AGAINST US.
NOW, LET'S GET EVERYMAN TO THE HOSPITAL.
WAIT A MINUTE, IS HE EVEN INSURED?
YOU MEAN TO TELL ME THERE STILL ISN'T UNIVERSAL HEALTH CARE?
WHAT HAVE HEROES BEEN DOING FOR THE LAST 30 YEARS?

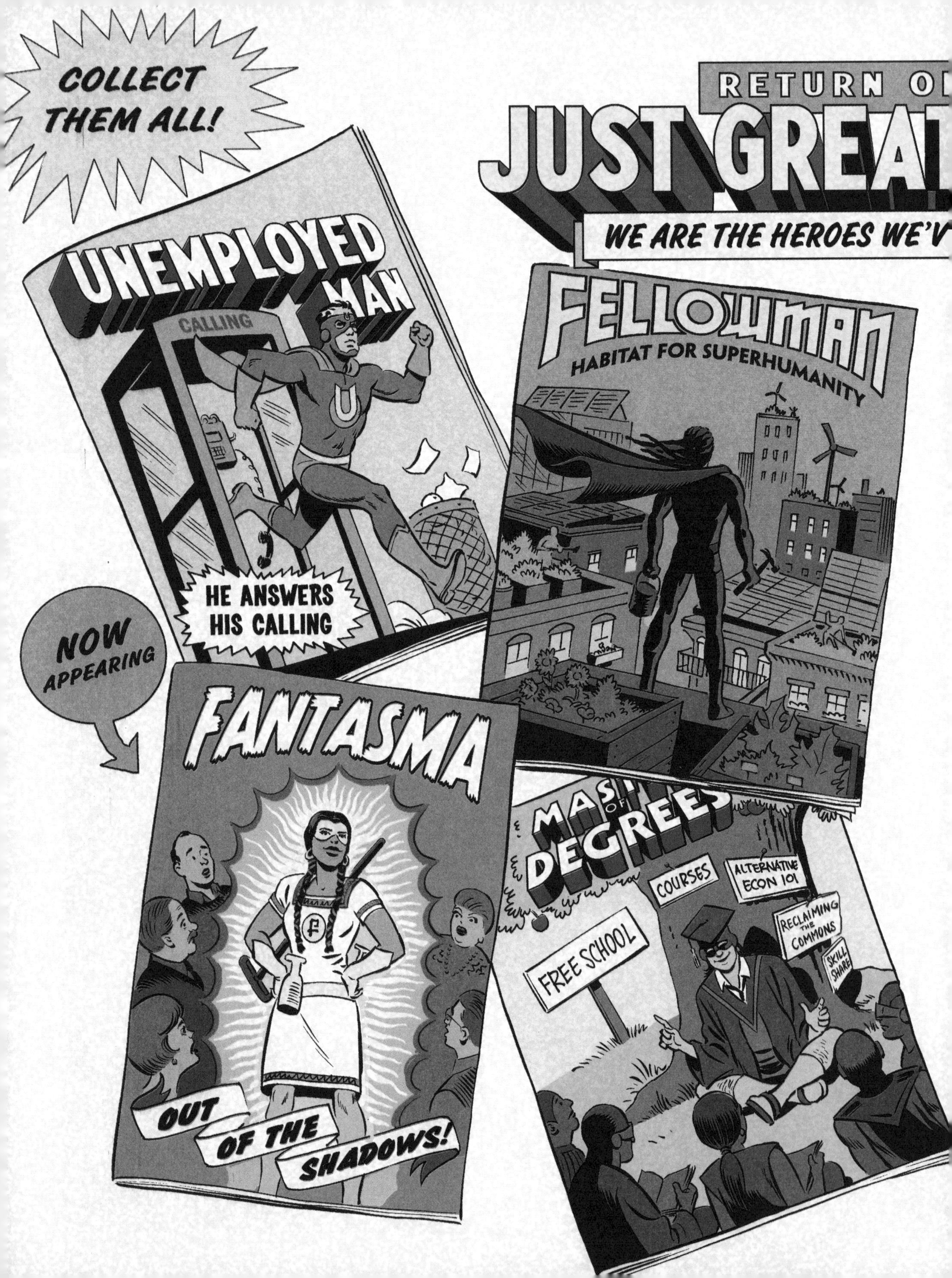
COLLECT THEM ALL!
RETURN O
JUST GREA
WE ARE THE HEROES WE'V
UNEMPLOYED MAN
CALLING
HE ANSWERS HIS CALLING
FELLOWMAN
HABITAT FOR SUPERHUMANITY
NOW APPEARING
FANTASMA
OUT OF THE SHADOWS!
DEGREES
COURSES
ALTERNATIVE ECON 101
RECLAIMING THE COMMONS
SKILL SHARE
FREE SCHOOL

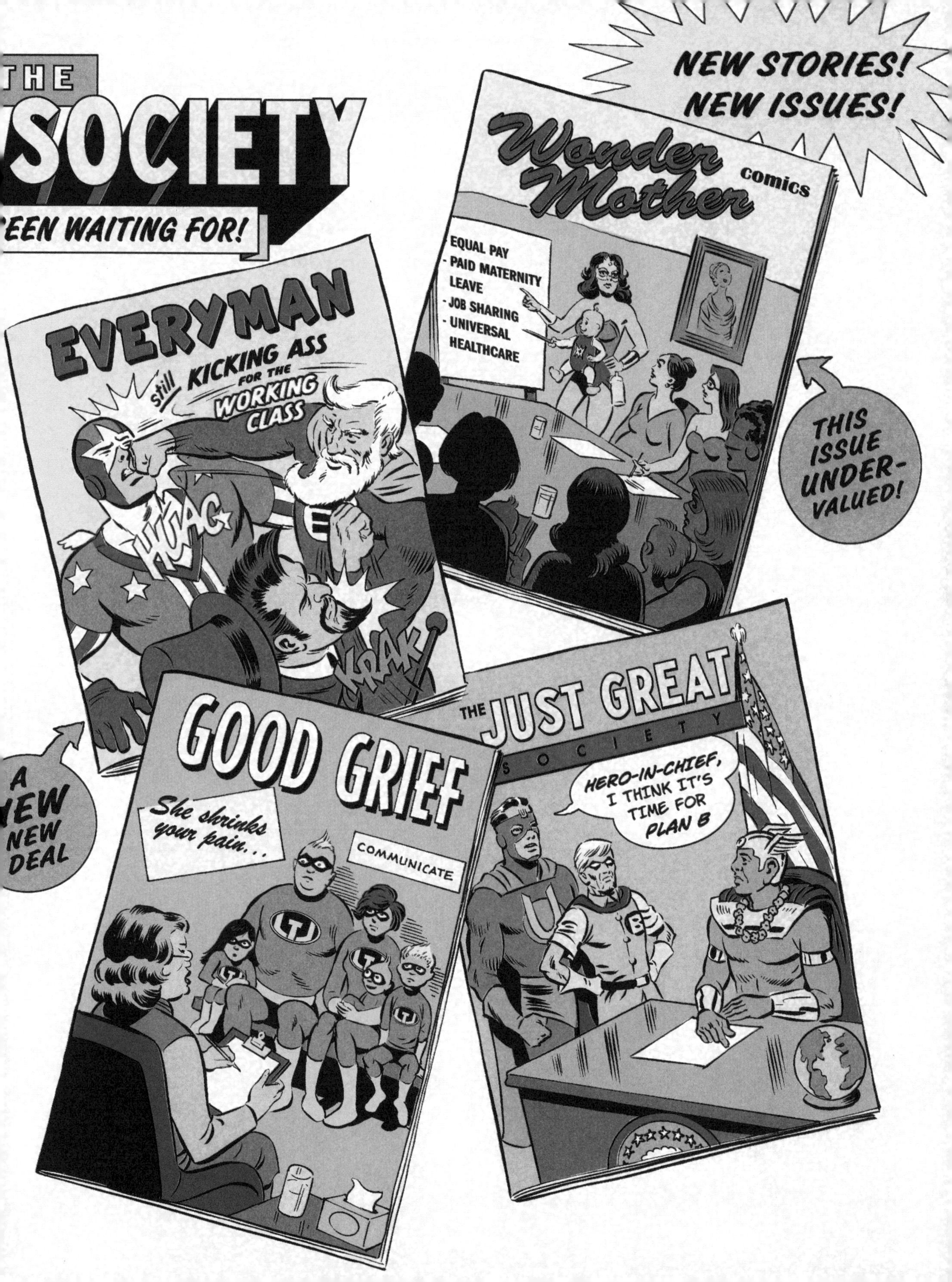

THE
SOCIETY
EEN WAITING FOR!
NEW STORIES!
NEW ISSUES!
Wonder Mother comics
EQUAL PAY
- PAID MATERNITY LEAVE
- JOB SHARING
- UNIVERSAL HEALTHCARE
THIS ISSUE UNDER-VALUED!
EVERYMAN
still KICKING ASS FOR THE WORKING CLASS
WOAC
KRAK
A NEW NEW DEAL
GOOD GRIEF
She shrinks your pain...
COMMUNICATE
THE JUST GREAT SOCIETY
HERO-IN-CHIEF, I THINK IT'S TIME FOR PLAN B

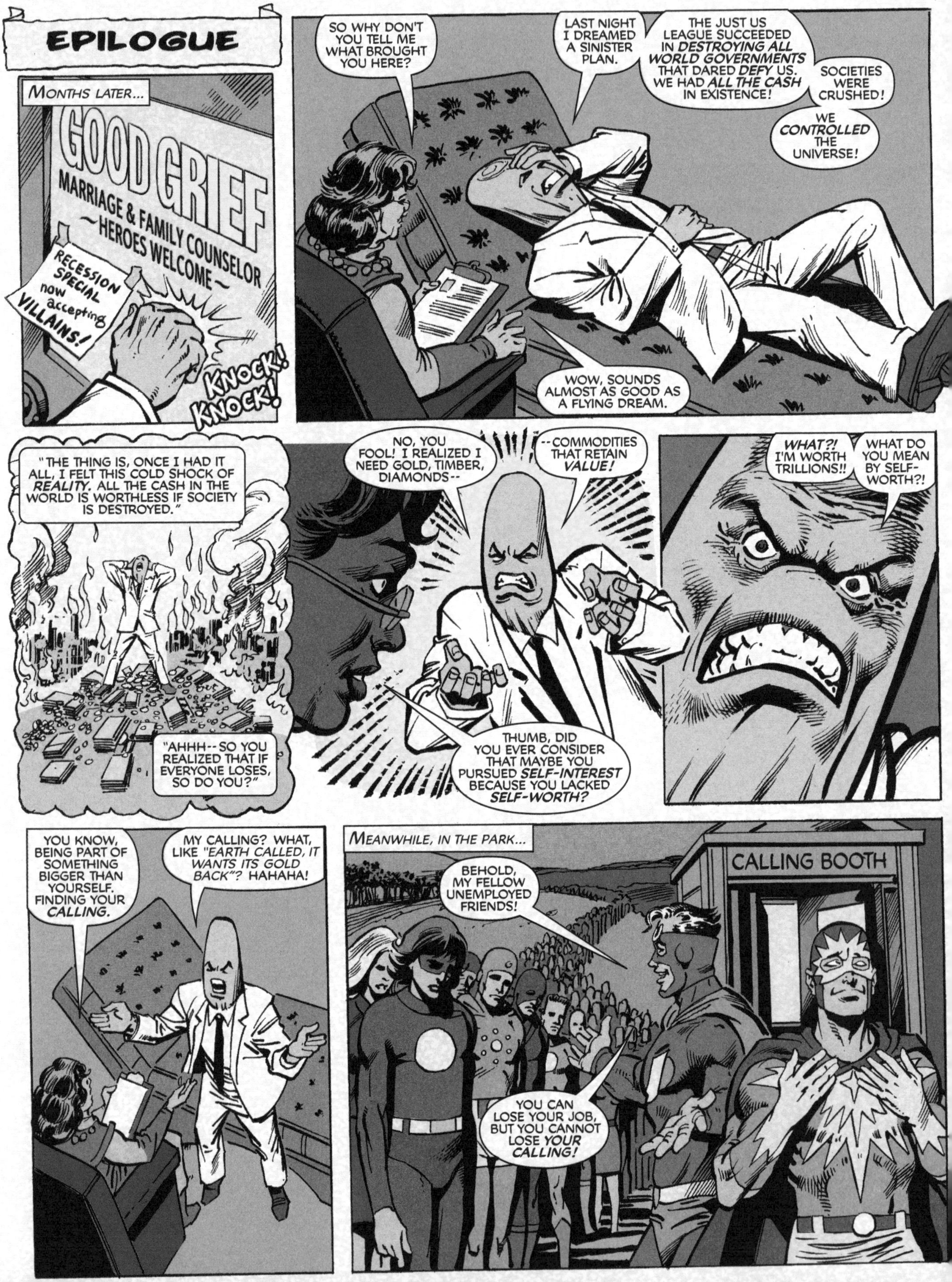
EPILOGUE
MONTHS LATER...
GOOD GRIEF
MARRIAGE & FAMILY COUNSELOR
~HEROES WELCOME~
RECESSION SPECIAL now accepting VILLAINS!
KNOCK! KNOCK!
SO WHY DON'T YOU TELL ME WHAT BROUGHT YOU HERE?
LAST NIGHT I DREAMED A SINISTER PLAN.
THE JUST US LEAGUE SUCCEEDED IN DESTROYING ALL WORLD GOVERNMENTS THAT DARED DEFY US. WE HAD ALL THE CASH IN EXISTENCE!
SOCIETIES WERE CRUSHED!
WE CONTROLLED THE UNIVERSE!
WOW, SOUNDS ALMOST AS GOOD AS A FLYING DREAM.
"THE THING IS, ONCE I HAD IT ALL, I FELT THIS COLD SHOCK OF REALITY. ALL THE CASH IN THE WORLD IS WORTHLESS IF SOCIETY IS DESTROYED."
"AHHH-- SO YOU REALIZED THAT IF EVERYONE LOSES, SO DO YOU?"
NO, YOU FOOL! I REALIZED I NEED GOLD, TIMBER, DIAMONDS--
--COMMODITIES THAT RETAIN VALUE!
THUMB, DID YOU EVER CONSIDER THAT MAYBE YOU PURSUED SELF-INTEREST BECAUSE YOU LACKED SELF-WORTH?
WHAT?! I'M WORTH TRILLIONS!!
WHAT DO YOU MEAN BY SELF-WORTH?!
YOU KNOW, BEING PART OF SOMETHING BIGGER THAN YOURSELF. FINDING YOUR CALLING.
MY CALLING? WHAT, LIKE "EARTH CALLED, IT WANTS ITS GOLD BACK"? HAHAHA!
MEANWHILE, IN THE PARK...
CALLING BOOTH
BEHOLD, MY FELLOW UNEMPLOYED FRIENDS!
YOU CAN LOSE YOUR JOB, BUT YOU CANNOT LOSE YOUR CALLING!

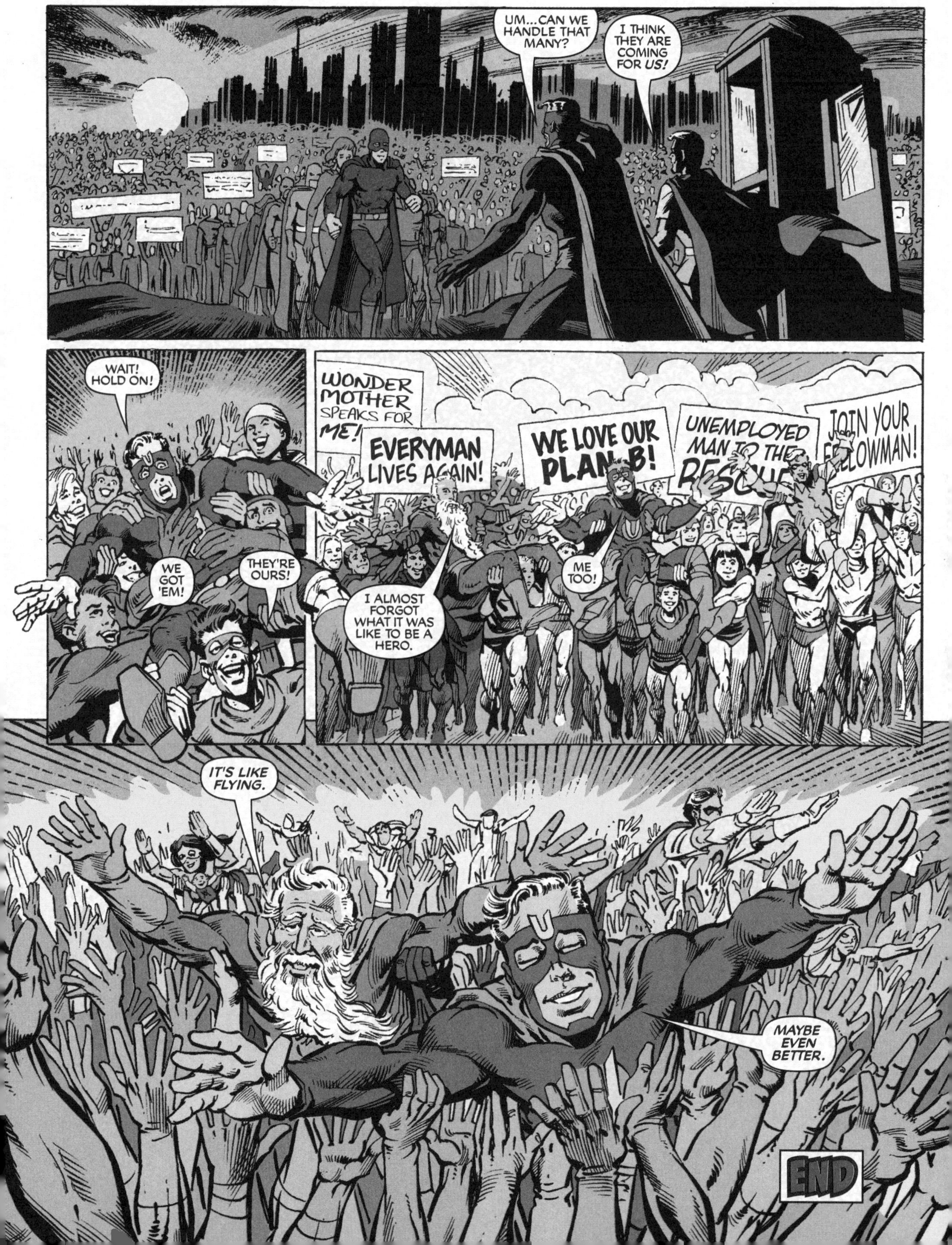
UM...CAN WE HANDLE THAT MANY?
I THINK THEY ARE COMING FOR US!
WAIT! HOLD ON!
WE GOT 'EM!
THEY'RE OURS!
WONDER MOTHER SPEAKS FOR ME!
EVERYMAN LIVES AGAIN!
WE LOVE OUR PLAN B!
UNEMPLOYED MAN TO THE RESCUE
JOIN YOUR FELLOWMAN!
I ALMOST FORGOT WHAT IT WAS LIKE TO BE A HERO.
ME TOO!
IT'S LIKE FLYING.
MAYBE EVEN BETTER.
END

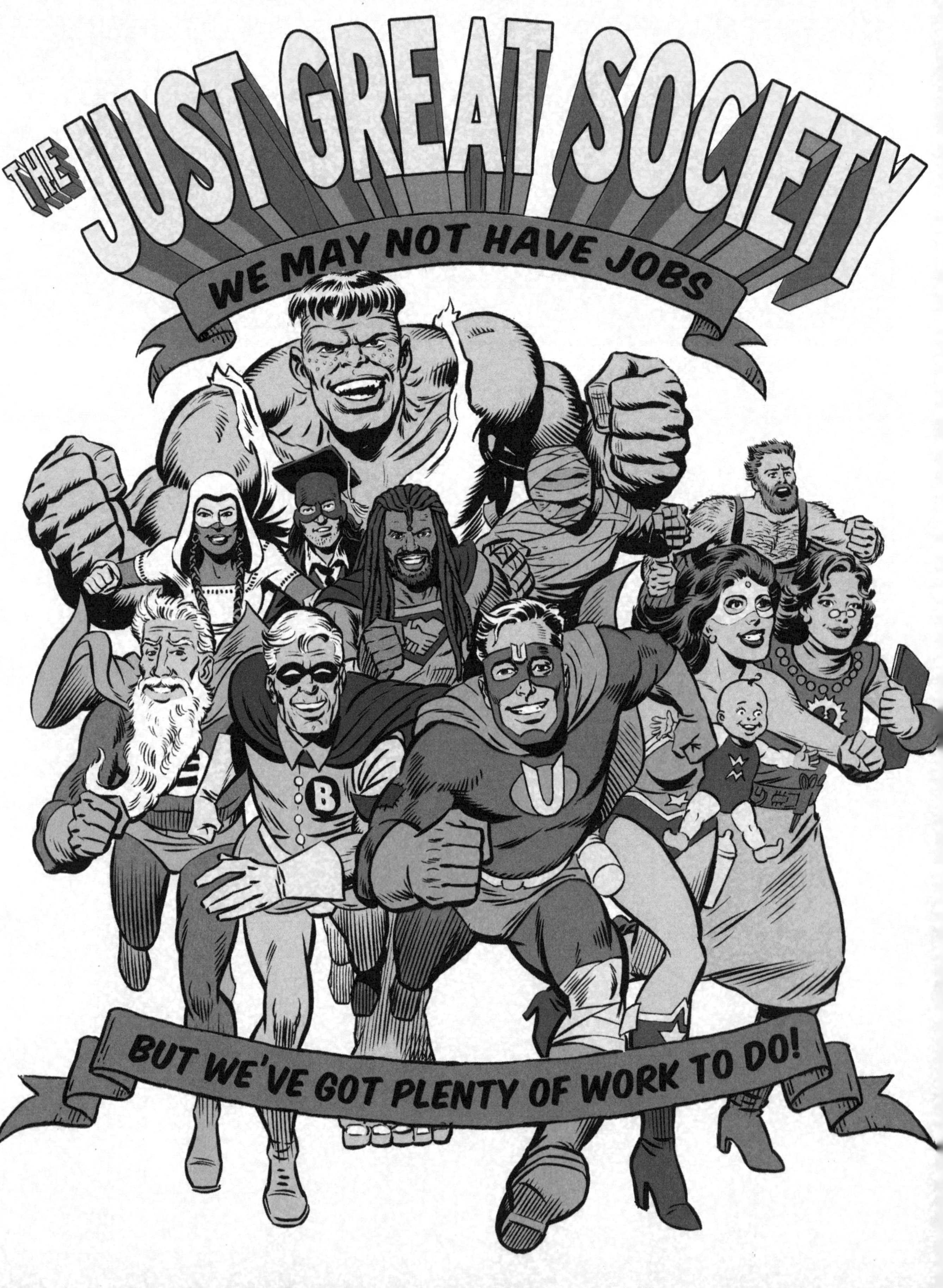
THE JUST GREAT SOCIETY
WE MAY NOT HAVE JOBS
BUT WE'VE GOT PLENTY OF WORK TO DO!

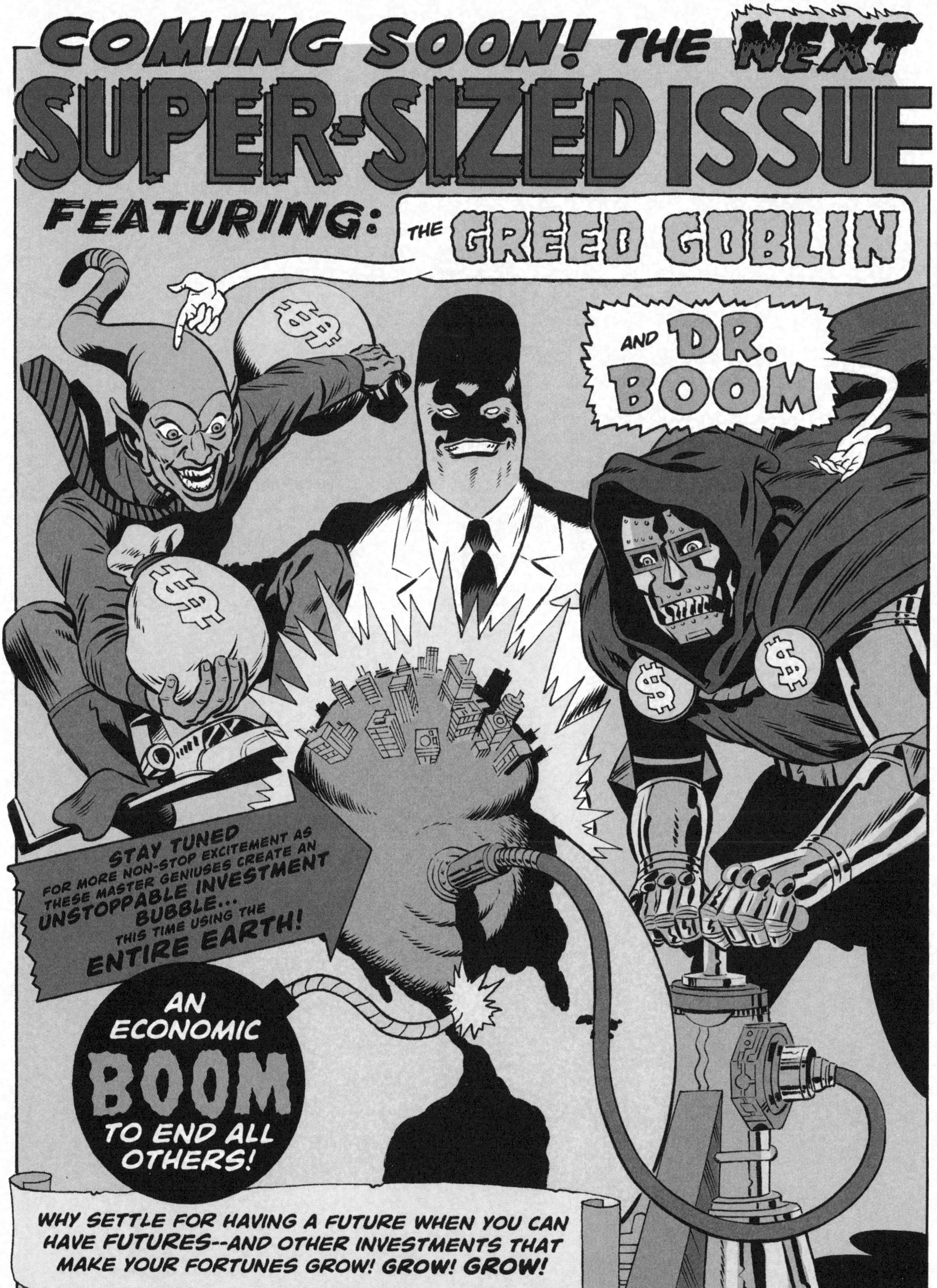
COMING SOON! THE NEXT
SUPER-SIZED ISSUE
FEATURING:
THE GREED GOBLIN
AND DR. BOOM
STAY TUNED FOR MORE NON-STOP EXCITEMENT AS THESE MASTER GENIUSES CREATE AN UNSTOPPABLE INVESTMENT BUBBLE... THIS TIME USING THE ENTIRE EARTH!
AN ECONOMIC BOOM TO END ALL OTHERS!
WHY SETTLE FOR HAVING A FUTURE WHEN YOU CAN HAVE FUTURES--AND OTHER INVESTMENTS THAT MAKE YOUR FORTUNES GROW! GROW! GROW!

SUPER HERO ROLL CALL

LISA "WONDER MOTHER" STONESTREET, FRIEDEL "THE SUSSURATOR" FISHER, TOM "THE IRISH INK GRENADE" SULLIVAN, JADE "THE MASSAGINATOR" RAYBIN, JUMANA "DYNAMICA" NABTI, ERIC "THUNDER" WILINSKI, ALLYSON "CUPCAKE" WILINSKI, RICH "FACTOTUM" KANTROWITZ, RICK "SOULCYCLER" GUNN, PREMILA "JOIE DE VIVRE" ANAND, FAVIANNA "FLAVBOT" RODRIGUEZ, JEFF "THE ICECREAMINATOR" DURITZ, MEIVER "TORBELLINA" DE LA CRUZ, CONAN "THE AVERAGE" MOATS, MARK "THE ENGINEERIUM" SCHEEFF, ARA "NOW YOU DIE" BARTOS, LYNDA "THE IMA" GOLAN, YUVAL "THE ABA" GOLAN, ELENA "SUPERSABTA" THURSTON, YASMIN "THE GRRRL WONDER" GOLAN, EMEK "EPID-EMEK" GOLAN, DAVID "DIRECT ACTION FIGURE" MEIEREN, NAOMI "ENDLESS SUMMER" ARCHER, ALEX "XRAYN" RATNER, YVONNE "TOUGH LOVE" CANNON, CHUCK "STRONGMAN" CANNON, LAURIE "LUMINA" LUSTICA, BECKY "THE LIVING SISTER" STARK, JAY "THE RELIABLE NARRATOR" BABCOCK, CHRISTINE "BOSS LADY" GAROFOLI, JOE "NEWSMAN" GAROFOLI, CHRIS "GOOD CALL" BEARDSLEY, ANOKHI "VISHKANYA" PARIKH, KENNY "THE ORANGACHANG" CHANG, MIKE "THE FLYING TACOMAN" McGUIRE, JEFF "THE CYNICIZER" GARNAND, JASON "THE SHADE" MILLET, LEE "NEON COWGIRL" LUCAS, WILLIAM "SECRET AGENT MAN" CLARK, JON "THE SAGE" HOSMER, LINDA "TUMBLEWEED" STONESTREET, JOHN "ROUGH JUSTICE" GLUSKIN, HEIDI "ACE" GLUSKIN, DEBRA "BONA FIDE" GLUSKIN, MIMI & POPIE, NEIL & MEL, AND THE AMAZING TRUMAN!

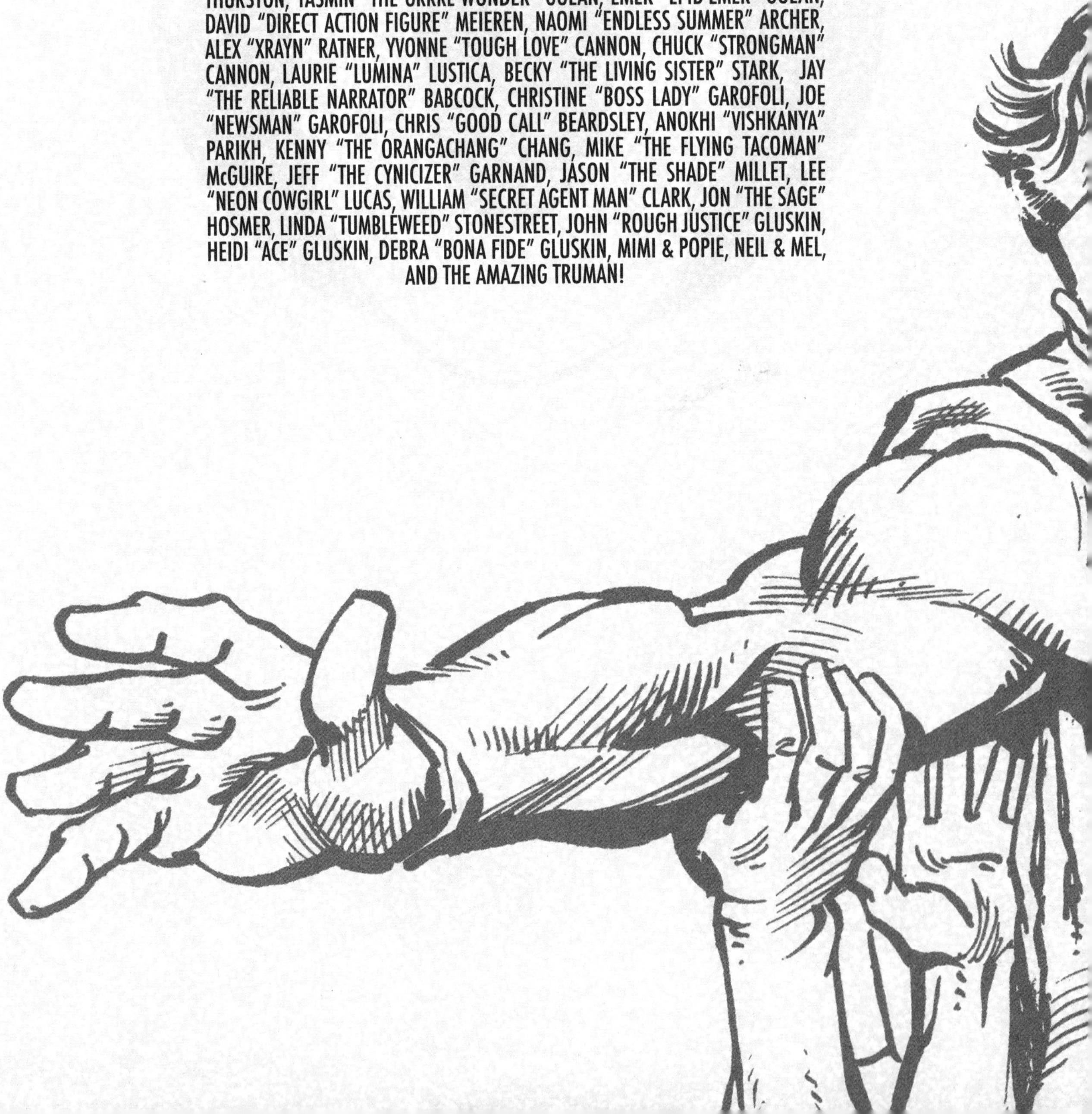